Tour de Farce

Anti-apartheid protest and South Africa's cancelled 1970 cricket tour of England

Mark Rowe

First published in Great Britain by
Association of Cricket Statisticians and Historians
Bedford MK40 4FG.
© ACS, 2020

Mark Rowe has asserted his rights under the Copyright, Designs and Patents Act 1988 to be identified as the authors of this work.

All Rights Reserved. No part of this publication may be reproduced, stored in a retrieval system, or transmitted in any form, or by any means, electronic, mechanical, photocopying, recording or otherwise without the prior permission in writing of the Copyright holders, nor be otherwise circulated in any form, or binding or cover other than in which it is published and without a similar condition including this condition being imposed on the subsequent publisher.

British Library Cataloguing-in-Publication Data.
A catalogue record for this book is available from the British Library.

ISBN: 978 1 912421 12 1
Typeset and printed by The City Press Leeds Ltd

Contents

Chapters (including interludes)

1	To 1965: 'Boycott plays for Yorkshire'	5
2	The sides	21
3	Summer of '69	54
4	Rugby: the first weeks	81
5	The stakes	106
6	Rugby: the last weeks	127
7	January and February 1970	155
8	March	189
9	April to mid-May	195
10	The last week	235
11	'The foul stink of success'	256
12	Verdict: the dreamers of the day	273
13	D-Day sixth of June	297
14	After the end	315
	Thanks and sources	327
	Index	335

Chapter One

To 1965: 'Boycott plays for Yorkshire'

> ... what has long been the central question of politics – the question of obedience and coercion. 'Why should I (or anyone) obey anyone else?' 'Why should I not live as I like?'
> Sir Isaiah Berlin, Two Concepts of Liberty, 1958

On MCC's first post-war tour of South Africa, the broadcaster John Arlott was the guest of another, the British-born South African Charles Fortune, in Grahamstown. Even in its name, Grahamstown had 'many of the qualities of a small English provincial town', Arlott wrote; until the evening that Charles Fortune drove his 'clean-as-a-pin and kindly native cook' to her home in the 'native quarter'. Arlott wrote:

> *Shame, hesitation, doubt, guilt struggled in the mind. Such conditions could, perhaps, exist on the edge of a too-rapidly commercialised city, but here, among the quiet houses and schools, beside a town where one could have grown up, it is not to be understood or accepted. In crawling filth, in houses made out of petrol tins hammered out flat, the people who live in that healthless quarter of Grahamstown are fortunate if they have a dwelling with one brick wall supporting a chimney. There are appallingly brave attempts to plant little gardens, to place tiny fences about the houses, but the floor space cannot work out to a square yard per person – probably less.*

John Arlott in a 1958 advert in The Cricketer for pipe tobacco.

That month, March 1949, the Nationalist Party won an election and began to make an institution out of the apartheid, 'separate development', that had appalled Arlott: '... the conscience cannot throw it off'.

Like others on that and other tours, Arlott gave the rest of his book – called, after all, 'Gone with the Cricketers' – over to the matches and the hospitality from white South African men and women; many from England that he and the players knew. Charles Fortune played on the common background in an article for Denis Compton's Annual in 1956. Fortune did not deny apartheid; '... teams are chosen from the European populations', as he put it. If all you knew of South Africa (and Rhodesia) was what you read in this book with Compton's name on it, there was no 'native' majority, because Fortune never mentioned them. Here was a paradox; the English and South Africans had personal stakes in each other – Compton on his first tour there met the woman who became his second wife; Colin Cowdrey met the woman who became his first wife, at the South Africa tour match at Canterbury in 1951. Yet all they had

A 1950s 'Visit South Africa' advert in an English magazine. White tourists drink wine in the open air, served by blacks.

in common - that made so many in English cricket wriggle to keep the tours going, against the odds and common sense by 1970 - included an innocent or wilful ignorance of apartheid. Let a story from 1991 sum up apartheid. On meeting Sunil Gavaskar, Nelson Mandela recalled he watched South Africa and Australia in 1950, 'from the segregated stand, and of course as always we cheered the visitors'. Apartheid made Mandela and the black majority foreigners in their own land.

A further paradox was that all sides could, and did, talk of morals. At the climax of this story, in May 1970, the cricket correspondent of The Times, John Woodcock, could write in The Cricketer magazine that he was 'convinced of the importance' of 'keeping this summer's tour going ... we have a moral obligation to see the thing through. This is something which can be most easily understood by those who have been to South Africa.' As Woodcock added, isolating South Africa could be the death of its cricket. As so often in any argument, what you left out mattered as much as what you said; what of the majority 'natives' without a vote? Woodcock might have added, as many did in many British newspaper letters pages for years, the wartime and other hospitality given them (like Arlott) in South Africa. Few asked why the South Africans were so generous that it obliged you to give something back.

* * *

Like so much that belonged to the 1960s, the protest against South Africa's sporting and other apartheid dated from at least the late 1950s. In 1959, while thousands were walking from Aldermaston to 'Ban the Bomb', so students in London and elsewhere marched, picketed Rhodesia House and gathered in Trafalgar Square. While a boycott of South Africa by jazz musicians ran from the late 1950s, by contrast sporting ties bloomed, thanks to rising wealth and ever-easier travel. The South African Trampoline Association paid (apart from the air fare) for a team of British men and women trampolinists to tour in 1965; Barry Richards turned 18 in England in 1963 as captain of

Daily Worker front page of March 16, 1959 reports students at Easter in Trafalgar Square, protesting against apartheid. Few others cared.

a South African schools cricket tour. That made sport an early and natural choice for anti-apartheid protest. Besides, the protesters without experience of apartheid – that is, near all of them – could grasp the grotesque pettiness of segregated sports pitches, like easily-photographed 'whites only' park benches, buses, or toilets.

Campaigning began against the South Africans' 1960 cricket tour. As the tourists landed at what was then called London Airport, at Heathrow at Easter, they nearly bumped into the Aldermaston marchers on their way to London; indeed, some placards had anti-Bomb slogans on one side, and anti-apartheid on the other. Senior members of Oxford University such as Sir Isaiah Berlin wrote an open letter that 'we ... deeply regret' Oxford playing the tourists. Such were the unassertive anti-apartheid and other protests then. Another professor who signed was the philosopher Freddie Ayer, who recalled in a memoir in old age that he chaired a committee against racial discrimination in sport: "It was a very weak organisation at that time and I cannot claim that we accomplished anything of practical importance."

Likewise nothing ever came of anything in the press. The 1960 tour manager Dudley Nourse, their 1948 captain,

Advert for Gray-Nicolls bats, in The Cricketer in June 1962. It seemed natural to place the South African Trevor Goddard next to the West Indian Frank Worrell, even though the two could never play international cricket under apartheid.

did face some pointed questions from journalists, such as: would his players be willing to play against the West Indies? ('We would go if we were invited and were allowed to play there.') A campaign through the newspapers to boycott the tour had begun months before. Some sounded apologetic. AE Benton, a councillor chairing Birmingham Labour Party's youth section and a Warwickshire county club member, told the Birmingham Mail in January 1960: "I don't suppose we shall affect attendance very much but it will be a gesture to help the people in South Africa know they have some friends over here." The Warwickshire secretary Leslie Deakins duly sent the newspaper cutting to Lord's, with an editorial from the local Sunday Mercury. You could read the Mercury's reasons for welcoming the South Africans countless times in countless places in the next ten years. The Mercury condemned racial intolerance (how did apartheid keep going? so few wanted it!) - anywhere: whether in Hungary (the morally wrong Communist bloc kept cropping up; why play them at sport, and not South Africa?) or Hitler's Germany (the obvious, no matter how relevant, historical comparison of the century). The South Africans were 'our guests' (the morality behind hospitality again), 'the selected representatives of their country', true, 'but they are in no way responsible for the selection policy' (another moral split, between the man and his nation).

A Londoner, WE Townsend, wrote to Lord's on March 22,

1960 'after the latest outrage', the massacre at Sharpeville: "... it is certainly time that we as a civilised nation washed our hands of these people ... how else are we going to let these murderers and fascists know what we feel? Until the South African people as a whole know what most of the world feel it will go on deluding itself that they are right. They should be ostracised by any possible means." These protesters were reasonable to a fault. Mr Townsend thought it was 'of course too late to upset the coming tour'. JL Burgess of Pateley Bridge told Lord's in April 'I shall demonstrate my disgust at apartheid by staying away from their matches'. The Huddersfield area of the fire brigade union, and the London branch of the national union of tailors and garment workers, were going to boycott. These and all the well-meaning lacked organisation. Some were highly informed; sixth formers at Stonyhurst reminded Lord's in March 1960: "There are brilliant cricketers like Basil D'Oliveira who have yet to be given a chance of playing for their country." D'Oliveira, so central to this story, would only land in England the next month.

Dozens of such letters reached Lord's before the 1960 season. Even at this early stage, the protesters provoked some strong feelings against. Colonel EV Ewbank wrote from Kent in April 1960: "I hope Father Huddleston, Lady Violet Bonham Carter, Labour MPs and others will not be

Protesters pass the Grace Gates at Lord's in May 1960, far outnumbered by the queue of spectators.

so dastardly as to try to interfere with this summer's Test matches by demonstrations or other manifestations of intolerance and pettiness. Should it appear that they are likely to do so and should you require any chuckers out for the Lord's Test matches please let me know. I should love to play some forcing strokes against the posteriors of that bunch of hypocrites." As in 1965 and 1970, you could never assume someone's view (if any) from their background or age. Gerald Palmer, a brigadier in Hampshire, did not agree that the South African team represented South Africa, 'as only whites are allowed to play'. Whatever the letter, MCC secretary Ronnie Aird answered complacently that for years the club had happy relations with the South African Cricket Association (SACA), welcomed teams, and had no reason to treat them differently.

No matter how fobbed off, some were too set in their ways, or not angry enough, to become less mild. In October 1969 Sir Isaiah Berlin was one of five heads of Oxford colleges to call on the university to say that the Springboks' rugby match against Oxford was 'most unfortunate'. As late as May 1970, Sussex University's South Africa committee wrote to the Sussex county club, regretting that it had not disassociated itself from the tour; the club replied by sending the Lord's leaflet 'Why the Seventy Tour'. The fact was that Lord's could reply politely to polite methods – petitions, and anything in writing – forever. In 1970, the Labour MP for West Lewisham, James Dickens, handed MCC secretary Billy Griffith a box holding 12,000 signatures in February; young socialists of Birmingham Labour Party handed Leslie Deakins a petition of 1500 in May. The petitions mattered from the time the secretaries took them from the steps of the pavilion to dumping them in a corner. Other campaigners too, such as the League Against Cruel Sports, would have to learn the lesson of the suffragettes and Irish republicans: that a spectrum of protest, from polite to terroristic, made most sense. It made no difference how fine your arguments were, or even who you knew. Roy Henderson, a vicar in the wealthy Bristol suburb of Stoke Bishop, wrote to the assistant MCC secretary Donald Carr in February 1970 rather than Billy Griffith, 'because we have competed so often on the cricket field'. Henderson understood Lord's had 'difficulties'; he made the smart point that there were 'bound to be opportunities for you to cancel the tour', such as South Africa's recent refusal to let the multi-racial Cavaliers tour. "The more one hears of the difficulties for non-white cricketers in South Africa ... the more one realises that we have an opportunity to do something to bring to an end the present injustices". Carr gave nothing in reply, only picking up Henderson's final point: "... there is no question of anyone refusing to rethink the whole issue ... exercising our minds for many months". These gentle Christians would never force change – such as the Methodist Rev Neville Wright, treasurer of the Stop The Seventy Tour Leeds group, who when told by the Yorkshire Evening Post in May 1970 that the cost to the city of policing the tour would be £100,000 (millions in 21st century money) said: "Good gracious me." Christians had consciences to think of. Also in May 1970, the General Assembly of the Church of Scotland refused to approve of anti-apartheid demonstrations. Few were as radical as the Rev Ian Reid of the Iona Community in Glasgow, proud to hold a banner 'where other banners said things like socialists object to apartheid – on which was written 'the World Council of Churches objects to apartheid' in a peaceful demonstration at Murrayfield', against the rugby Springboks the previous December. "It is not only weirdies who are concerned," Reid added. The politics, and looks, of protesters were enough to put off other clergymen. In Birmingham in November 1969, the Rev PN Hayward, who called himself 'a bitter opponent of South African apartheid over many years', described the demonstrations against the Springboks – to be more exact, the 'catchphrase slogans and mindless chanting' – as 'valueless and misguided'. Once they had shock value, he reckoned; now they would 'needlessly divide the nation'. In other words, older people might feel more disgusted at the demonstrators' bad manners than by apartheid; or as Hayward put it, 'the subjugation of the black man in South Africa is far too serious and tragic a matter to be reduced to the level of young people with time on their hands working off surplus energy'. Anti-apartheid was splitting; even clergy disagreed in public. In Leicester in November 1969 the Rev WA Stewart complained of another vicar who argued for the Springbok tour as 'building bridges' ('surely his love of sport has dulled his judgement').

The most famous cricketing cleric was David Sheppard, the Sussex and England batsman who publicly (and with impeccable manners) refused to play South Africa in 1960. Harry Grimes, a Cambridge solicitor, wrote to Lord's that Sheppard was right: "For the first time in 40 years since I started playing at the age of ten I shall read no report on matches, listen to no broadcasts or television and attend no grounds at which the South African team is playing." His very syntax gave away that Grimes' protest was purely negative; who would notice?! At the other extreme, the Rev PDS Blake, a former Oxford University captain and Sussex batsman, wanted *more* links with South Africa; the UK to send, and invite, non-white teams. In a letter in the Daily Telegraph in November 1969, Peter Blake said South Africa's fine sportsmen represented a twisted society: "Unfortunately it is often difficult to make it clear that by rejecting the antics of these protesters one is not supporting apartheid." Viewing from the 21st century, when few people even know of apartheid, we must not assume that anti-apartheid was as sure to win as the young were sure to replace the old. In the 1960s, older and old-fashioned people were still around – the decade belonged as much to Neville Cardus as Paul McCartney; Larkin as much as Lennon. As the rise of protest in general and anti-apartheid in particular showed, the 1960s in Britain were as much about the death of things – Churchill, decorum in crowds, respect for authority - as beginnings: of football hooliganism, Sunday and one-day cricket, and short skirts.

* * *

In old age John Woodcock remembered, on MCC's 1964-65 tour of South Africa, visiting the black township of Soweto, 'when they were building a cricket ground ... but I am ashamed to say one took apartheid, one accepted it as a fact of life.' Woodcock was at least in company: of household names in business; and emigrants, including the greatest English cricketer of his time, Wally Hammond. On Hammond's death in 1965 Woodcock wrote in The Cricketer of fielding at slip beside Hammond, in his last match. Woodcock recalled it again more than 50 years later in conversation:

At a place called Richmond, near Durban. He hadn't fallen on hard times exactly; to some extent he had; he was in South Africa because when he went to South Africa as England captain, or captain of MCC, in '38-39, he had met his to be wife. In '56-57 he was rather dour, gave nothing away, and didn't fraternise with the party, with the team at all; and yet in '64-65 he was a new man; and it was put down to the fact that he had a very bad road accident and he had a bad knock on the head which can apparently, so they say, change a man's personality.

A 'grand country', Leslie Ames called South Africa. 'Always a pleasure to have the South Africans with us' wrote another Kent and England wicket-keeper, Godfrey Evans, of their 1947 tour of England. By 1960 Doug Insole, a tourist of 1956-57, was admitting in his memoir that 'because of the colour problem South Africa has infrequent visits from touring teams'. Insole's choice of words was curious (who was causing the 'problem' – the whites; or the 'native' majority for refusing to die out?!) and he was avoiding the truth: most cricketing countries did not tour South Africa because they were not white-skinned and not invited (so much for South African hospitality). Tourists could bump into apartheid. David Sheppard in his 1964 memoir told how his Sussex teammate and 1956-57 tourist, Alan Oakman, knocked over an 'African' on a bicycle, while driving. A crowd of whites wanted Oakman's autograph and ignored the injured man. Mike Brearley, one of what proved the last MCC-England tourists of South Africa, in 1964-65, did look around and 'was appalled': "It was much worse than I had imagined and that was what made me feel that I did not want to have anything to do with it again." More common however was Jim Parks, who commented in June 1965 as one of several England players to receive 'extremely well written' letters urging him not to play South Africa. Parks saw it as a 'clumsy way of bringing politics into sport and a way of life that has always been far above such things'. The previous winter he had been 'lucky enough' to tour South Africa: "Without entering into political argument let me say that I have never received such wonderful hospitality and saw no incidents whatsoever." As Parks implied, he could have entered into political argument, but chose not to.

* * *

A few, only a few, were choosing to. In Bristol a branch of the Anti-Apartheid Movement (AAM) began with keen support from some churches and (on paper at least) from some of the city's Labour MPs; not from trade unions and the Co-operative movement. The South African exile Joe Slovo told the branch's first public meeting in September 1964 that the British were doing more than any other country, to protest against apartheid; and, were investing in it. The same was true for cricket. The novelist RF Delderfield was wrong in June 1970 when he despaired of 'the obsession the British (in common with most other Western tribes) have with sport, as though kicking or knocking a ball about a field is likely to solve the least of our social problems'. Men played sport not to solve problems; but to avoid them.

* * *

The crowd booed while the South Africans were fielding in their first tour match of 1965, at Queen's Park, Chesterfield – only because umpire Syd Buller called the Derbyshire fast bowler Harold Rhodes for throwing. Demo organiser Tony Pendry, an AAM member and full-time trade union official, had hoped for help from the Labour Party and miners outside the ground on the first day, Saturday, June 26. Instead, spectators entering the ground passed 'with hardly a glance' at the barely 30 demonstrators. By lunch they and their banners such as 'apartheid is not cricket' had left. The South African tour manager JB Plimsoll could joke: "What bothers us more than the demonstrators is your very cold weather." In truth –a feature of this story is that so

To 1965: 'Boycott plays for Yorkshire'

Advert for Rothmans King Size cigarettes, from a brochure sponsored by Rothmans for the 1965 South African tour. The advertising copy linked Durban, Auckland, Sydney and London – all white cricket-playing nations.

An advert in the Yorkshire Post in June 1965 for Barclays DCO (Dominion, Colonial and Overseas) had a Caribbean boy supposedly addressing former West Indies captain Sir Frank Worrell. What went unsaid was that the bank also invested in southern Africa – where the boy would have had less cause to smile.

many in authority said one thing in public and another in private - Plimsoll was more nervous than that. On the Sunday the tourists visited nearby Chatsworth, closed to the public 'in case of demonstrators'. Usually the tourists would watch a Sunday afternoon match on the estate. While Derbyshire did play a Duke of Devonshire eleven in aid of Laurie Johnson's benefit, the South Africans did not attend – not because Johnson was West Indian, but 'because of fear of demonstrators'. The West Indian Learie Constantine, contracted to write a newspaper column for that summer's Tests, told a press conference organised by the AAM that he would not watch any South Africa match. What Alex Bannister of the Daily Mail called 'earnest looking people' had already carried anti-apartheid posters outside the South Africans' London hotel. A Labour Party MP, David Ennals, urged people to stay away from the matches, only to draw bile from the Mail columnist Bernard Levin (defining a cricketer as 'very nearly as stupid as a dog'). The tourists went next to Bramall Lane, Sheffield, that had readied stewards and a few more police than usual for demonstrations: '... trouble that never came.'

What protests the South Africans faced ('of a minor character', Wisden sniffed the year after) came mainly on Saturdays, as at Bristol on July 10. Gloucestershire had hoped for a crowd of 5000; only 3000 came, blamed on the overcast sky. Even if the threat of a demo (front page news for the Bristol Evening Post beforehand) had put some people off, how could you tell? The letters to the press, the standing with banners at gates (only done to make the organisers feel virtuous, sneered Levin) were not working. Worse; they became a laughing stock. After the Chesterfield match, the diary column of the Yorkshire Post recalled one banner had said 'Boycott South Africa'. "Nay, lad," said one of some miners going into the ground. "Tha's got it wrong. He plays for Yorkshire."

* * *

Cricketers like Jim Parks had the confidence of men with their culture on their side. In June 1965 he even lectured the

Cover of South African 1965 tour souvenir programme.

protesters: "Know exactly what you are talking about before you condemn. This means visiting a country, not listening to others or reading what they say." By that logic, did you have to visit Russia or Germany in the 1930s to oppose Stalin or Hitler? Parks did not believe in bringing politics into cricket, 'and I trust that the English cricket public is sane enough to have the same principle'. In any case, Parks suggested, the South African players did not necessarily believe in apartheid: "I know for a fact that they would dearly love to be able to play against West Indies, India and Pakistan." Here for once the apologists for apartheid had facts on their side. At the end of the 1964 season, Parks captained a Hastings Festival eleven against the Australians; including Eddie Barlow, the South African all-rounder, and Basil D'Oliveira, 'a coloured cricketer now playing for Worcestershire who hails from Cape Town'. "So why can't we do all in our power to welcome these cricketers?" Parks asked, showing again what a hold the giving and taking of hospitality had on such men; misused, as so much else was, by apartheid. An answer came days later in the same newspaper that ran Parks' column, the Sheffield Star, from MJ Ball of Bolsover, one of the Saturday demonstrators at Chesterfield. He called Parks naïve and had a question of his own: why did D'Oliveira come to England? D'Oliveira's gifts, character, and good fortune would make the world face that question in 1968. Meanwhile, Sheppard stuck to the cause. Asked for his hopes for the 1970s in the February 1970 issue of The Cricketer, he hoped that cricketers would make plain where they stood, on racialism in cricket ('the most important issue it has ever faced'). In other words, it was one thing to boycott South Africa (in 1960, Sheppard had only turned down the Duke of Norfolk's team for a day; a professional might have to risk his career); it was another to go public and upset others in the small world of cricket. Sheppard, by 1970 a bishop, stuck to his methods too: "The cause ... can and should be promoted by reason not violence." Peter Hain in his 1971 book of the affair, Don't Play with Apartheid, was right to point out that these tactics, 'of polite and reasonable persuasion', 'simply had not worked'. The men of Lord's, who picked the likes of Parks who were so glad to tour, would go on doing what they wanted, the same as British governments of whatever political colour went on making more and larger atomic bombs, while the Campaign for Nuclear Disarmament made fine moral arguments, respectfully printed in newspapers, until CND withered. By December 1969, in the thick of the demos against the rugby Springboks, the Sheffield Morning Telegraph was among those to see the change, 'between the lawful, however forceful, and the knowingly unlawful'. If the new tactic succeeded, 'it will not be a measure of changed hearts but merely the old assertion that might is right,' the newspaper warned.

While Hain and the new breed of protester would face plenty of such opposition, even hatred, so did Sheppard; except that English cricket, with its mania for keeping appearances, hid it better. One sign is in the records of the Nottinghamshire county club committee meeting of December 1968. When discussing who to invite to their annual dinner to speak, the former captain Reg Simpson seconded, 'and it was agreed that Mr Sheppard should not be invited'. Suggested instead were the more conservative broadcaster Brian Johnston; and Leslie Deakins of Warwickshire, who attended.

* * *

The Cricketer hailed the 1965 season 'as the one in which England lost one of the best post-war Test series to South Africa'. English cricket was managing to ignore the politics behind South Africa. Just as South African mines and businesses were rewarding British capital, so the attractive South African cricketers ('clearly worth a full tour', commented The Cricketer, after South Africa had shared the 1965 summer with New Zealand) thrived from English investment. South Africa's young players at the 'major [fee-paying] schools and universities' were coached by English players in their winter; private tours gave the likes of Colin Bland and the Pollock brothers Peter and Graeme 'experience of English conditions'. John Woodcock noted 'high jinks' after the South Africans won the Test at Nottingham; they 'ceremoniously consecrated' the pitch 'in cold South African beer'. Later generations of winners would do worse. That generation of South Africans had no way of knowing they would never return.

Left to right during the 1965 Test series: batsman Eddie Barlow, Ken Barrington, MJK Smith at short leg, Colin Cowdrey at slip and keeping wicket Jim Parks.

Chapter Two

The sides

> *... we should attempt from the start to place the event in which the crowd participates in its proper historical context; for, without this, how can we hope to get beyond the stereotypes and probe into the crowd's outlook, objects and behaviour?*
>
> George Rude, The Crowd in History, 1964

You could tell this as the story of Peter Hain, the youth suddenly famous for leading a cause, like Joan of Arc, only with a happier ending. Whether to belittle him, or as a compliment to his skill in making his case, some claimed the media made Hain. As early as November 1969 PT Rippon, the honorary secretary of the Rugby Football Union, commented: 'It is my private opinion that if only the Press would lay off, the whole thing would perish from inanition.' Surprisingly, Hain seemed to agree. In his 1971 book, he said he had not bargained on the 'fantastic interest'. He recalled being only a 'spokesman' when Stop The Seventy Tour (STST) launched in September 1969; the next day's newspapers called him chairman (of the press confernce). 'Elected by the press', Hain described himself. Perhaps the reporters were better judges of who was in charge of STST than the founders.

He gave the press, radio and television alike what they wanted; written or spoken words easy to quote and in good time, and a well turned-out image. Ian Hamilton in the London Illustrated News of May 9, 1970 predicted cynically that 'the trendy demo will win ... because of the informal but effective working arrangements between 'militants' and those TV executives for whom civil disturbance is, short of actual warfare, the most precious raw material'. Tellingly, Hain was giving an interview in a BBC studio when news of the cancellation came through.

In the early days of the Springboks rugby tour, in November 1969, Peter Spence, President of Leicester University Union, said: 'If we stop this tour and the cricket tour in the summer, South Africa will no longer be able to kid themselves that they are tolerated in the world.' A demo, of whatever size, done well or not, sent a message; if the media picked it up. It only took a few banners to make a newspaper photo or to fill a TV screen; on Tuesday, May 19, the day that cricket's authorities confirmed the tour for the last time, the Daily Telegraph for one reported 'only a handful' of demonstrators were outside Lord's. Hain's family in 1969 briefly interrupted a Springbok training session near their Putney home, which brought 'massive press and television coverage', Hain recalled. Once STST had won, the Daily Telegraph's future editor Bill Deedes told its readers that the protest had more publicity than it deserved (it 'might otherwise have languished through lack of attention'). Paradoxically the Telegraph, and other newspapers, reported day after day ('at times what Fleet Street calls 'blanket coverage'', Deedes admitted) and thus made credible what they hated politically. The reason: journalists relished conflict. 'A clash seems inevitable today between police and anti-apartheid demonstrators,' said a front page report in The Scotsman before the Springboks played in Aberdeen in December 1969. By comparison a morally impeccable letter to the press signed by 55 Church of Scotland ministers and elders in November 1969 was naively wrong in what it thought made the news: ' ... perhaps the most effective protest is simply to stay away from the match,' it claimed. 'Empty spaces in stand and terracing speak as pointedly as rude placards and crude harassment.' In a front page story in the Aberdeen Press & Journal, about the first Springbok match at Twickenham on November 5, the reporter sounded disappointed: 'Not since Guy Fawkes was caught sitting on a keg of gunpowder has there been a damp squib as the much vaunted anti-apartheid demonstration ...' The more violent and large the demo, the 'better' (in terms of news) the story, just as Parliament blown up would have made an even better story in 1605 than caught conspirators.

Editorials approved some sorts of protest and not others. In December 1969 the Glasgow Herald condemned the 'arrogant minority' of 'self-righteous rowdies', 'as much the enemy of peaceful protesters as they are enemies of the public at large'. The Glasgow Evening Times likewise had no time for 'mindless protest' and praised the torchlight march before the Springboks played at Murrayfield as 'much more dignified and useful ... Unfortunately these do not receive as much television coverage as mindless exhibitionism on the field'. As that suggested, newspapers looked down on their new rival, television. It took a newspaper to print an intriguing insight into TV. On the eve of an anti-Vietnam demo in London in November 1968, The Observer quoted a London Weekend Television spokesman that LWT had cameras at 'strategic spots' to see the most 'action':

'If things are quiet, we'll switch to the studio where a panel of people representing all shades of opinion will discuss the events they have seen. When something happens on the march again we'll switch back to it. It will be like a sports report.'

While controversy sold newspapers the same as it attracted viewers, the press was mainly conservative, and backed Conservatives. On the eve of cancellation the Glasgow Herald reckoned that would 'indirectly smooth Mr Wilson's electoral progress', days after Labour Prime Minister Harold Wilson had called a general election. This explains why the media reported so much against cricket's authorities, while giving them a good press. Wilf Wooller, the easily-upset Glamorgan club secretary, told a committee in March 1968 that their county was 'very well served by the press and the BBC'. Cricket was starting to play the protesters at their own game. A February 1970 memo by the former England batsman turned public relations consultant Raman Subba Row and MCC assistant secretary Jack Bailey told Lord's of the first mailings of the official point of view 'to as many people as possibly involved in the game'; and petitions and letters to the press. They admitted: 'The nature of BBC coverage continues to cause the gravest concern and it might be considered that the time has been reached for a complaint to be lodged at the highest level. Mr Hogg' – Quintin Hogg, a Tory home affairs spokesman in the House of Commons, who handily was the local Marylebone MP – 'can advise on that point.' Besides such work in private, Subba Row had made a public case for better public relations, for example in an article in The Cricketer's 1967 spring annual. Subba Row set out the basics of PR ('to build up a good situation and where possible to play down a bad one') as an essential 'modern business technique', like advertising, and made a rather blatant offer to be English cricket's PR specialist. Others saw the need for, as Michael Melford put it in the Sunday Telegraph in April 1969, 'an expert hand in presenting the MCC's case, not least on television', while recalling that in 1967 the counties had voted against MCC's idea to appoint a professional public relations officer. Cricket's relations with the press were usually bigoted and unfriendly. Soon after Tony Greig's debut 156 for Sussex at Hove on May 3, 1967, Pat Marshall of the Daily Express told the off the field story to The Cricketer. As Marshall and two other journalists interviewed Greig, a Sussex committee man told Marshall to 'break it up'. Later the Sussex secretary Colonel Pat Williams – obviously under orders from his committee, or a committee member, Marshall shrewdly guessed – went into the press box and asked to see any copy written about Greig. Marshall told Williams it wasn't allowed (and, any journalist could have added, was insulting to ask). 'Good chap that he is, he accepted our word that Greig had not been asked any tricky questions about apartheid! Though what this vexed political issue had to do with a youngster scoring a glorious maiden century in county cricket is beyond me.' The episode showed how touchy cricket already was about apartheid and how little it trusted journalists who were giving daily free publicity. Sussex also told off committee men who spoke to the press, even if it sounded good for cricket. In the Brighton Evening Argus of January 1, 1970, Geoff Cornford, chairman of the Sussex membership and publicity sub-committee, said he had spoken to one of the four (secret) men on a Test and County Cricket Board (TCCB) sub-committee preparing for the tour. 'Amazed' at the detail, Cornford believed the tour would not have 'very much bother'. On January 5 Cornford had to apologise to another Sussex committee that he had been 'grossly misquoted'.

County committees wanted to keep the power that came with control of their affairs; for example at a Sussex committee meeting in May 1970 about contracts, the chairman EE Harrison deplored 'leakage of information' to the press and radio after the previous meeting. Cricket's phobia against telling others its business hobbled its response to the STST, or any, challenge. 'No other Iron Curtain is more difficult to tear down or pull apart than that which Yorkshire county cricket officials always put up whenever controversy concerns their domestic affairs,' complained Dick Williamson in the Sheffield Green Un in September 1968. He was not joking. John Thicknesse at Lord's in Decmber 1969 for a TCCB meeting complained in the Evening Standard that Jack Bailey - the man at Lord's with the title of press secretary - repeated 'the familiar words': 'We will issue a statement this evening.' Lord's was ignoring one rule of PR; giving journalists things in good time (despite its title, the Evening Standard had afternoon deadlines).

Gubby Allen.

TCCB members refused to comment to journalists on their way in and out of meetings. To 'put the least pressure on you all', the chairman of the May 18 emergency meeting of the Cricket Council asked members for it to be 'in as great secrecy as possible'. Leading officials such as MCC treasurer Gubby Allen worked privately, through men with influence. In December 1969 Allen told another emergency meeting that he had contacted Ian Macleod, the senior Conservative politician, and was seeking to meet Quintin Hogg for advice on police protection of grounds,

Daily Sketch cartoon of the 1960s, cleverly setting out how conservatives in the House of Lords, and at Lord's the centre of power of cricket, were the same.

costs, and possibly raising cricket's point of view in the House of Commons. Cricket lost journalists' goodwill by passing up chances to offer even good news. In mid-May, Colonel Charles Newman, chairman of the fund for the tour, refused to say how much money it had raised; Thicknesse rightly called it a 'mistake', because after all the money had come from the public. Counties copied this tyranny at the top. HT Milnes attended a TCCB meeting in December as Nottinghamshire club chairman. He told his committee that 'he did not propose to refer' to the tour at the club's annual meeting, 'unless a question was put, in which case he would reply as per his prepared statement which with slight amendments the committee approved'.

In fairness, government also worked this way. In February 1970 the Ministry of Defence and Foreign Office fretted about a dinner in a London hotel to mark 50 years of the South African Air Force. Foreign Secretary Michael Stewart wrote that the FO did not object to a senior airman attending, besides the South African armed forces attaché and British aircraft makers: 'We trust that you will attempt as far as possible to avoid publicity ...' More to the point of this story, in December 1969 a South African journalist wanted to put questions to the FO about the rugby tour. JA

Pugh of the FO's central and southern African department admitted it would not be helpful to answer some of the questions frankly: 'There is quite enough attention focused on Anglo-South African relations as it is.'

* * *

'Come along, children,' said Peter Yarranton, the official rugby union announcer at Twickenham, over the loudspeaker at a Springbok match in November 1969. While condescending, he had a point about the demonstrators. In a letter in the Bristol Evening Post in January 1970, Roberta Cook, press officer of the Bristol Federation of Young Conservatives, deplored 'the action of those people of our generation who seek to foist their views on to others'. In 1960, while to be anti-apartheid was an acquired taste, the chief constable of Birmingham – and Warwickshire cricket club committee member – EJ Dodd felt demonstrations most likely were by 'intellectuals'.

Who were the demonstrators? As so often, many comments said more about those who said it. Pithiest but least credible was the leader of the Nationalist Party in the Transvaal, Ben Schoeman, during the South African election of April 1970: 'Long-haired scum and fugitives from South Africa under Communist leadership.' Some in Britain, and Ireland, did take up those insults. 'Hoodlums and blackguards' the Limerick Leader called them. 'Started by the Communist Party of South Africa,' an Axbridge man said in a letter to the Bristol Evening Post. 'Revolutionary minded fanatics', said conservative historian and Illustrated London News columnist Sir Arthur Bryant, after cancellation. 'Louts' said Telegraph man Michael Melford. 'A horde of violent and non-violent agitators', according to a Daily Telegraph editorial, on May 20, in the week of the affair's crisis. Many abused those protesting for their looks, whether because it was an easy shot, or some felt genuinely offended. Or, it was a fact: a police witness statement in January 1970 described an 18 and 20-year-old student, arrested for sticking anti-tour posters to Lord's gates at night, as 'untrimmed'. The same month, angered by the weed-killer on the outfield of the County Ground, Bristol, Gloucestershire county chairman Mike Jarrett called the unknown vandals 'long-haired spotty youths'. ER Eriksen, team manager of Wilfred Isaacs' private tour by promising South African cricketers in summer 1969, at least saw his demonstrators, who mostly 'wore long unkempt hair and were generally scruffy'. In looks, anti-apartheid demonstrators were like any other 'filthy long-haired dropouts', that the Police Federation complained about at their annual conference in May 1970. Some comments in the papers were wittier. An ex-serviceman in Sutton Coldfield mocked 'boys' for 'whiskers which a decent sea breeze would blow away'; a Manchester man who was one of George VI's bodyguards on the king's tour of South Africa sniffed at 'soapless wonders'. Robin Prescott, secretary of the Rugby Football Union, was briefest: 'twits'.

It was enough to give all students a bad name. Michael Denny was a 25-year-old fined for briefly hijacking the Springboks' coach outside their London hotel in December 1969. The Sunday Telegraph diarist Albany told the story of how Denny told a sergeant behind a police station desk that he had a pass degree from Oxford. The sarge replied: 'That is the sort of degree you pick up with two tops from a cornflakes packet.' That remark, and the newspaper's glee in repeating it, may have been mere envy of students with government grants, and the young in general. Yet it never does to generalise. After a pensioner complained in the Oxford Times in November 1969 of students wasting tax-payers' money, another reader objected to paying tax towards universities that played apartheid teams. Students did not think alike. The Oxford Union vote was split 391-400 on a motion for disrupting the South Africa tour, amid allegations of rigging; less famously at a debating society meeting at Oxford College of Technology, a motion calling for a ban on Russian and South African teams in international sport lost 62-42. As always, most students liked a quiet life and did not march. Even after 92 were arrested and 100 more detained after the Springboks match in Manchester in November 1969, Lancashire chief constable William Palfrey called most of the demonstrators 'nice young people'. Few took the trouble as he did to separate them from 'a minority of anarchists who were out to cause trouble'. One of the tragedies of this story is that the two sides – like those fighting the two world wars - so seldom met each other. After the Springboks-Ireland match at Lansdowne Road, Dublin, on Saturday, January 10, as spectators and protest marchers alike walked back to the city, a man wearing a 'South West Africa 1965' blazer debated with, then eagerly shook the hand of, an Indian demonstrator, and said 'I am glad to shake your hand, sir'. As other marchers became angry, police had to usher the South African away.

As in that case, it's surprisingly hard to name and trace who the demonstrators were. A few made the official record. Edward Bailey went to a Leicester police station to arrange the route for a march before the Springboks' match at Welford Road in the city in November 1969. He had already been one of 'ten to 20' Leicester students protesting on the terraces at Twickenham. At Swansea, he had trespassed on the pitch – according to Bailey, to escape violent stewards and vigilantes as much as to 'stop the tour'. Bailey sounded like a sixties student stereotype: a bearded 19-year-old from Surrey studying sociology, five feet nine, ginger collar-length hair, and wearing a brown corduroy wind-cheater, blue jeans and brown suede lace-up boots. We have fewer details but a larger sample of those arrested at the second Springboks match at Twickenham, on Saturday, November 22. Some 178 gave their particulars and another 13 refused. Although the most aggressive protesters may have chosen to be nearest to police, they were mainly young men, including Hain; only three were women and only seven aged over 30. The mode (most occurring) age was 20, and the average 21.1. For addresses, several gave universities or Oxbridge colleges. Frank Williamson, an inspector of constabulary, after the Springbok match at Swansea, likewise reported that most of the 62 arrested were aged 18 to 28, except for a 41-year-old welder. Besides students or unemployed, other occupations given were electrician; PR officer; and steelworker. They came mainly from Wales.

Likewise of the 26 in court after the Murrayfield match in December 1969, several that gave their age and occupation were students aged 17 to 20 from lowland Scotland or northern England, besides an electrician and a silversmith. Another, smaller, sample – of ten injured at Leicester – included three Leicester students, and others from the Midlands, another sign that people usually demonstrated in their own region. Already by the Leicester demo, small groups (such as one of 'about 20 Maoists from Nottingham') were part of a larger small world, with medical attendant ('a veteran of Grosvenor Square') and comforting 'rights of arrest' leaflets from the National Council for Civil Liberties ('you shall not be alone'). This was no mob – but it could turn into one, as when Michael Stewart was shouted down at the Oxford Union and had to flee in May 1970. An Oxford Times editorial condemned 'rabble tactics'.

'The fact that anybody says something in a loud voice does not influence me at all,' Labour minister of agriculture Cledwyn Hughes told the press in an Exeter hotel in January 1970: 'It is the still small voice of reason which influences me.' That was humbug. He left the place by back stairs because farmers were waiting for him at the front door, having heckled his hour's speech. More revealing still was Harold Wilson's response to five anti-American demonstrators as and his wife left a Hampstead church's jubilee service in May 1970: 'You send me a letter, I will write to you and tell you about it.' Politicians, like Lord's, wanted politics on their terms: polite; impersonal; at a distance. In a victory speech, Hain said: 'We have intimidated no cricketers. We have threatened no violence – only direct militant non-violent action. Violence has played no part in it.' It was an odd non-violent movement that had to deny violence so much. Amos Cresswell, a Methodist minister in Cheadle Hulme, agonised at length in the Manchester Evening News in November 1969 about whether to take an invitation to march against the Springboks. He chose not to, hating more than apartheid 'anything which disrupts the relationship of one man with another'. He was frank enough to admit the political fact that Cledwyn Hughes did not: '...

he who makes the most noise is listened to. Yet he may not be right.' As a Conservative MP, Bill Deedes regretted that 'direct action', 'allied to liberal opinion' was now common. 'Direct action' was all the rage; Bristol Polytechnic students voted for it in February 1970, against the 'terrible food' in their canteen. What did 'direct action' mean? As with many things, whatever you made of it. Hain in his 1971 book defined it as 'the actual disruption of matches, rather than the more traditional picketing or demonstrating outside', though STST did plenty of pickets, even when given the choice. Direct action could sound military and daring. According to Special Branch in November 1969, LSE students were planning three 'commando groups', two to enter Twickenham and one to stay outside. By April 1970, Special Branch was hearing that 'since many of their proposed actions for disrupting the [cricket] tour verge on the criminal, they [STST leaders] are becoming increasingly anxious as to how they can contain and control their more militant supporters'. Hooligan acts, too 'direct', might lose moderate supporters and the public generally, so STST feared. Some said so in public. Ian Thomson, secretary of the sports union at Stirling University, during the Springboks' Scottish matches rejected 'violent demonstration' and was 'fed up with the small minority' behaving irresponsibly, taking the public away from the main issue.

Society is always weighing what is lawful, or at least acceptable, and not. A Leicester Mercury editorial in November 1969 disagreed with a reader's letter of complaint that courts fined Leicester City Football Club hooligans less than the city's Springbok demonstrators: 'soccer louts do it for kicks' and students 'for conscience', and some students 'weren't too particular about how they did it, either', the newspaper said. Others in the 1960s weren't too particular. Police protected the Beatles, leaving Heathrow in June 1965, from the 'customary mass hysteria'; some disappointed girls staged a 'sit-down protest' in the Fleet Street offices of the Daily Express. Counter-demonstrators could behave worse than the original demonstrators, as when Welsh students protested in March 1969 outside the Aberystwyth

University hostel that Prince Charles was due to stay in. British patriots poured buckets of water over them from the roof and sang God Save the Queen.

As that suggested, a demo ran the risk of coming second if others showed themselves. Better, then, to warn of a spectrum of threats, keep the more extreme in hand, and present yourself as moderate. Hain was telling the press in November 1969 'our plan is for passive protests and sit-downs, but when these fail, there are many who will call for more violent methods'. Here the enemies of STST saw a weakness. In an editorial of December 2, The Times asked if lawful demonstrators were 'providing cover for anarchists'. Maybe some were. In late January 1970 at a Western Federation of Young Liberals (no less) meeting in Bath, national executive member Gordon Lishman backed the recent vandalism of ten county cricket grounds and said Young Liberals might dig a pitch up. While such outright criminal damage seldom happened, the Springboks had already been 'in a state of siege' in their hotel in Dublin, one reviewer of the tour recalled, facing 20 bomb scares, and taunts from loudspeakers until 3am of the day of their game against Ireland. Australian protesters did much the same against touring Springboks in the Australian winter of 1971. 'Direct action' was not new. The May 1968 'revolution' in Paris had already made it famous. In December 1938, men of the National Unemployed Workers' Movement lay around traffic lights on Oxford Street. It only took a few people – if your cause had thousands, you marched. 'Direct action' in that sense was a sign of weakness.

Everyone was doing it. Peregrine Worsthorne in the Sunday Telegraph listed, besides the Springbok demos, strikers, students occupying university buildings, Welsh and Scottish nationalists, 'even farmers and teachers'. The Tory Worsthorne saw disrespect for the law. You could put it another way; people with grievances, for or against something, progressives or conservatives, wanted to get their own way. Keeping to the rules did not pay; and was less fun. Hence the 'guerrilla action' of slow farm tractors stopping traffic around Newton Abbot in December 1969;

sheep (on their way to slaughter) and a mock coffin at Exeter against Cledwyn Hughes; thousands of chanting farmers blocking Whitehall in February 1970; and jeering at Jim Callaghan on a visit to Cardigan. At Aberystwyth, demonstrators chanted at Callaghan in Welsh. 'No popery,' shouted demonstrators angry that Liverpool's Anglican Cathedral let in Roman Catholics in January 1970 for a unity service. A cry of 'Lord deliver us from popery' stopped a guest from the Greek Orthodox Church addressing the General Assembly of the Church of Scotland in May 1970, before three arrests. Younger teachers and college lecturers, as a rule, struck and marched; older ones would not. Before Northern Ireland fell into near-civil war, the civil rights movement marched and picketed. After Edinburgh Town Council voted in November 1969 to add fluoride to water, a dental student leapt on the stage at an anti meeting; stewards pulled him off. All these campaigns, some more selfish, important and popular than others, had to ask: did the ends justify the means? The former president of the Oxford Union, the philosopher Bryan Magee, said after Michael Stewart was shouted down that many agreed with anti-apartheid protesters' aims, 'but are repelled by their methods'. Earlier, after the vandalism of cricket grounds of January 1970, the Liberal MP John Pardoe said the 'attacks ... have gone too far'. A December 1969 letter writer to the Glasgow Herald favouring protest said the best was 'non-violent and hardest hitting'; sport provided 'a unique opportunity'. Such muddled and opportunistic anti-apartheid thinking allowed George Gale in The Spectator in February 1970 to denounce 'demo-mobsters'. Glamorgan's West Indian fast bowler Tony Cordle appealed to coloured people to stay away from the demo against the Springboks at Newport,

'because they aren't doing any good. People in this country do not appreciate the South African problem. In Britain we have plenty of people not wanting coloured enterprises. Is apartheid any worse than this? Everybody pretends to be rooting for the black man but they are using sport as a lever.'

Like the metaphor in the Gospels of looking for the speck of sawdust in your brother's eye, instead of the plank in your own, Britain pointed at faults abroad yet took years to face Cordle's challenge to its own racial injustices; if it ever did. Tories had their own reasons for slighting demonstrators. Eldon Griffiths – made minister for sport after the Conservatives won the June 1970 election – was in South Africa in November 1969 when he began an article for the Sunday Telegraph sarcastically: 'So this time it's South Africa. With Ban the Bomb out of fashion and Vietnam off the front pages, I suppose it was inevitable that our demo enthusiasts would turn their attention to the Springboks ...' Some of the demonstrators, at least, felt strongly. Ron Press, the science lecturer and anti-apartheid organiser in Bristol – one of so many South African exiles – typed in a newsletter to a local Labour Party: 'It's about time people got angry.' All the argument about demos – was the 'anarchist element' negligible as one letter-writer to the Glasgow Herald claimed? – showed that violence in public was a taboo in Britain, despite (or perhaps because of) two recent world wars. When shouts of 'Remember Biafra' interrupted the bugling of the Last Post at the Cenotaph on Remembrance Sunday in 1969, the most telling detail was not that police hustled the offenders away, but that police clamped their hands over the protesters' mouths, to protect the annual silence for the dead.

* * *

Someone could do violence, then, to more than your body; to your hearing, even your sense of smell. A game of cricket was as easily broken as silence. In January 1970 as the Springboks drew with Ireland in Dublin, the Irish Times noted someone made a loud noise, and spoiled 'the reverent hush that traditionally precedes the taking of a penalty', angering some in the crowd. When Lord's met its South African equivalents, president Jack Cheetham and vice-president Arthur Coy, in November 1969, the English administrator CGA Paris called cricket 'vulnerable'. That went for the physical surrounds, besides the actual play when, to state the obvious, as Bill Bowes did in a column in his Leeds newspaper in May 1970, 'one ball can completely change the state of the game'. English cricket had seen the threat coming. In Playfair Cricket Monthly in April 1968, Denzil Batchelor could write a long article on 'A Crisis in Cricket' without mention of South Africa; the occasion was bottle-throwing crowds and tear gas stopping play during the second Test on England's tour of the West Indies. Other sporting events, pop concerts and even Miss World contests were as insecure. Young Liberals handed out anti-apartheid leaflets outside the Albert Hall in November 1969, because Miss South Africa was there; either they or 'militant feminists' also protesting 'phoned anonymous threats and threw smoke bombs. Billy Griffith, in an interview on his retirement by David Frith in 1974, claimed to have been bothered about 'crowd control' as early as the Australian summer of 1962-3, when some spectators ran onto the field at Sydney. Griffith could understand the enthusiasm, 'but often there is an element of exhibitionism, and there is the added danger of damage to the pitch. We want the people here at Lord's to stay on the grass and enjoy the game.' As Griffith did add, by 1974 it took police ejecting invaders of the pitch, to enforce the rule. An unspoken, and taken for granted, respect for the field of play - unless a voice over a loudspeaker gave you permission to promenade at tea-time - no longer worked,

Punch cartoon from July 1939. The joke was that people commonly tried to watch cricket that way, without paying, more often by standing on a bicycle; it also showed weak perimeter security.

even though nearly all still obeyed. Special Branch as early as November 1969 was naming groups keen to confront authority and support any demo at Twickenham, such as the Working People's Party of England ('a small militant organisation oriented towards Maoism with a predominantly coloured membership'). Small in mass, they might still make a large force. The novelist RF Delderfield said why it mattered in November 1969:

... what the apologist doesn't tell you is that it doesn't need more than a small percentage of louts in one assembly be it protest march, football crowd or down town Saturday night larkers to convert that assembly into a maelstrom mostly composed of people trying to keep clear of it.

Ronnie Delderfield was writing about 'the blue screen between you and anarchy'; which brings us to the police.

* * *

Leicester chief constable John Taylor was proud to be a British bobby after the Springboks' match at Leicester. 'We permitted a demonstration and at the same time ensured that people could enjoy a rugby match,' he said. His assistant John Webster had said much the same more fully in an operational order beforehand. Police were also there to 'maintain order', and 'safeguard players and officials'. Significantly, the demo and march through the city centre had to be 'peaceful', Webster had written. The ranks that had to do the actual work were more cynical. The Police Federation magazine in October 1969 asked 'Why waste words on weirdies', hailing the ejection of squatters from a building on London's Piccadilly. The anonymous article laid into 'hippies' as workshy drug-takers, with bad hygiene and good public relations, 'as developed by all protest groups genuine and spurious over recent years'. Also condemned were newspapers for hypocritically complaining of hippies on the editorial page and 'spreading these same sickening antics across the front page'. Right wing police were claiming to stand with 'the vast majority of the British people', against the weird and their media friends. That slant did not sit well with the Edinburgh deputy chief constable RMM Campbell's statement on the eve of the Springboks' match at Murrayfield: 'The police will act strictly as the guardians of law and order in all their dealings with the supporters of rugby and with demonstrators alike.' According to those in charge, police knew best. Before the Springboks' match at Leicester, the local Mercury reported that police would 'shepherd' the march. That word, that the newspaper presumably took from the police, implied that the marchers were sheep. By December 1969 police had a routine for the part of a town hosting the Springboks. At St Thomas in Exeter, police sent thousands of letters to shops and residents, about roads closed and cars banned on the day around the rugby ground. The local Express & Echo called it 'one of the biggest public relations operations ever mounted by the police'. The locals the newspaper quoted sided with police rather than 'hooligans who have made such tight security plans necessary'. Some police forces, whether with a different aim in mind or simply less competent, worked differently. Hain in his 1971 book complained that at Swansea in November 1969 police had used 'apartheid methods', that is, violence, 'to protect an apartheid team'.

Apart from showing good manners, demo leaders shared their plans to stay lawful. Ron Press wrote to police before collecting signatures outside Gloucestershire cricket ground in June 1969 for a petition. While a Special Branch report in November 1969 described Hain and other organisers as 'uncooperative', Hain did approach police. A rare and touching insight into the young man is his typed letter (and typed address on envelope, with 5d stamp) asking police for permission for a rally at Twickenham on December 20; which he could not attend because of a Young Liberals conference in Leeds. Hain first mis-typed the letter o for the zero in 20, then over-typed the zero correctly; evidently not a perfect typist, and careful with typing paper, he preferred the slight error to starting on a clean sheet. Police and protesters each wanted to learn about the other; an STST committee 'action sheet' of January 1970 stressed that the movement was gaining experience of police 'and their tactics'. When police stood at turnstiles to check tickets before the Springbok match at Bristol, and elsewhere, they faced the profound problem of modern British policing. The operational order drawn up two weeks before said 'great discretion must be exercised', by the bobby, that is. The chiefs, for all their fine principles, had to rely on constables to judge thousands of people, in an ever more anonymous and well-travelled world. Police by asking to see tickets could offend 'obvious rugby supporter types' if police were too suspicious; just as police not suspicious enough could let in known demonstrators with tickets; as the operational order told officers to. Police had to confiscate poles and banners, and get the carriers to sign a receipt; and all this in time for kick-off ('there should be no undue delay'). As the orders admitted, plans could only work 'so far as practicable'. Likewise in October 1969, police left Oxford University to decide against hosting the Springboks, after local police described the Iffley Road ground as 'vulnerable'. Police would only do what was 'reasonable or possible' against public disorder. What was 'reasonable', police kept to themselves; they too wanted to keep control of their business. That included concealing when things went out of control, as at the Swansea match in November 1969 or indeed Hillsborough in 1989. At root, like any institution the police looked after their own interest; what police regarded as 'order' was not the demonstrators'. On the terracing at Murrayfield, a reporter saw 'about ten SRU [Scottish Rugby Union] stewards wearing red armbands stood shoulder to shoulder with the solid line of policemen facing the crowd'. Actions spoke louder than words.

* * *

It may appear obvious who were the men of authority in cricket; their names were in Wisden each year; 'men of integrity', as Gordon Ross, editor of Playfair Cricket Monthly, wrote in the November 1968 issue of the magazine, on the Basil D'Oliveira 'affair'. Few in cricket were free enough of conflicts of interest – or sure enough of their standing – to ask too many questions of authority. Rex Alston in that issue of Playfair for example denied that 'MCC' (like Lord's,

'Men of integrity': MCC committee meeting at Lord's, September 24, 1968, on the South Africa tour. Right: Brian Sellers and Colin Cowdrey. Nearest the corner, Donald Carr.

a shorthand term for the few men in charge) were 'bumbling amateurs'. Alston however was an MCC member 'for many years'. He did describe the MCC committee as 'a self-serving oligarchy ... the pool from which new committee members are chosen is extremely small and no one outside the ranks of former first-class captains and ex-amateurs has much chance of being nominated'. That left out most of the 14,000 members; many, as Alston said, eminent, and cricket-loving, 'who would bring a fresh approach'. An anonymous typed letter to Arthur Gilligan – MCC president in the 1968 season at the age of 73, committee man and Sussex county club chairman during the STST protest – sums them up. The December 1967 letter was probably from Sussex vice-chairman FG White. They were formal men often with a military outlook, even vocabulary. The Sussex club secretary Colonel Pat Williams, named solely as 'Williams' was 'on leave'. White wrote:

What oppressing times we live in! One hardly dares open the morning paper for fear of what the latest news is. But I cannot see the Socialist Government resigning before their time is up simply because politics is now a very well paid career. I am convinced that most of the world's troubles stems from the unforced termination of the Pax Britannica – those were the days, weren't they?!

These were old men, intelligent, even self-aware, telling each other 'those were the days'. They saw the worst in politicians in general and Labour (or 'Socialist', as White old-fashionedly insisted on calling them) in particular. Paradoxically, these men with power felt themselves oppressed, because what to them had been the certainties of empire, monarchy, church and cricket were changing, for the worse, so they believed. Important besides the usually unspoken mental assumptions of these men was how they knew each other. Again, evidence is hard to find. As good a source as any is the memoir of a publican, Tony Hackett. Through a sporting friend he went to a dinner of the Corinthian Casuals Football Club in the early 1970s:

It was there that I met, among others, Sir John Waldron, Commissioner of the Metropolitan Police, a six-foot-six ex-centre half, Denis and Leslie Compton, [football broadcaster] Jimmy Hill, Doug Insole, Richard Hutton, Bob Willis, Graham Roope, Hugh Doggart, Trevor Bailey, Ken Barrington and Mickey Stewart all past and present CC players and Jim Swanton, Brian Johnston and John Arlott, the cricket commentators.

Hackett attended Corinthians matches, was 'introduced' to WCT Webster, who became MCC president in 1976, and who proposed him for MCC membership (seconded by Doug Insole). This story shows how 'it's not what you know, it's who you know'. Men socialised and made friends across sports, and their shared love of sport included the likes of Sir John Waldron. Police, having to be physically fit, were natural sporting enthusiasts. They, and journalists, liked a drink, too, which made the likes of Hackett welcome. He recalled once after an England-Wales rugby international out-drinking 'an illustrious company' including broadcasters Peter West and Wilf Wooller, a former Welsh rugby international. The hotel bar at Cowbridge outside Cardiff was near Wooller's home. While not falling for any conspiracy theories, we can at least say that police, sport and media figures in this story had informal connections that may have added a personal angle to their public work, whether it influenced a decision or made it easier to pick up the telephone and get put straight through.

* * *

At a cricket club dinner in Burton upon Trent in December 1969, Brian Bolus the Nottinghamshire vice-captain said: 'Let's keep politics out of sport – I should be delighted to play against the world's most attractive team, and I am sure they will prove a tremendous draw.' Many playing and following sport felt the same. Others have wondered whether religion, or doing business, should mix with politics; although strangely no-one ever asks if we should keep politics out of the writing of history. The likes of Bolus were assuming that sport was ethically good (enabling man to pit himself against others and do his best, entertaining to watch, harmless) and politics bad (deceitful, only getting things done through grubby compromise, harmful). As an editorial in the Sunday Telegraph in May 1970 put it: "Sport after all or most of it is good clean fun, so long as the politicians can keep their hands off it. Unfortunately they cannot ... anything that stirs up the people soon gets caught up in the political maelstrom." The Telegraph too was cynically implying that politics was something best avoided; yet if we define politics as public affairs, even to deny that sport (or anything) is political, is itself political, if it means you accept the settled way of doing things, making you conservative. In any case, from the letter to Gilligan, we can see that cricket administrators happily made strident political statements among themselves. In a televised debate at the Cambridge Union in November 1969 Wilf Wooller said: "If you bring politics into our sport you are going to destroy the last bastion of sanity we have." Yet he, John Arlott and former England captain Ted Dexter were speaking alongside Labour sports minister Denis Howell; they were all being political. Arlott accused Wooller of 'political naivety'. Just as the Yorkshire spin bowler's saying, 'if t'batsman thinks it's spinning, it's spinning' is true enough, so if enough people say something is political, it is; even if you are not one of them. MCC seemed to realise it was folly, as a famed British institution, for it to have international dealings as if it were above politics. In a 1969 book Basil D'Oliveira recalled a panel on ITV. Billy Griffith said: "We tried desperately hard to keep them [politicians] out [of the decision first not to pick D'Oliveira for a tour of South Africa in September 1968, then to pick him]. We might be naïve about this and it might be impossible to do it but God knows we tried hard enough." To state the obvious, the politicians and their officials knew sport could be political. Paradoxically that made the Foreign Office, for one, careful of what they sent in writing to Lord's, in case cricket published a 'dossier' as evidence of political pressure. As JC Macrae of the Foreign Office did write to Miss EM Riley, honorary secretary of the Women's Cricket Association, in October 1969, it was 'not for us to advise you officially in this matter', namely a possible invitation for an English women's team to tour South Africa and Rhodesia in 1972. Macrae duly set out his arguments and suggested the women put off a decision ('1972 is some way away'). Not deciding, however, was a decision of sorts; and suited the FO.

* * *

Interlude

Harold Wilson

When John Warwicker, a Special Branch bodyguard, first met Harold Wilson in 1974, the prime minister 'asked a few, low-key questions to someone apparently hovering over my left ear'. Warwicker realised Wilson was speaking to him, though not at him. Such a side-on action might have fitted Wilson well to be a Yorkshire fast bowler, as in interview he said he wished he had been; although he would not have played South Africa; so he said. Whether to look people in the eye, to trust them, obsessed Wilson. Put another way, the man in Downing Street until May 1970 was 'an incredibly complex person' according to the anti-apartheid campaigner Frank Judd, one of 16 Labour MPs who signed an anti-apartheid letter to the Times in November 1969.

So many of his own party let alone outside enemies raged against Wilson as a 'pragmatist' that the judgement stuck. They must have seen something. Of his allies, Richard Crossman was one of several Cabinet diarists who at least touched on the tour. Once in passing Crossman noted

A collage of photographs of Harold Wilson, sold among his possessions at auction in 2019.

Wilson's and fellow ally Barbara Castle's 'fanatically hostile attitude' to South Africa, and fascist Spain. To oppose those countries was impeccably left-wing, and would offend few if any voters. Perhaps there – in the very fact that apartheid, and sport, and apartheid sport were fairly simple and unimportant, free of the compromises of everyday politics – lay their appeal.

Wilson could match a clever phrase to his grasp of the game. Interviewed by David Coleman on Sportsnight on BBC TV on Thursday, April 30, 1970, Wilson hoped the Cricket Council would think again: "... after all we always respect a sporting declaration in cricket. We respect the man who starts to walk to the pavilion without waiting for the umpire's finger." Three weeks later, Labour did indeed give cricket the equivalent of the umpire's finger. Just as some batsmen resent ever being given out, so English cricket felt Labour, and Wilson, were on the protesters' side all along. At the most extreme, Arthur Coy of the South Africa Cricket Association (SACA) in a bitter letter of June 1970 to his MCC counterpart Donald Carr lashed out at Wilson ('who never fired a shot in World War Two'). While true, you could say the same of Hammond, Sir Donald Bradman, and many others.

Harold Wilson famously smoked a pipe.

The last Cabinet meeting before the tour was cancelled – on Sunday, May 17, that only covered the dissolution of Parliament – gave an insight into Wilson as a politician, and how he saw the tour. Wilson was calling an election months before he had to because otherwise his government would 'lose the power of initiative'. Wilson prized the ability to control events; and the deadlines of the tour and the Commonwealth Games, forced him, through Home Secretary James Callaghan, to take sides so publicly. It was not his fault that if the Church of England was the Conservative Party at prayer, the MCC was the Conservatives at sport.

James Callaghan
Nor can Jim Callaghan have warmed to cricket after England batsman Ted Dexter stood for the Tories against him in Cardiff (not an obvious place for the Sussex captain) in the October 1964 election. Dexter then went on MCC's winter tour ... of South Africa. In the Sunday Telegraph after the cancelled tour, the columnist Peregrine Worsthorne called Callaghan 'Hain's puppet'. Either Worsthorne was rude for effect or he was blind to the ability and ambition in the man who (eventually) succeeded Wilson. That Callaghan and Wilson spoke by telephone on the night before, and the

"It's morally disgraceful that the M.C.C. should be free to demonstrate that I'm incapable of defending this wicket during the Election!"

A clever Sunday Express cartoon had a worried-looking Harold Wilson defending the outsized stumps of 'law and order' with a bat with Home Secretary James Callaghan's head on.

morning of Callaghan's crucial May 21 meeting with Cricket Council members, said much about both men: Wilson for how carefully he managed even senior ministers (at least on issues he saw as most important), and Callaghan for going along with it. Callaghan had shown himself well able to manage the police and press in previous similar controversies, such as the rise of football hooliganism of the late 1960s; actual problems proved less manageable.

* * *

Denis Howell, as minister of sport, had opinions, for example about three-day cricket ('which I love'). However as he added in that January 1970 interview, he would do no more than express views. Politicians could take sides; when Callaghan said he would not watch the Springboks, the cricket tour was doomed, Deedes reckoned after the cancellation, without explaining why the rugby had gone ahead.

Politicians did at least take note of public opinion, which 'seemed to be moving' against Lord's, so Callaghan told the Cabinet on April 30. Officials noted public opinion for their political masters. JH Waddell, deputy under-secretary of state at the Home Office, in a memo offering 'some material' for Callaghan ahead of a November 1969 meeting with chief constables, wrote of the demonstrators' opposition to South Africa's racial policies: "Most people in this country share this opposition ...." These were only guesses; the biggest was by Sir Jack Nicholls, the about-to-retire British ambassador in South Africa, who told the local press in November 1969 'a noisy minority wanted to stop the [rugby] tour and that the majority wanted it to continue'. Such arrogant men believed what they wanted to see.

Labour junior minister Denis Howell.

You could interpret even mass expressions of opinion,

such as the 'long, loud applause' by the Aberdeen crowd after the Springboks thrashed the North of Scotland 37-3 in December 1969, different ways. Did these rugby watchers, roughly one-hundredth of the town, stand for the whole? Any more than did the four-foot high message written in weed-killer on the Iffley Road playing field in October 1969, 'Oxford rejects apartheid'? Letter-writers to newspapers went out to bat for the 'quiet' or 'silent majority', implying that the media and their country did not reflect the average man. Marchers to the Springboks' match in Exeter in December 1969 passed 'a few local lads pretending to be skinheads', chanting 'Enoch [Powell] for prime minister' from the pavement. Were any who made such an exhibition of themselves the exception, compared with the indifferent (or outright right-wing) majority? As 'Salford Englishman' put it to the Manchester Evening News in November 1969: "Let's face it, what Englishman in his right mind cares about what is going on in Timbuctoo?" Men grateful for South African hospitality while on troopships in the 1939-45 war repaid it when they wrote to newspapers. Those writers did not consider that South Africa had institutionalised apartheid since, or that times had changed. DL Sutton of Oxford did; 'as a legless ex-serviceman', in October 1969 he resented the Springboks' visit. He wrote to his local newspaper: "If coloured people were good enough to fight and die alongside us in time of war, then they are good enough to be given equal rights and to play alongside us in times of peace." The more famous Jim Laker had enjoyed South Africa in 1941 and returned as a coach and MCC tourist, but learned the 'horrors' of apartheid. Just as men could have the same experience and draw opposite conclusions, so they could change their opinion. Some did; after cancellation the Daily Telegraph reported a Gallup poll that showed 46 per cent agreed with the tour, while 36pc disagreed and 18pc didn't know. In February, the percentages had been 52, 29 and 19; and in mid-November, 62pc had been for the rugby tour, against only 25pc for cancelling. As ever with polling, it depended on who you asked, and what question. A Harris poll for the Daily Express after cancellation found still 49pc for the tour going ahead, and 37pc opposed and 14pc of no opinion. More approved political demonstrations against the tour (50 to 43pc), a question that let people leave aside what they thought of apartheid; yet only 7pc approved of demos inside cricket grounds. A May 1970 poll for a charitable trust that included the anti-tour campaigner Sir Edward Boyle found a majority, 58pc, for calling the tour off; and 53pc were against the invitation in the first place. Whichever you chose to prefer, the country was plainly divided; as it was over what was politely called 'race relations'. In a survey of Sun readers in March 1970, 23pc admitted they were 'very prejudiced' against people of a different colour. A Daily Mirror poll of British teenagers meanwhile claimed to find an 'overwhelming majority had no racial prejudice'. While John Arlott spelt out on a BBC TV Panorama debate on April 27, 1970 that the tour threatened race relations and 'the whole social future for us and our children', the Sheffield Morning Telegraph in a December 1969 editorial warned the opposite, that the anti-apartheid protests were 'likely to create a positive backlash'. Certainly SH Smith of Exmouth was angry when he read in the Daily Telegraph in June 1970 that Peter Hain objected to Sir Cyril Hawker, chairman of a bank with interests in South Africa, becoming the next MCC president. It 'almost made me explode', Smith wrote, '... what the hell has it got to do with him?' The longer the controversy, the more some tempers frayed. Each side got enough backing to feel in the right. Days after Bristol was among county grounds damaged in January 1970, secretary Grahame Parker told Gloucestershire's AGM that the club had received a dozen letters 'decrying their support for the South Africa tour', yet the vandalism had prompted 'far more letters and numerous phone calls offering assistance'. People cared about their county club; more than cared about Soviet discrimination against Jews, for instance. Glasgow University student Alan Shroot complained in May 1970 that a silent, non-violent demo by Jewish youths of Glasgow against the Red Army Choir, singing in Motherwell, had scant publicity. He could not face the fact that demo causes were a beauty contest.

* * *

To win a beauty contest, you have to enter. The BBC in Bristol, replying in November 1969 to a letter by local anti-apartheid campaigner Ron Press, gave what amounted to a tutorial in getting publicity. "Of course we will be reporting the [Springboks] visit and any demonstration that may or may not be taking place. Obviously what appears on the screen or on the air depends on us having reporters and camera-men at any event or incident. Like all news organisations we depend upon tip-offs to get the news when and where it happens." The BBC or any newsroom could not read minds; Press would have to give them a call (the letter helpfully gave the hours, 6.30am to 10.30pm, Monday to Friday). Howell got a tutorial in the opposite. On Sunday night, October 19, 1969, he gave his view on an ITV sports show that the South African cricket team should not visit. The Thursday morning after, Howell went to see the Foreign Office minister Lord Chalfont, who politely told Howell to cool it: 'it would therefore be wiser if as little as possible were said publicly on the subject by ministers'. This was the old anti-democratic trick by the FO and all those established in power; keep it all within the elite. Chalfont noted later: "I said that I thought the MCC ought by now to have got the message about the tour and that they should need no further ministerial prompting." Howell agreed, at least according to Chalfont, and also agreed not to take part in the Cambridge Union debate: 'and said that he would try to arrange with the government chief whip for some business to be arranged that would require his attendance in the Commons on the day ... he would probably arrange for a backbencher to take his place'. Howell went ahead and spoke at Cambridge, because as the only elected politician of the two, he knew that once you stopped pressing for something, everyone would forget it; for it no longer mattered. Chalfont was either ignorant or cynical.

Sir Jack Nicholls meanwhile worried to the Foreign Office about South Africa's reaction to demos against the rugby tour, 'not so much the demonstrations themselves as to

UK press, TV and radio comment and especially statements by individual ministers'. This was a rum comment from a diplomat who was supposed to represent a government. Yet the very fact that South Africa reacted angrily showed, as Nicholls admitted, that a sports boycott was apartheid's 'Achilles heel'. The white break-away regime in Rhodesia sided with South Africa; the British High Commission in Lusaka reported home that Radio Rhodesia repeated with 'great relish' commentator Wilf Wooller's 'notorious attack on lefties, weirdies and odd bods' and broadcast some of the Springboks' first tour match.

*　*　*

All along we have assumed the protesters wanted to 'stop the tour'. Appropriately for such a divisive affair, not everyone could agree on that, even. The Daily Telegraph editorial on the eve of cancellation claimed 'the object of many of the demonstrators is not the cancellation of a tour or even the end of apartheid but nothing less than the overthrow of our society. Take away one issue, they will find others.' The Telegraph had a point; some seemed to be looking for causes to occupy a weekend. After the shooting of students at Kent State University in Ohio, about 500 marched in Bristol on Saturday afternoon, May 9, 1970, 'the biggest street demonstration seen in Bristol for several years'. Was it worth stopping traffic for? All the uproar that made Michael Stewart flee the Oxford Union, the student shouts of 'Ho, Ho, Ho Chi Minh' and 'Stewart, we want you dead' ... what did a war by the United States in Vietnam have to do with Britain? Surely *that was the point*; the more irrelevant and distant the cause, the less need for demonstrators to do anything about it, and the prouder they could feel that they cared about the far-away. Except for the motivated few expelled from South Africa, apartheid was only a name.

The cause could feed off itself. Students campaigned at Bristol University for example, after it fined some students in May 1970 for an anti-apartheid demo. Other causes and campuses likewise became caught up with general unrest against university discipline and file-keeping on activists. A cause was simple to find; Sheffield Polytechnic in April 1970 for instance wanted removed any member of the board of governors with a business connection with South Africa. Newspapers fed off themselves the same, British newspapers quoting South African newspapers that the Springboks tour was in 'danger', which then quoted the British newspapers; and so on. Yet for whatever reason – the (pardon the pun) black and white, right and wrong, starkness of the cause, South Africa's very similarity to Britain, guilt over a student's easy life - apartheid gripped campuses more than any other issue, and 'probably more often and with greater heat', so Douglas Baker, deputy dean of students at the University of East Anglia, wrote in the Evening Standard in December 1969. "The Springboks tour has stirred up a hornet's nest and many students up and down the country are debating whether to ban South African goods from the campus or even whether to use funds for freedom fighters." Such widening of the campaign promised more impact, and threatened to weaken the focus of 'stop the tour'.

* * *

The English (and Welsh) cricketers that would meet the South Africans from May to August 1970 would face the protests as much as the tourists. What did they think? David Sheppard in his 1964 autobiography counted several of the South Africa team as friends. In the 1967 spring annual of The Cricketer, the South African bowler Peter Pollock chose a 'world eleven' – Bill Lawry, Eddie Barlow, Hanif Mohammed, Gary Sobers as captain, Pollock's brother Graeme, Tom Graveney, Bobby Simpson, John Murray as wicket-keeper, Wes Hall, Charlie Griffith and Lance Gibbs. He named two South Africans and five non-whites. Peter Pollock called the West Indies the 'unquestioned world champions'. Such an international-class cricketer was a man of the world, rating West Indian and Indian sub-continental men by their ability, not their skin colour. What they had in common gave them reason to be more tolerant than most of their countrymen – of whatever colour. D'Oliveira in his 1969 book recalled meeting several South African Test players at a double wicket competition in Australia; after some embarrassment they 'talked and talked and talked'. In 1964, as a Worcestershire player but before he could play for his county regularly, D'Oliveira was one of a Hastings Festival eleven, including South African Eddie Barlow, captained by Jim Parks. "So why can't we do all in our power to welcome these cricketers?" Parks said in June 1965, of that summer's South African tour. The International Cavaliers

Cavaliers team flying BOAC to Kingston, Jamaica, February 1970, dutifully advertising a make of Scotch whisky.

team, while long forgotten, drew crowds in the mid-1960s and routinely mixed races. In July 1969, after the 'D'Oliveira Affair', Graeme Pollock captained the Cavaliers eleven including West Indians Lawrence Rowe and Alvin Corneal at Witney Mills blanket factory in Oxfordshire, to mark its 300th birthday; the local side included Tom Graveney and D'Oliveira as guests. The Cavaliers filled gaps in the 1970 tour calendar, again running mixed-race elevens, such as West Indians Bernard Julien and Deryck Murray and Rhodesian Brian Davidson at Bristol in late May. This counted for something in a land where The Black and White Minstrel Show, of white singers appearing in black face paint, was popular television, and when a Daily Mirror poll of British teenagers found near one in ten (nine per cent) 'would rather not have someone of a different colour sitting beside them at school or work'. The Pakistani all-rounder Mushtaq Mohammed's best friend at Northamptonshire was the white South African, Hylton Ackerman; two Cavaliers. Yet in January 1970, Mushtaq told his county 'that I would prefer not to be available for selection for the South Africa match on June 13 ... my objection is entirely a matter of my conscience and principles. I have absolutely nothing against individuals.' As a 'patriot' he objected to the South African government not allowing a Pakistani team in their country. Derrick Robins had invited Mushtaq to play for him against the tourists in April: "I can hardly do that." It sounded like international politics.

Chapter Three

Summer of '69

Selectors, like the rest of us, are not infallible.
   Wally Hammond, Cricket's Secret History, 1952

One of the many oddities of apartheid South Africa was that alongside the secret police ran what looked like democracy (for some). Thus Prime Minister John Vorster got angry, so the Rand Daily Mail reported, in front of a crowd of 1500 at Brakpan town hall, near Johannesburg, in November 1969, when an English-speaking questioner said Vorster had made a mistake when he tried to pick the MCC team in September 1968. Vorster replied that the MCC only included Basil D'Oliveira after pressure from anti-apartheid groups. If Vorster believed that and was not simply trying to escape the question, it showed how warped the apartheid view of Britain was; if anti-apartheid protesters asked for something, Lord's was more likely to do the opposite. Vorster had got angry because the man had told the truth.

* * *

The 'D'Oliveira affair' was, as the Irish Times rightly said after cancellation, a 'moment of truth'. "Sixty-eight was hard," John Woodcock recalled in old age. "Nobody came out of '68 well, really." The Foreign Secretary Michael Stewart told the British embassy in Pretoria in November 1969 that the British opponents of apartheid believed ('rightly or wrongly', Stewart added weakly) 'that it was Mr Vorster's refusal to accept D'Oliveira which has put sporting contacts squarely into the political arena'. Meanwhile Lord's managed to annoy everyone – Vorster and his kind, and the anti-apartheid movement for standing by white-only South African cricket.

Let us tell the story briefly, told so many times – a 'fairy story' as D'Oliveira called it years later. He appreciated, for all the strain, how unlikely his success had been. A failure

(BBC commentator Norman Yardley's word) on the West Indies tour of 1967-68, D'Oliveira did not play for England for much of the summer of 1968. He only made the last Test because a batsman, Roger Prideaux, dropped out with bronchitis. D'Oliveira took his chance, made 158 and took an important wicket, as England won and drew the series with Australia. Had someone else on the fringe of the team that summer, Dennis Amiss, Keith Fletcher or Barry Knight, made that 158, they would surely have made the touring 16; and indeed D'Oliveira played in England's next Test, in Pakistan in February 1969. That the MCC selectors did not choose him on August 28 made front page news. While many felt outrage - Conservative MP for Worcester, Peter Walker, called leaving out D'Oliveira 'blatantly wrong' - you can always find reasons for picking or not picking someone. The 'right decision', John Woodcock called it the day after. Looking back in 1970, Michael Melford wrote that the passing over of Colin Milburn had been a 'far more heinous omission'. Yet the very fact that you could argue for or against D'Oliveira made for controversy. It did not help that according to convention the selectors did not explain themselves fully in public. Even if they had, could they have assured even themselves that they did not leave out D'Oliveira in case of political trouble, on purpose or subconsciously?

Nor did the selectors say, and nor can we trace now, how informed they were of the politics behind picking D'Oliveira or not. In April 1969, Britain's ambassador Sir Jack Nicholls wrote to the Foreign Office after a 'long and uninhibited' conversation with Vorster, 'in which I extracted from him a statement that he did intend to modify the convention about the inclusion of non-whites in visiting teams'. Vorster however had to balance opinion overseas with pleasing apartheid-loving voters at home. He reserved the right to refuse admission to a team, if anyone tried to make political capital out of it (defined by him). It sounded as if Vorster in 1968 may have let in D'Oliveira, if picked in the first place. However, the News of the World asked D'Oliveira to tour as their reporter. That alone – as the Sunday newspaper no

Colin Cowdrey.

doubt reckoned – would bring controversy. As Woodcock pointed out at the time, no 'Coloured' man had ever been in a press box at the major South African cricket grounds ('except in a menial capacity'). In a statement on September 9, 1968, Colin Cowdrey said he only agreed to be the tour captain when the selectors assured him that they selected the team on ability alone. He described D'Oliveira as a 'possible reserve'. One of the 16, Tom Cartwright, had been unfit for weeks. When Cartwright cried off, Lord's chose D'Oliveira. Vorster banned the team.

"I feel a stand should have been taken then," sports minister Denis Howell said in interview in January 1970. Once the apartheid regime chose to feel offended – 'the idea of D'Oliveira being greeted as a hero playing against the country of his birth was not to be tolerated', EW Swanton commented in The Cricketer 1968-69 winter annual – only time ('a decent interval' as Swanton put it) could heal wounds. Even an impeccable conservative such as the former Sussex amateur captain Robin Marlar saw 'all the signs of a permanent and complete break in our cricketing relations with South Africa'. There was no such thing. Few had an appetite to 'sever relations with friends after 80 years', as another, anonymous columnist put it in the annual.

EW Swanton.

Through a notice in newspapers some MCC members seeking reform of the club met, and formed a steering committee, 'and as the youngest of this group,' Robin Knight chuckled at the memory, 50 years later, 'I ended up being the secretary'. The MCC committee agreed to meet them at Lord's:

We thought this was the prelude to some sort of compromise but when we got to this meeting we were presented with this Berlin Wall. Where no compromise was going to be agreed about anything and we were the ones who were going to withdraw and no attempt whatsoever made to discuss the issue.

On the reformers' side, besides Knight ('I can't remember opening my mouth') were Peter Howe, the actor ('a very eloquent speaker'), Mike Brearley the Middlesex batsman ('a rather hesitant speaker'), David Sheppard ('a good speaker, but rather earnest') and Jeremy Hutchinson ('one of the leading QCs of the day, and a notable champion of liberal causes'). On the MCC side, 'the whole committee were there and they lined themselves up at this long table'. They included the most eminent public figure among them, Sir Alec Douglas-Home, the former Conservative prime minister and MCC president, who had flown from Scotland. 'We were basically told,' Knight recalled:

we were essentially letting the side down by proceeding

with this. That was an impossible position to take, especially with David Sheppard. So they [MCC] handled it very badly. But essentially they handled it badly because they were truly convinced they were right. So they weren't going to compromise.

The reformers left Lord's and went next door to the pub:

... and concluded the only thing we could do was demand a special general meeting. And in those days – the MCC has made this ten times more difficult now, you didn't need too many signatures to call one. And so we did. And we had the meeting at Church House [Westminster]. Quite intimidating [venue] really. The committee completely controlled events. It was a fix from beginning to end. I mean, one boorish speech after another on the side of the committee. We lost the vote, but in the hall itself we actually did quite well in the circumstances.

That December 5 special meeting drew 1000 full members. One reporter, Rex Alston for Playfair Monthly, reckoned MCC 'triumphant but not entirely unscathed'. The first resolution, that members regretted the club's 'mishandling' of the affair, was lost by 4357 votes to 1570. David Sheppard afterwards said he was glad ideas were aired; so all failed reformers consoled themselves.

The authorities ignored those ideas. In their 'Why the Seventy Tour' leaflet in spring 1970, they could claim the special meeting of MCC members showed 80 per cent were for continuing with South Africa. The paradox was that MCC insisted to all that it chose its teams on merit, yet stayed in power not on the merit of its actions, but by relying at Church House on the votes of what the outspoken reformer Rowland Bowen mocked as 'backwoods members'; men (because MCC did not let in women) who sent their vote by post and who always supported authority. Cricket would soon start facing enemies who did not play by MCC rules.

* * *

As so often in life, inaction – letting things carry on – soon amounted to a choice. The MCC tour had been due to begin in November 1968; before Christmas a first MCC schoolboy tour left for South Africa, to play on Test grounds.

An England women's team was due to break its journey to Australia in December 1968 'for a few days in South Africa', so captain Rachel Heyhoe recalled in her 1978 autobiography, and play a couple of warm-up matches, 'but the Sports Council presumably under direction from above told us in no uncertain terms that it was not a good idea'. The Women's Cricket Association (WCA) had needed the government's Sports Council grant to afford the tour. Heyhoe was right to suspect politics. In a paper for a February 1971 meeting, the Conservative sports minister Eldon Griffiths noted 'in effect the Sports Council under Howell's chairmanship applied a political boycott on all British teams seeking to play in South Africa – except of course on those who can afford to pay the whole of their expenses'. Perhaps Rachel Heyhoe felt hurt pride, then, besides naturally resenting being told what to do ('it was the first time ever that my sporting life had run head into a political barrier and I didn't like it at all'). In October 1969, when the WCA was wondering whether to invite South African and Rhodesian women to tour England in 1972 and wrote to the Foreign Office, JC Macrae of the FO had ended his reply: "I realise that the decision before the committee is a difficult one." What mattered was that cricketers, South African and English alike, were as keen to carry on as ever.

On January 23, 1969, the MCC Council, meeting for the first time as the new governing body for British cricket, confirmed by letter its invitation to South Africa to tour in 1970. In February MCC sent a proposed itinerary to its South African counterparts. Life was going on because Lord's had sympathy for those running South African cricket, whose position EW Swanton had called 'thoroughly unenviable'. Political people – whether the apartheid regime or anti-apartheid activists – were a burden the two cricket authorities had in common. As Arthur Coy of SACA put it in a letter to Billy Griffith on September 22, 1969 – they were on first name terms – SACA had no say in South African politics any more than MCC; 'probably less, because no cricket administrator in South African cricket is a politician or in close touch with politics'.

If you define politics as public affairs, plenty of cricket men were, in truth, political. Wilf Wooller on Monday, February 17, 1969 was telling Glamorgan's finance committee darkly of 'organisations designed to isolate South Africa on the sports field' including one in Cardiff 'which had a distinct Communist background':

... a new assault from a Mr Dennis Brutus a full-time official of SAN-ROC [South African Non-Racial Olympic Committee] had been received. In recognising the method of their operation Mr Wooller stated that he had taken steps to find out the background of Mr Brutus. It was thought that SAN-ROC derives its funds from the international defence and aid fund of which Mr Brutus is alleged to be a director. A similar South African organisation was declared unlawful in the terms of the Suppression of Communism Act. Mr Brutus is a Cape Coloured born in Rhodesia in 1925 but whose family migrated to South Africa where he was educated and qualified as a teacher. He claims South African citizenship and also claims to be a British Subject and obtained a British passport in 1963.

Wooller went into yet more detail. Billy Griffith the MCC secretary 'had been similarly plagued by Mr Brutus and that the matter would be discussed more fully at the next meeting of the TCCB. Mr Wooller thought it right that certain of these activities should be exposed otherwise the unwary were misled'. Wooller's bizarre sniffing into Brutus's past ('in a personal capacity', the club's minutes noted) set the tone for Wooller's calamitous influence on this story. The committee had no control over Wooller, supposedly an employee. It 'agreed that the less said officially by the county on this matter the better' (why not, if Brutus was such a threat?). Wooller would write to Brutus that Glamorgan 'thought it in the best interests of cricket to continue to play South Africa and advise that further correspondence would serve no useful purpose'. SAN-ROC letters, deploring the decision to invite South

Africa to tour in 1970, presumably went to all counties. At Nottinghamshire, one club committee member, Jack Elliott, 'spoke strongly in support of the views expressed and suggested we should not entertain them [South Africa] until such time as their policy was altered'. He made this a proposition, 'but received no seconder. The matter was left on the table.' The likes of Brutus would not let it stay there.

* * *

The British ambassador Sir Jack Nicholls warned in April 1969 that MPs or 'the Bishop of Woolwich' (David Sheppard) with 'strong personal views and quasi-official positions may in the vacuum exercise a quite disproportionate influence'. He meant that 'things might snowball'. Already in The Spectator magazine that month Simon Raven was looking forward to the 'exciting' 1970 season, while foreseeing 'bickering' from 'the predictable voices'.

The Daily Mail in April 1969 revealed that Lord Cobham – a former MCC president and, as Charles Lyttleton, a Worcestershire amateur captain in the 1930s – had met Vorster in March 1968 to be told that D'Oliveira would not be acceptable. Cobham wrote a letter with this crucial news (marked 'private and confidential') to an unnamed senior member of the MCC committee; who passed it on to Billy Griffith, secretary. As a mere employee, Griffith gave it to the president, Arthur Gilligan, and the treasurer, Gubby Allen ('the dominant personality at Lord's', Robin Knight recalled, '30 years, nothing happened at Lord's without Allen agreeing to it').

Lord's had tried to play politics in 1968; badly. Vorster was able to tell his parliament lordly that he had spoken with Cobham ('for a few minutes') and separately Sir Alec Douglas-Home ('again, not on my initiative'). "Neither of them was competent to speak on behalf of the cricket organisation or did speak on behalf of that organisation. As far as those talks are concerned, then, they were personal, private conversations between gentlemen and it has never been my policy to divulge personal, private conversations between gentlemen across the floor of this house, to newspapers, or to any person." That allowed Vorster to say that South Africa had not tried to influence MCC; in his warped words, the tour party had become 'the team of SAN-ROC'. MCC's amateur, secretive diplomacy had let Vorster pose as a man of principle. It left Sir Alec Douglas-Home, who noticeably had not attended the Church House meeting, looking the shifty one.

As David Sheppard wrote in the Sunday Telegraph of April 13, 1969, it meant the MCC had concealed 'vital' facts, basic for judging the D'Oliveira affair, from the December meeting of members. Sheppard wrote charitably that 'the real villain' was not the MCC committee 'but the pervading South African policy of all things separate', that South African cricket 'lamely acquiesced' in. "Men of goodwill at Lord's have been pushed into positions they have felt they must conceal because they have tried to compromise with a set up which is basically wrong." Although Sheppard did not make the comparison, the obvious one was with the Nazis 30 years before; appeasing them only made you as bad as them.

New Zealand rugby meanwhile showed English cricket how to treat apartheid. In 1967, South Africa invited New Zealand to tour, without Maoris. New Zealand rugby stood their ground. Fifteen months later, another invitation came; with Maoris. In May 1969, New Zealand rugby asked for assurance that South Africa would treat Maori supporters like any other New Zealanders; and got it. This did not come thanks to any insight into apartheid; New Zealand had no diplomats in South Africa and in May 1969 the Foreign Office was agreeing to give the New Zealand High Commission in London details of developments in South Africa 'on the All Blacks tour'.

William Watson of the Foreign Office's southern African department was admitting on Thursday, April 24, 1969 that his government would not want a cancellation of the tour 'pinned on them': "On balance, however, a cancellation might well cause less damage than a tour which secured nothing but bad publicity." Such was the typical FO view;

not of what was right or wrong, or even in Britain's interests but what looked good. That day Denis Howell fielded questions in the House of Commons about the tour from Labour MP David Winnick ('disgraceful') and Tory MP and former rugby international Captain Walter Elliot ('juvenile to cut off these contacts'). In parliament, on television, and on the following Tuesday, April 29, in conversation, Howell left Billy Griffith 'in no doubt about his [Howell's] own personal view that the South African tour should not take place'; so the Foreign Office heard and passed on to Nicholls in Pretoria. The government did not wish to give any formal advice, Howell told Griffith, having just given him some informal advice. MCC duly issued a statement on April 30 that it believed continuing to play South Africa served the best interests of the game and kept open 'essential channels'. Cancelling was a 'minority feeling', it reckoned. Howell, as a sports minister keeping out of sports politics, accepted that, 'provided', so the FO noted, the MCC kept it under review, 'so that whatever decision was subsequently reached was not reached at pistol point'. Howell had uncannily foreseen what did happen, 13 months later; what any sensible politician sought to avoid; events out of control.

Letters went back and forth between Lord's and SACA in the summer of 1969, as they did the year before any tour. One issue was money; because South Africa had cancelled the previous tour, Britain did not want to give more 1970 tour profit to South Africa than it had to. In May 1969, Griffith passed on to South Africa an invite from Derrick Robins for an early tour match at Eastbourne from April 29; similar to one for the West Indies that had just finished. Robins would pay for the hotel and expenses, and share profits with the Eastbourne club. To most administrators of English cricket, 1970 was a normal tour. For instance in a letter dated May 29, 1969 the secretary of the Minor Counties Association, Frank Crompton, asked for their tour match at Norwich, instead of Durham, as it was unreasonable to ask the South Africans to travel north and then to Glamorgan. Griffith evidently felt concerned enough about possible demonstrations to raise it with SACA, only for its secretary and treasurer AS Frames to reply complacently on June 23 that 'we are heartened by the fact that the general UK cricketing public is such that its enthusiasm for good cricket will overshadow possible extraneous acts'.

The counties, too, were only thinking of money. At a Glamorgan general committee meeting in August 1969, Wilf Wooller said 'he had been endeavouring these last 12 months to get counties to repudiate the agreement' with South Africa over proceeds. As Glamorgan let its members into the tour match free, after giving some to the tourists Glamorgan 'would be left with the cost of running the game'. The committee 'discussed this at great length and decided that in view of the goodwill attached to members this year' – membership had passed 14,000, a record – 'there was nothing to do but write the loss and admit members free as usual and to advertise the fact as much as possible'. They said nothing about possible protest.

Yet protest against South African sport had begun. In July, Ron Press the Bristol anti-apartheid campaigner appealed to Herbert Willcox, the Lord Mayor of Bristol, not to give the customary civic reception to the South African Davis Cup tennis team. The mayor gave him a civic brush-off ('I have carefully considered your suggestion'). On Thursday, July 17, Peter Hain and two female fellow Putney Young Liberals drove to Bristol 'with the vague intention of interrupting the game by sitting on the court. We were inexperienced, undecided about tactics, and rather apprehensive', Hain recalled in his 1971 book. He was too modest. The three had chosen well because the tennis was live on BBC television. The protest at Bristol Tennis Club in Redland, and reactions, looked strikingly like protests in the rest of this story. The spectators had no time for the protesters, shouting 'get off'. Nor did the press the next day; the local Western Daily Press condemned the 'puerile antics'. The flour bombs were arguably puerile; downright nasty was a telephoned warning of a timed bomb, found to be three bottles wired to an old radio transmitter. Outside, about 60 demonstrators hissed and shouted the Nazi 'Sieg Heil' at

South African players. Some felt the protest did harm to its cause; the Western Daily's sports reporter Graham Russell called it 'an embarrassment even for the principals as they waited to be carried off', by police.

Afterwards, Ron Press sent a typed report to the Anti-Apartheid Movement in London. It's worth dwelling on, as a rare description by a protester for other protesters, unlike what they said in public, where they naturally sought to look good. The report came at a watershed. Students, with new, bolder tactics, were joining the movement of a devoted few.

Press judged his protest against the tennis 'a goodly success'. Labour, Liberals, Communists and the local trades council had co-operated. They started the Saturday, the third and final day of the match, with a meeting outside the ground - speakers included Dennis Brutus - and handed a letter to a tennis official. They had a 'small sing song' outside the gates, marched around the ground, finished with a 'small meeting, then dispersed'. In the evening, placards outside the civic reception at the Mansion House at nearby Clifton Down. Letters to the newspapers; some published. All proven and useless tactics. Bert Willcox told the press he enjoyed the civic reception, which included the South African ambassador, Dr Hendrik Luttig; and claimed not to notice a 'small demonstration'. Hain and the other Young Liberals, and a young communist (Mike Williams of Swindon, who didn't make it into Hain's memoirs) had sat on the tennis court 'on their own initiative'.

In other words, Hain had come uninvited. Press raised sensible questions: were they hoping to influence the spectators? Did they just want to stop the sport? Or get publicity? Should the protesters turn militant, when 'we were incited to this by the national publicity media'? Was militancy in the movement's interests, when public reaction was 'mixed'? "I feel that we must be careful in our approach," Press concluded. He recalled that most of those at the tennis 'were quite beyond being convinced that apartheid was bad, and in fact were from their remarks and attitude as bad as the white South Africans that we in the anti-apartheid movement oppose'. Likewise the tennis and local cricket officials were 'most reactionary and unco-operative'. Press was working out his own and his movement's profoundly new attitude to their enemy. Just as football hooligans in the 1960s showed a new malice to others – because they came from another town, or for no reason at all – so the protesters were sloughing off the respect for people and property that society took for granted. Press was a convert to 'militant action', that he called 'suitable'; tellingly he said nothing of law, or morality. As tellingly, he understood that he was running the risk of anarchy. He urged 'care and discipline'; and drew the line at 'permanent damage to the facilities of the tennis or cricket grounds as this surely is not our aim'. The old, reasonable protest methods had some success, paradoxically with those thinking in a new way. In late 1967 Press had written to Bristol University against its athletic students hosting South Africans. The university passed the letter to the Student Union. A referendum of those students halted the visit. In a letter to Press, Roger Berry of the student Liberal Association agreed it was 'indefensible for the Athletics Union to engage in supporting visitors with racially segregated teams'. By contrast the Lord Mayor, a city politician, unhelpfully had nothing to say about the athletes. By now he, like the MCC, had showed whose side he was on. Consider that some British civic leaders were still refusing to greet Germans, because of war a generation before.

The Anti-Apartheid Movement had already lost patience and was speaking more sharply. Ahead of a March 1968 march in Bristol, it sought 'an end to collaboration with apartheid' by British banks. By November 1969, when Press appealed in a letter to Bristol Rugby Club, not to play the Springboks, his demands had a new strident confidence: "You must surely realise that the strong feelings which have been aroused by the tour will find expression in the area before and on the day of the match." It was the confidence of a man on the right track.

Interlude

Peter Hain
The Tory journalist Peregrine Worsthorne savaged him as 'a young immigrant supported by nothing more than his righteous passion and the threat of violence'. Here as so often Worsthorne was entertainingly wrong. Hain was young, turning 20 in February 1970. A Special Branch report of June 1970 speculated that 'the real instigator behind Hain was his mother, who constantly drove him on'. If the police were implying that Hain, living at the family home in Putney, west London, while a first year mechanical engineering student at Imperial College, Kensington, was his mum's mouthpiece, his long career in Liberal and then Labour Party politics proved otherwise. In April 1970 Wooller called Hain 'a dangerous young foreigner'. In truth the danger came from others; in his 1971 book Hain admitted 'that the public distinction between militant non-violence and violence became very blurred'. Conservative cricket-lovers, or simply older men without illusions, such as Tony Pawson, deputy editor of The Cricketer, felt no sympathy. In a January 1972 review of Ashes to Ashes, a film raising money for Hain's legal defence, Pawson began: "For Peter Hain cricket was merely a pawn in a political battle, a stepping stone in a political career." Everybody was using somebody, or something, else, like the 'stereotyped politics' that STST avoided and in his 1971 book Hain deplored, and duly thrived in.

* * *

English cricket had a taste of protest in the summer of 1969 against a private South African tour captained by Wilfred Isaacs. The tour manager Ronnie Eriksen sent Lord's a memo halfway through the tour on July 25. Every match but one was interrupted. Most demonstrators were 'relatively passive', offering leaflets, scattering stones, and squatting on the pitch, although 'our captain was spat on' and once Eriksen and public relations man Cyril Biggs 'were threatened with a violent demise by a drunken Ugandan'.

'How about sitting down between El Salvador and Honduras?' says the cricketer to the long-haired protester, in the Sunday Telegraph cartoon of July 20, 1969, referring to the brief 'football war' between the two countries in the previous week. In truth, the Oxford demo showed cricket was helpless.

Isaacs began at Basildon against Essex on Saturday, July 5. Hain was among ten Young Liberals who, so Hain recalled, 'planted themselves on the pitch'. Essex captain Brian Taylor – in an early example of where English cricketers stood – called on the bowler Keith Boyce to bowl at the protesters. Boyce did not, 'and', according to Hain, 'Taylor had to content himself with kicking one of the demonstrators in the back'. Police dragged or carried them off. Next came three days at Oxford University from the Wednesday, July 9. On the Monday morning, Jack Burton, Superintendent of the Parks, found a 45-yard trench dug across 17 cricket pitches, even though a guard and dog from the private security company Securicor had been on duty from the Saturday. Billy Griffith's comments were revealing. While respecting those against the tours, the digging was 'a most absurd thing to do', 'because it hurts so many people not connected with the game who do not deserve to be hurt. As far as next season is concerned such behaviour will make no difference to our plans.' Griffith saw the threat to 1970; yet naively he assumed that the protesters were reasonable like him. In truth men like Press were losing their respect for property, or, if students, they had yet to learn to be an adult in the first place. How many of the bedsheets, with slogans on, that they marched with, belonged to them, and how many to their university?!

Heavy rolling repaired the field. Late on the first day's play, after Graeme Pollock made 231 not out for the South Africans, and Oxford's opening bats went out, a whistle blew and scores of men and women sat on the pitch.

After 40 minutes, after police promised to release the three arrested, 'the demonstrators suddenly rose to their feet, linked arms and walked off'. They had proved that if protesters outnumbered those on cricket's side, they made play impossible.

Isaacs' itinerary showed how highly English cricket thought of him: next they played Denis Compton's eleven on a Sunday at Gerrards Cross (free of demo), Warwickshire at Edgbaston, Surrey at the Oval; Combined Services at Portsmouth, Standard Bank at Elmers End in Kent; and a Derrick Robins eleven at Eastbourne. At the Oval, players and spectators helped pull about 20 demonstrators off the field. In a letter to Griffith in May 1970, Surrey secretary Geoffrey Howard recalled how Isaacs' fielders, the two Surrey batsmen - Younis Ahmed had just walked out to join Mike Edwards - 'and of course the umpires' behaved impeccably. "I wish I could say the same for some of our members and a young South African who were disposed to put in the boot!" While Howard made light of the day, more to the point was that police made no arrests; the demonstrators were free to do it again. Like others with less physical power - the civil rights movement in the American South, even the Vietnamese Communists - one of their weapons was public opinion. JL Manning in the Daily Mail called the news of the trench at Oxford 'a searing wound in the jolly dee appeasement of very sporting apartheid' and urged South Africa to cut its losses and leave international team sport.

Journalist JL Manning.

As effective as any protest was on Saturday, July 19, the first day of Isaacs' three-day match against Ireland, at Rathmines in Dublin. Smoke bombs and a sit-down on the pitch sent the players to the pavilion. The minutes lost (some said 45, others 75) could have made the difference between a result and the actual finely-balanced draw. Two men went to court: Kevin Myers, a 19-year-old student (later a distinguished journalist) and Henry Kelly, a 23-year-old journalist (later a presenter of TV's Game for a Laugh). It only proved how hard it was for the law to pin anything on protesters; Myers had his charges of assaulting a policeman and carrying an offensive weapon (a piece of wire) dismissed; Kelly denied an assault of a policeman but was fined a mere £2 for a crime that even the judge called 'technical'.

Still county cricket raised no qualms; counties wrote to Lord's in August 1969 confirming which grounds would host South Africa the next summer. Surrey assistant secretary MN Romer queried playing South Africa on a Sunday, 'in view of the obvious political considerations'; probably he meant the Christian opposition to sport on the Sabbath, not apartheid.

Isaacs' team was South African propaganda, reckoned Rowland Bowen in his 1970 history of cricket, one of 'a flood ...of club teams and schoolboy teams' visiting England and in turn inviting teams to South Africa; somehow no-one ever invited South African non-whites. One problem, that would crop up for the rest of this story, was that people who wanted to keep playing South Africa, too used to getting their own way, saw and wrote about only what suited their case. Michael Melford for example, writing in Sunday Telegraph on Isaacs' tour and later in The Cricketer winter annual, condemned 'a tiny minority' and spied Communists ('singing the Internationale' as they left one field). Likewise Isaacs on his return to South Africa in mid-August 1969 complained of 'disgusting' demonstrators ('their language was filthy') without drawing any moral. In his private report to Lord's, Eriksen did. He suggested no matches in Scotland or Ireland ('from our own experience demonstrators in Ireland are more emotional').

He summed up that the 1970 tour would be a success, 'with reasonable security measures'. Yet if, as Eriksen believed, the demonstrations the next summer would be larger; and because, as he noted, on average it took three policemen to remove one demonstrator, to defend a cricket field against demonstrators ran the same risk as a coast at high tide; you built your wall, then had to watch if it held.

* * *

In September in Britain, summer sport ends and politics after its holiday begins. When someone stood at the Liberal Party annual conference at Brighton and said 'if the South African tour goes on next year, there's going to be a great deal of trouble', the hall cheered. Days earlier, Hain, Brutus and others had launched their 'Stop The Seventy Tour' group in London. At a National Party congress in South Africa, Vorster said that his government would not insist on the whiteness of every sportsman (which looked like hypocrisy; why then keep out D'Oliveira a year before, and if the colour of a sportsman's skin didn't matter, why should anyone else's? Vorster was making apartheid up as he went along). In a weekly column in mid-August, Norman

Norman Yardley.

Yardley – former Yorkshire and England amateur captain turned commentator, a more important figure than he may seem in the 21st century – hinted that 'certain people' were 'trying to push South Africa into including one or two coloured players, regardless of their quality, in the touring side, to appease apartheid factions here'. That may explain the letter of Arthur Coy of SACA to Griffith a month later, setting out his 'unofficial' (in other words, deniable) views. He claimed SACA always selected on merit; but, 'there are no non-whites who are good enough to be selected'. This was rank humbug – why then had D'Oliveira left for England? – because apartheid law segregated the sports field, the same as white and black could not be neighbours or married. Even in his letter, Coy admitted 'no local interracial cricket in South Africa' was allowed. What efforts were SACA making to scout non-white talent? What crumb could SACA throw to British public opinion? None, judging by Coy's letter; if tours stopped, he claimed, it would drive 'countless numbers of people into the segregation camp' (where he and his sport were, in truth, already).

English cricket had all winter to await, and debate, the 1970 tourists. On October 7, RA James of the Home Office saw Griffith for 'a fairly long talk', so he reported to the Foreign Office. James found Griffith had 'considerably changed his general thinking about the proposed tour since our meeting in April', when (according to a Foreign Office record) the MCC was already 'having second thoughts about the advisability of the tour'. The Isaacs tour was one reason:

it is recognised that hundreds of demonstrators can interrupt play almost indefinitely. Moderate opinion within the Cricket Council appears to have begun to doubt the wisdom of going ahead with the tour. Griffith said that in recent weeks GO Allen, Aidan Crawley [former MP, future MCC president] *and Wilfred Isaacs had all for the first time expressed this view to him.*

Here was a window on Lord's that it never opened to the public. Finance was another reason; what if, after ruined matches, South Africa had to fly home early? James reported Griffith 'moving to the view that the prudent course would be to call off the tour', despite the blow to South African cricket. Griffith was already thinking past the tour: "He told me that an alternative would be to organise a tour by a Rest of the World eleven, probably under the captaincy of Gary Sobers (or possibly the Nawab of Pataudi) which might include South African players like the Pollock brothers and Bland. He thought that such a team would be popular and profitable financially." James, so he told his FO counterparts, 'thought it right to nudge Griffith circumspectly along those lines of thinking', for example reminding Griffith of the cost of policing. That first, detailed, mention of the Rest of the World can explain why its first 'Test Match' against England began only 26 days after cancellation of South Africa. Griffith told James of a Christmas deadline, as afterwards the tour had to go ahead. Griffith saw conflict coming, 'as I understand', James wrote, 'that more than a few members of the [Cricket] Council are determined to continue with plans for the tour come what may'.

Another Home Office man was blunter. John Clift wrote to the Foreign Office, the day before Griffith and James met, that 'we must, I think, expect there to be a succession of actions on which cricket has to be abandoned or is so badly interfered with as to cause a scandal', such as people on the pitch 'or interference with the ball etc'.

Some cricket men could see no further than their county. At the Nottinghamshire club, one committee man at a meeting on October 27 was worried about how much Gary Sobers cost the club, 'particularly if the South African tour did not materialise', which suggested that the Lord's idea for a Rest of the World team had soon reached the counties. The tourists would play their first county game, by tradition, at Worcester. On October 29, the daily Worcester News ran a long letter by local vicar Malcolm Richards, who said he would give the match a blessing; 'it is time now that we segregate politics from sport', he wrote provocatively, claiming British sport had a 'proud heritage of race relations and the time has come for it to stand and defend itself against snivelling critics'. Another vicar the next day pointed out that 'four-fifths of South Africa's population are being denied basic human rights'.

Wilf Wooller, John Arlott, Ted Dexter and Denis Howell debated, with much publicity, at the Cambridge Union on November 10. That day, Cheetham and Coy of SACA went to Lord's. MCC committee man and a future president, Cecil Paris, while claiming that 'public opinion at present [is] on our side', feared the cost of police at grounds. On Monday, November 17, Mr James went to see Griffith, 'at his request'. According to James' report for the Foreign Office, Griffith was worrying about the cost of protecting grounds, 'and the possibility of acts of sabotage putting a cricket pitch out of use for a whole season'. James, no doubt still wanting to nudge Griffith towards cancelling, suggested police would cost 'upwards of £2000' for a three-day game. To give a few comparisons as an aside, £2000 was two years' pay for a workman; a football club spent about £2000 on Saturday afternoon policing; a shire county club spent

At a February 12, 1970 meeting at Lord's: Billy Griffith, Cecil Paris and Maurice Allom.

about £50,000 a year, a Test-hosting county like Surrey or Lancashire £100,000. As English cricket relied on profitable tours, usually by Australia, to stay in business, it could not afford many extra bills. Nor could police guarantee play. Griffith told James of the visit of Cheetham and Coy, 'and he said that the South Africans had indicated that they would be prepared to pay half the expense charged to any club for providing police protection. Griffith told me this in confidence and I made no comment in reply." The South Africans plainly wanted to tour so badly – suspiciously so – that they would go beyond the norm. Would someone pay the bill for SACA; would apartheid be paying for British police? No wonder James was cautious. Sooner or later, the press had a habit of finding out, if only because someone scandalised and in the know fed them. By December 1, the MCC was having to admit that it was looking into the costs of protecting grounds, and that two South African officials had met the Cricket Council for talks, but denied (in other words, lied about) any South African offer to pay. Asked to comment in Manchester, Lancashire's chairman Cedric Rhoades admitted a ground would need protecting for days before a match, besides the match days: 'of course the tour is still on and we should know just what it will cost at next week's meeting of the TCCB [Test and County Cricket Board]'. In those days, The Scotsman among other newspapers speculated that police costs would force the MCC to give up the tour, and that Home Secretary James Callaghan had rejected a 'tentative request' by MCC for money.

On December 10, previewing that two-day TCCB meeting for the Times, John Woodcock correctly noted that several county secretaries had 'misgivings' about hosting the South Africans, 'for practical, not political, reasons'. Protection of grounds, he said knowledgeably, would be 'prohibitively expensive': "I have yet to find anyone who holds any generous hope of a happy tour." He wondered in print if the TCCB would prefer an 'abbreviated' tour or one by a 'World XI'. John Arlott in the Guardian offered those same two alternatives. He wrote as dubiously of the tour as Woodcock: difficult to see it as practicable; 'harder still to believe that it could be financially successful'. Inside the Foreign Office in mid-November, Sir John Johnston had been even more definite; that the MCC could not run the 'financial risk' seemed to him 'inevitable'.

Why, then, when EE Harrison met his Sussex club committee, the week after that meeting at Lord's, did he report that 'the most important item concerned future cricket structure', namely the mix of one and three-day games? Was he a fool, or a liar? As for the tour, the TCCB agreed unanimously to a sub-committee, 'to examine ways and means'. John Thicknesse for the London Evening Standard, having faced the 'determined silence' of committee members, reported once it was all over that the final Test could last for eight days, in case of hold-ups by weather or demonstrators. JL Manning, now in the Evening Standard, accused the TCCB of 'idealistic bunkum' that the public would subsidise – through their taxes for the police. He summed up: "No good will come of it, at a time cricket needs all the goodwill it can get."

Between October and November when Griffith and others had sounded the alarm, something had happened – or had failed to happen. Sir John Johnston in mid-November had shrewdly noted 'we have not much room for manoeuvre', meaning that soon Lord's had to set the tour calendar; agree the cut of profits; print tickets. As early as October 7, John Clift at the Home Office had set out how the prospect was 'pretty gloomy either way'; if the tour went ahead and 'antis' disrupted it, 'we [the British government] shall no doubt be considered "soft"'; if MCC did cancel in advance, 'it would cause widespread dismay', in South Africa, and some would suspect, 'however falsely', the Labour Government put pressure on MCC.

Perhaps the 'anti' campaign might fade? So Sir Dennis Greenhill at the Foreign Office wondered in mid-November, 'as I am told it may well do for lack of funds'. Counties had enough reasons to stand by old friends in South Africa; 'blind faith that everything will come right in the end', as

Thicknesse put it; hatred of 'lefties', he might have added. Crucially, the counties at the TCCB meeting had to do nothing, and the tour would proceed. Griffith, Allen and any 'moderates' urging cancellation – oddly, no-one seemed to suggest putting it off a year – had to do more; they had to convince their fellows to change their mind, and agree to something different. Instead, to judge from Thicknesse's report, the TCCB hoped to avoid paying for police on a technicality; to muddle through. He ended with foresight that may have come from a tip-off about something already discussed around the TCCB table: "The one way it can be protected cheaply is by barbed wire fencing around the edge. And I would sooner no tour than that."

Another sceptical journalist, Arlott, wrote of 'surprise' that the TCCB was unanimous; it seemed to make no sense, as Griffith admitted that counties would have to 'dig deep into their pockets'. Arlott found it noteworthy that besides the usual Griffith and Jack Bailey, MCC employees, the TCCB chairman Cecil Paris and the former England batsman now Surrey and TCCB committee man Raman Subba Row, fielded questions; as if the administrators sought strength in numbers.

The press was already speculating about the cost of policing cricket; 100 policemen costing £10 a day, for three days, made £3000. John Clift at the Home Office had gone into detail as early as September 29. The Metropolitan Police charged £10 9s 9d a day for hire of a constable (more for higher ranks), or £1 6s 3d an hour, and you had to hire for at least three hours. A policewoman was slightly cheaper, £9 5s 9d an hour. Time and a half for all on public holidays. Clift speculated that public order, and the cost of keeping it, were 'not likely in themselves to justify calling off the tour'. In other words, to cancel, someone had to take a political decision.

That was not Griffith's to take; in any case, he seemed to be planning for the tour. At a Nottinghamshire county committee meeting on December 8, club secretary Ron Poulton read out two letters from Griffith, about 'the problems of grounds security which were likely to arise'. Griffith was looking for estimates of police costs. Poulton had already discussed it with a senior local policeman, who (totting up 200 men during the match, some out of hours besides, and beforehand) came up with a minimum £20,000. That was a suspiciously round number; yet for a club that had lost £4000 in the last year, making a total deficit of £30,000, any such sum was madness. "The committee felt that with the added risk of irreparable damage, this alone made the tour impracticable," the minutes read. A comment by one committee man, Michael Dennis, explained why English cricket was carrying on regardless: he was for the tour, 'if at all possible, for the good of cricket'. Why let a few noughts keep you from seeing the most exciting team in the world?! Reg Simpson, the former captain now committee man, likewise was for, 'if any guarantee was forthcoming to make good any damage'. In January, after Sir Arthur Snelling the new ambassador in Pretoria did some canvassing of what money South African cricket could stump up, JA Pugh at the Foreign Office wrote that the 'financial impracticability will emerge naturally'. It already had, at committee tables around England; and men had ignored it.

Raman Subba Row was one of a younger generation of more commercially-minded cricket administrators. In a letter to Griffith on October 22, as Subba Row was retiring as chairman of the TCCB's public relations sub-committee, he wrote:

I am more than ever convinced that our problem is one of public relations. We are mostly agreed that 1) we dislike apartheid in sport. 2) we cannot alter the laws of the land in South Africa. 3) the best method of exercising our influence is by continuing to play against South Africa most of whose cricketers agree with our way of thinking.

Subba Row then applied his PR mind to how to win the public over. "What we must do is to create news which will make it clear that the SACA has its heart in the right place." Could SACA select a coloured player or manager?

Here inside Lord's was the idea Yardley had already scoffed at. Or, Subba Row went on, 'a mixed side of lesser ability sponsored by SACA', as 'a practical demonstration of good faith on the part of SACA'. Needless to say, neither happened (and why couldn't SACA come up with these ideas?). Subba Row, the son of an Indian, who, had he flourished for England a few years earlier or later might have caused his own D'Oliveira-like 'affair', could have been as powerful a voice against white South Africa as David Sheppard. Subba Row was clear-sighted about South Africa: "If they want to have their cake and eat it," he added, meaning if SACA wanted to tour without giving something to other races, "then we are taking a considerable risk by defending them. This would invariably reflect on MCC who have surely taken enough blame for other people's actions already."

Talking of South Africa, sport mattered to the whites. Their foreign minister Dr Hilgard Muller, on a courtesy call to the Foreign Office while on a (private) visit to London in June 1969, significantly raised sporting contacts during a talk on commercial relations. Muller's meaning; if South Africa was good enough to trade with, it should be good enough to play with. That was one sign of how those in authority in apartheid would never compromise, unless made to, politically; and how hollow was Subba Row's talk of 'public relations'. In fairness, the Labour Government was sending at best mixed messages. Foreign Secretary Michael Stewart sent a telegram to the British embassy in Pretoria in November 1969, sharing its 'concern' at sporting contacts (or lack of them) having an 'adverse effect on Anglo-South African relations'. He asked the embassy to stick to his government's 'policy of official neutrality'. Stewart repeated his assurance made at that June meeting with his South African equivalent; 'that the government will not seek to influence' a sport's decision to play South Africa, 'in any way'. That went further than Howell, who was only promising not to pressure sport 'officially'. That word – as used by Stewart already in his message - made all the difference, as it allowed politicians to be 'unofficial'; Stewart's lack of attention to detail would embarrass him later. As politicians were giving so weak a lead, officials did as they pleased. The Foreign Office in mid-September 1969 spotted that the 1970 tour would have a match against the Combined Services; the FO wanted to 'clear this' with the Ministry of Defence. The MoD had written the day before to the FO that the Combined Services 'of course would very much like to arrange such a fixture' and one of its officials could see no reason why not. The junior defence minister Roy Hattersley wrote to Harold Wilson on November 3, proposing to tell the Portsmouth commander-in-chief not to allow the match. Wilson agreed. A hitch was that the services had arranged the match as far back as early 1968, at Aldershot. That now appeared too hard to defend (ironically, for an Army site) against demonstrators. Hence the move to the Navy ground at Portsmouth, whose walls could keep demos out better. Hattersley argued that it would look as if the government was co-operating with the South Africans; but, as the fixture was long agreed, Hattersley – while publicly against the tour – was 'more relaxed' about it. Hattersley, ambitious enough to be careful, had discussed it with Howell, who agreed.

Who in power was doing a thing against apartheid? In November 1969, people without power started to change that.

Chapter Four

Rugby: the first weeks

Every people, the proverb has it, loves its own form of violence.
   Clifford Geerte, Notes on the Balinese Cockfight, 1973

While some newspaper headlines called it a 'quiet welcome', the demonstrators were there, about 20 of them, from Reading University; booing at the Springbok rugby team at Heathrow on Thursday morning, October 30, 1969. Their captain Dawie de Villiers said: "We had a few demonstrations when we were last here in '65 so we do expect some trouble." Just as the change between (say) a 15-year-old and a 19-year-old is obvious to a distant relation, and not to parents who see their child every day, the Springboks were about to see how Britain had changed. The Springboks did not know where they would play Oxford University in their first match.

In mid-October Thames Valley Police chief constable TCB Hodgson had written to the university's Rugby Football Union, warning of 'severe public disorder' and 'severe strain on police resources', if the RFU played the Springboks on the open Iffley Road ground. The university took the hint, and looked for another ground. The week before the Wednesday afternoon, November 5 match, Greig Barr, the Oxford club treasurer, said that clubs 'up and down the country' offered to host, 'but I don't think it's really possible now ... it would have to be an all-ticket game and there wouldn't be time'. The night after the match, on ITV, Roy Hattersley defended himself and the police from fellow guest, the pro-rugby Wilf Wooller. Hattersley said 'the police were responding to people with rather more sophisticated views than you, Mr Wooller'; when Oxford tried to use the Services's Aldershot or Portsmouth grounds, Hattersley as minister refused to take sides; so he pretended. As he well knew, by not helping Oxford, he was taking the side of protest.

With about 30 hours' notice to police, Oxford arranged to use Twickenham. Two demo coaches came from Reading, two from Oxford; other students were from Essex, Leicester, Cambridge, Leeds and Manchester. Met Police Deputy Assistant Commissioner (DAC) John Lawlor recalled in January that only the west stands and terraces were open. Only a four feet high metal fence stood between rows of benches and the west terraces, and the field of play; police kept spectators off the benches and still struggled to keep order at the fence. While Lawlor sent officers onto the terraces 'to break up' trouble-makers he could see, he chose not to arrest any as it 'would have led to far more trouble'. As with football hooliganism, police could not do their job fully. Much of the match sounded unpromising for the protest cause. Of the 540 police commanded by DAC Lawlor, Twickenham only had to pay for 79. Most of the crowd (estimated from 5,000 to 15,000), evidently on the Springboks' side, gave them a 'tremendous reception', so Barry Newcombe reported for the London Evening Standard, and 'far outweighed the volume of demonstration outside the ground'.

Barry Newcombe's words two days before were significant, when rugby union asked club members to show their membership card at the turnstiles, or pay ten shillings, without knowing yet where the match would be. Rugby union according to Newcombe had been 'frightened out of Oxford by threats' and were 'farcical', a 'laughing stock'. Hain likewise on the day told reporters the aim was to turn the match into 'a farce'. STST succeeded, as reporters such as Newcombe saw, as they sat in the otherwise empty east stand. Wire blocked their stand and terrace, the north end, and their tunnels. Mounted police stood by in case of emergency; a loudspeaker van outside said it was from 'the fireworks day committee against racialism in sport', claiming to support 'all the people who are suffering under apartheid'. Rugby was powerless against this enemy on its doorstep; it lost face. Thus although, as Hain admitted in his 1971 book, that first match's actual protest was 'not all that successful', 'in fact it was a triumph for the movement'.

Merely for protesters to show they were still around could count as success. At Twickenham again on November 22, Newcombe reported how more than 100 demonstrators sat on the middle of the field; police and stewards took five minutes to remove them; players meanwhile stood in a corner, passing the ball to each other: "It was a ridiculous atmosphere for a major rugby match." The rugby authorities saw it too. After the November 5 match, at an RFU meeting, the treasurer WC Ramsay said a demonstrator invading the pitch was not chased, in case it was a 'source of ridicule'. Instead the invader was 'allowed to settle' and a steward, attended by police for legal reasons, 'asked him to move'. If he refused, police removed him. Otherwise, a steward led him off. The protesters had found, literally and metaphorically, a level playing field. They stayed the course; on January 30, previewing the last match of the tour, Newcombe called it a 'bizarre winter'.

Students were using these tactics already. At Oxford in October 1969, the university vice-chancellor – the historian Alan Bullock, who kept out of the rugby protest – left the Sheldonian Theatre to meet 'a crowd of singing, dancing, and jeering anti-matriculation revellers' who were showing their dislike of the ceremony for new undergraduates. Noise, even dressed up as a carnival, was a weapon.

Protesters made a stir; sometimes childishly. The only invader of the Twickenham pitch on November 5 was a 60-year-old Surrey teacher, Bill Laithwaite. He walked on before the second half, wearing shorts and striped socks (and spectacles) as if the referee; took his sweater off to show the words AA (for 'anti-apartheid') on his back, and kicked the ball away. The protesters and others had to reckon whether the fuss amounted to success. The Oxford Times at Twickenham reported the demonstrators 'were often drowned out by the cheers and clapping' from people in the ten shilling seats, 'who included a large South African contingent'. The protesters were always in a minority inside grounds, sometimes in danger from the rest who resented having their entertainment spoiled. With a title of Stop The Seventy Tour, the likes of Hugh Geach, a Reading University student and secretary of STST, were aiming high, and he was only stating the obvious when he said before the first match: "We would like to make sure that no games take place." That the game did happen meant the Mirror could reasonably print the headline, 'Springboks protest flops'. John Tarver, treasurer of the Oxford protesters' Fireworks Day Committee, also talked big. They had chased the Springboks out of Oxford, he said: "We have got to keep them running." Less reported was what those watching the rugby had to say. One exception came from Peter Jenkins of the Guardian, who watched on November 5 from the west stand, not the press box. He reported that 'rugger men' cheered as police 'manhandled' a 'coloured student'; 'sportsmen' (he wrote ironically) shouted 'put the boot in, you coppers'. "What I saw was an organised contingent of South Africans waving flags and urging on the police to suppress a peaceful demonstration by British citizens against unwelcome visitors from a detested country." Two sides were drawn up; in public, which made it political. As Jenkins put it uncomfortably, the rugby only went ahead, 'to the satisfaction of Dr Vorster, by kind permission of the British Government and its coppers'.

As that implied, protest was only half the story, at most; as were the forces against them; the police, how they kept the peace, and how they defined it, also counted. Tellingly, the Twickenham loudspeaker announcer, Peter Yarranton, asked the crowd to leave control 'to our friends, the police'. Newcombe afterwards wrote that the police 'did quite competently' at Twickenham 'what', he added shrewdly, 'others throughout the country will have to do to safeguard the tour'. The next match was on Saturday afternoon, November 8, at Leicester. While every county or city police force had its own ways, they would learn from each other. Leicester and Rutland chief constable John Taylor invited two inspectors of constabulary to watch; Gwent Police chief William Farley sent three senior officers to Leicester, days before they hosted the Springboks, and 'drastically revised' his arrangements afterwards, one of the inspectors, Frank Williamson, reported.

Leicester demo organisers days before agreed a march, led by a police van, around the city centre at lunchtime on the day. Police had time to divert traffic. Marchers were supposed to turn into the park beside the Welford Road rugby ground, hear speeches and disperse. Instead those at the front (presumably the most motivated) tried to march to the ground. Mounted police went into the demonstrators, throwing some of them, Saturday shoppers and Sunday Telegraph reporters Gerald Bartlett and Barrie Mattei against walls. A policeman was doubled up in pain, 'after a hefty kick in the groin'. Ambulances forcing their way through to pick up the injured; skinheads, Hell's Angels, 'black power' banners; no wonder such anarchy made the front pages. Reporters, lacking experience, fell back on vague phrases such as 'really tough skirmishes' (Leicester Mercury) and 'running battle' (Observer). The force of numbers ruled. Right-wing scufflers from the National Front had their banners smashed. The demo broke one line of police and surged for the ground, only for a second line

Aerial photo of Leicester looking north, showing the rugby ground at Welford Road. Trouble arose when marchers would not turn into (and, police hoped, soon disperse) into the park, at the top of the picture.

with horses to force the protesters into a side street. Police at the Welford Road gates stood shoulder to shoulder, checking tickets. Inside were 15,000, by far the biggest group of the day, which explained why protesters tried but failed to stop ticket-holders walking to the ground 'after one or two angry scenes'. Michael Melford for the Sunday Telegraph and other reporters noted the crowd gave the Springboks 'an enthusiastic ovation'.

Court cases added detail to the story later. Stuart Roach, an 18-year-old London student described as one of the organisers, denied a public order offence but was fined £25. He told magistrates that he grabbed the lapel of a policeman who he thought was using unnecessary force, to find out his number – which he shouted, and which demonstrators around him began shouting too. More outrightly violent were unnamed 'student leaders' who tried to get people to charge the police. In fairness, those leading the march had asked by loudspeaker for it to turn away from Welford Road, only to provoke 'a mass cry of no'. The demo was deceptive; the crowd was not united. Someone threw red paint. Some took their shoes off and threw them at police. Others more peaceable, though still risking an arrest for a 'public order' offence, sat in the road. The students from several universities, trade unionists, and Communists had never met; they had too many tactics and targets (the police, or the rugby?) or none.

Hain, in what was already becoming a pattern, reckoned to the London Evening Standard that simply having so many police there was a victory. Even in the thick of the rugby, he was thinking of the cricket tour, which he claimed was already off: "Nobody in their right mind can say otherwise …. what we can do to rugby we can do 100 more times to cricket." Hain's point hit home, though he did not know it. Days later, Billy Griffith told RA James of the Foreign Office that the secretary of Leicestershire County Cricket Club, Mike Turner, told him that after seeing the recent Springboks match 'he [Turner] was in no doubt that a cricket match against the South Africans could not be held in Leicester next year'. So much for the unanimous TCCB vote weeks later.

Frank Williamson, one of the inspectors of constabulary, made the best witness, if only because he was well placed and could report at leisure. He watched some of the day on the city corporation transport department's new closed-circuit television. Of the 990 police on duty (Leicester police's operational order said 1080) only 75 were inside Welford Road; of the 2000 estimated demonstrators, only 20 had to be removed from the field of play. Significantly, Williamson in his report felt he had to cover 'reasonable force' by police, which as he said 'depended on physical reaction of each demonstrator'. That did imply that each policeman had to judge, in an instant, on a charged day, what was 'reasonable'. Williamson reported that he did not see any 'untoward physical force by any police'. He soon would.

* * *

How important was the Leicester (or any) match, whether as an experience for those there, or in the overall, three-month tour? The day before, the Leicester Mercury built up the 'battle of Welford Road'; police were planning at their London Road headquarters, students in coffee bars. As in warfare, many of the police, for much of the time, may have felt bored. Most came from outside Leicester; those from London came by coach up the M1, carrying their lunch with them (not to be eaten on the journey) in boxes with cutlery (to be returned to the Met Police catering branch). Significantly, police chiefs and students alike were talkative about their plans for the day: police, to inform spectators, shoppers and visitors to the nearby infirmary to leave themselves more time for journeys; the students, simply to rally their side. Before the internet had pictures of the famous, and while it was easier to keep a secret, the Mercury did not know, or at least did not say, where the Springboks were staying. While a handful of demonstrators were outside the tourists' hotel, some Springboks 'strolled around the city in their distinctive green blazers', without trouble. Just as that implied the protesters were not looking that carefully, nor were the anti-antis. An anonymous Leicester Mercury man inside Welford Road recalled a man behind him was 'out of his seat screaming blankety blank thunder' at a banner, raised at half time. "I pointed out that it appeared to be a 'Welcome Springboks' banner. Oh, he said, disappointed, that's all right then."

One responsibility of leaders was to have more of a grip on reality. Ged Murray, vice-president of the Leicester Students Union, admitted afterwards: "We lost control of the demonstration once we got outside the prison," next door to the park and Welford Road. Revealingly, Murray went on to measurable things – he was pleased at so few arrests, and injuries; and suggested the cost of policing alone might stop the tour ('they are going to have to do this every time'). However, leaders also have to express the unmeasurable – how people feel (or ought to feel, for the good of the cause, and to turn public opinion their way). Hain did give followers unmeasurable things, such as hope. Williamson the inspector of constabulary picked up a phrase of Hain's after Leicester ('we are determined') to end his report on Leicester: "There is no doubt about his determination to continue the protest." Here was the most profound question of modern life: how to measure, and so master, the intangible things, like determination, and how to put a value on them, to compare the qualitative with the quantifiable? Value for money, for one thing. Police found it hard enough to put a price on their work; the chief constable John Taylor told one newspaper the cost of policing the Leicester match was £10,000, another, 'more than £5000'. The marchers cared more about how good was the police service. How could you weigh people's experiences? At Leicester as at other tour matches, for every complaint – of a police kick on the ankle, or knee in the face when you were down – you had an anonymous five pound note pressed into the hand of a policeman on duty; and police horses fed with sugar and apples. Out of a thousand policemen, or marchers, or anyone, you would have all characters – some would relish a scrap, or turn a blind eye. Some actions were hard to interpret – when a copper dived into a mass of demonstrators, was it to do hurt, make an arrest, or rescue someone crushed? Success, for either side, rugby and the antis, was both quantifiable – the tour stopped or it did not; the tour would make a profit or loss – and it was not. The same sight could provoke opposite feelings; noisy protest could spoil the match for you, or make it special; a bystander could identify with the police or the protest.

Special Branch, at Leicester to identify 'various prime movers', faced this same problem as it spied on STST – how to measure the unquantifiable, to tell which activists were full of wind and who meant business. A November report that called Hain 'the young Rhodesian liberal' was only two-thirds accurate; he and his family had been exiled from South Africa. Police evidently had an intimate source; their October 30 report gossiped sourly that 'only a few more heroic supporters' had volunteered to attend Springbok fixtures in Wales, because the Welsh 'are thought to be, to say the least, hostile to rugby matches being interfered with'.

* * *

As early as the third match of the tour, at Newport, south Wales, on Wednesday, November 12, the security around Springbok matches had matured. Securicor was patrolling the rugby ground that had a telephone line installed direct to the police station. Steel barriers in the streets around the ground made a checkpoint for police to check for weapons and only allow through ticket-holders. At Leicester, demonstrators inside the ground had worn armbands like the stewards; Newport's stewards wore rugby jerseys. Newport was not as violent as Leicester, Williamson reported; and if the at most 400 protesters had broken through, the 20,000 spectators would have been violent, 'and possibly beyond the ability of police to control'.

Williamson's report on Swansea, the next match, on Saturday, November 15, showed that the police and the rugby club could have seen trouble coming. The club let terrace spectators pay on the day, 'a freedom of access ...

which is clearly undesirable'. The St Helens club had 'several weak points'; at Bryn Road for instance (where students had lodgings, next door to the new campus) you could reach the ground through gardens. Williamson warned that the Swansea march from the town's civic centre would want to stand outside the ground; it would not go the nearby beach as agreed. It moved off at 2pm, 'orderly', and had 'some strong but good-humoured banter' with spectators walking the same way. As the marchers in files of four on the bayside road reached the length of the grandstand, they halted. Police walking in line with them joined arms. Williamson, watching out of a window in the stand, noted a red and black 'Swansea Anarchists' banner at the front of about 60 'mostly young men'. Things quickly turned nasty, from pushing against the police to 'physical force ... in both directions'. Williamson saw – what, he was too polite to say, the local police supposed to be in command did not – that the march had to move on, or police had to break up the trouble-makers, because the marchers behind wanted to walk on and were causing a crush. Williamson went outside and took charge ('as far as was possible') and after ten minutes of arrests, the fighting stopped. The column went onto the beach; police re-grouped and linked arms.

It was 2.45pm; the match began at 3pm. A fresh column came from the other direction, the university. In a 'lesser confrontation', someone threw a smoke canister as used on farms. The match's first half passed with shouts from outside, and demonstrators inside trying to hand out leaflets ('not many accepted') until some demonstrators tried to scale the fence between Bryn Road and the terraces. Soon after half time, about 100 people ran on the pitch from the 'cash enclosure'; that is, those paying on the day, not club members. One of them was Hugh Geach. He told the Guardian: "Three policemen took hold of me, one of them by the groin, and chucked me into a crowd of vigilantes." From now, Williamson's proper, police-English, by habit or on purpose, did not capture the scene. Reporters at Leicester the previous Saturday had foreshadowed it. What if the rugger crowd takes the law into its own hands, the

Mercury asked; a demo was 'liable to get more than they bargain for'; while Michael Melford wrote in the Sunday Telegraph: "It needs no great imagination to picture a large crowd of unpolitical responsible British citizens addressing themselves forcibly to a rabble which tries to prevent them watching an important rugby match ..."

Williamson described the next three or four minutes as 'extremely confused'; the pitch invaders were 'roughly handled' by stewards, police, and even spectators ('taking direct action', Williamson wrote, possibly ironically, given that was Hain's prized phrase). From the tunnel in the stand, Williamson saw 'unnecessary force'. The slack policing all day went as far as the 'confused and not satisfactory' detaining of the 62 arrested at the civic centre – as usual on the tour, more or less all demonstrators - because police were not matching an arresting officer to a prisoner, as they were supposed to by law. Was the policing so weak because the police were incompetent, or they wanted the protesters to take a hiding; or both? The rugby commentator and demonstrator John Morgan saw police punching and kicking. He asked a senior officer to stop it 'and his reply was, "It's persons like yourself who cause the trouble by putting people like them on television."'

From the press box above the tunnel in the stand, reporters could only take in so much. Richard Streeton of the Times saw 'a milling mob'; pulling of hair, spitting: "Twice I saw demonstrators being hit over the head with their own banner."

Edward Bailey went through the turnstile at 3.30pm, one more example of how Swansea was slacker than Leicester; would any rugby fan have been half an hour late? He found some fellow Leicester University students behind one of the goalposts. They chanted such slogans as 'apartheid out', 'and probably Sieg Heil'; as he was making a statement to police, he may have felt embarrassed to admit using the Nazi salute as an insult. The stewards shouted back, 'shut it' and 'go home' and the crowd behind threw grass and moss. Bailey and the other protesters faced stewards with orange armbands, who at half time handed out several armbands to 'enthusiastic spectators'. About ten stewards entered the crowd and jeered and jostled the demonstrators who, if they had not realised by now, were about to realise that if you tried to get your own way by force of numbers, you ran the risk of your enemy having their way, if they had the numbers. The stewards attacked, 'using their fists and feet'. Bailey ran. "One steward grabbed hold of me. I pushed him away. As my path was blocked to the left by other stewards and to the right by a metal fence and above me by the crowd I jumped over the wall and ran on to the pitch." The second half had begun. Had Bailey, ironically, invaded the pitch to save himself? If so, did he have to run to the opposite goalposts, turn, and run past the players to the middle? In any case, Bailey let a policeman grab him. Police half-carried, half-dragged him off the pitch, through a door, into a lobby, 'where we were pushed from one policeman to another until a last policeman pushed me out through a door into the street. I landed on my face." Bruised – Bailey listed the physical bruises, not the psychological ones – he returned to Leicester by coach.

A sure sign that Swansea rugby club was in the wrong and that police had blundered was that Dai Price the club secretary would not comment. The Home Secretary Jim Callaghan called for reports, and a meeting of chief constables for November 24. In the House of Commons, Michael Foot (MP for Ebbw Vale, due to host the next match) complained of 'vigilantes'; Richard Streeton in the Times commented that Swansea set 'a dangerous precedent'. In his 1971 book and 2012 memoir, Peter Hain, who was not at Swansea, dwelt on the hurt done to demonstrators. At the time, he sounded aggressive, telling reporters that Ebbw Vale 'could make Swansea seem like a tea party'. Hain in his memoir claimed he and STST leaders had 'a fearless idealism'; their focus on ends ('our cause was just') could appear indifferent to casualties (including, in fairness, themselves). Their January 1970 newsletter for instance coldly urged protests to be 'effective', by going beyond the rugby grounds, such as sitting in front of the Springboks'

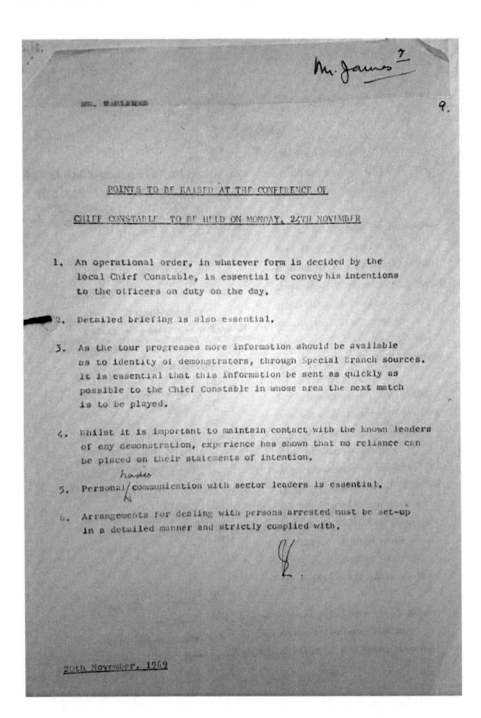

From a Home Office file, 'points to be raised' at the November 24, 1969 meeting between Home Secretary James Callaghan and chief constables, including identifying demonstrators 'through Special Branch sources'.

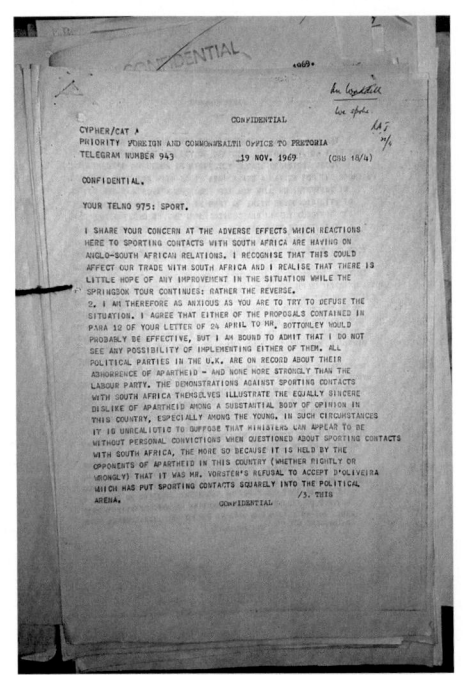

First page of a telex dated November 19, 1969 from Foreign Secretary Michael Stewart to the British ambassador in South Africa, 'anxious … to try to defuse the situation'.

coach, or 'harassment in the hotel'.

Sports terraces could be crowded, rough places. Derby County FC in December 1969 used marshals, for the popular match against local rivals Nottingham Forest, to organise 'the packing of the crowd' by loudhailer. At a Glamorgan cricket club committee meeting in March 1969 – inside the pavilion at the St Helens ground – committee member Oswyn Davies complained that the stewarding of Glamorgan matches 'at the football end had not been too good'. Davies saw a steward let his friends in. Stewards, then, were untrustworthy ('always a problem') and clubs could do little about it ('one can only rely on plugging the holes as they were seen'). Just as some of the stewards at Swansea had been smiling as they beat students, so Wilf Wooller relished it all. Denis Howell passed on a story from Thursday night, December 11 at the BBC sports review of the year; there Wooller had told him Swansea hadn't been charged for police, and Cardiff (about to host the

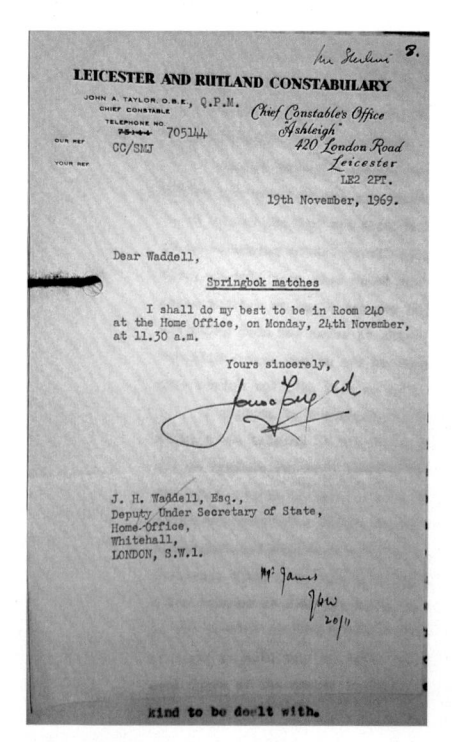

Before the age of email or even fax machines, Leicester chief constable John Taylor sent a letter to accept the invite to the November 24 meeting at the Home Office.

Springboks on the Saturday) would not need police in the ground, because the club would use stewards; and 'this issue would in itself be likely to bring the government down in an election year'. This was far from the last time Wooller pressed his wishful, right-wing views on others. The irony (that escaped Wooller) was that in his mind Labour would fall because it could not keep law and order, whereas the worst breakdown in order came on Wooller's patch, at Swansea.

How violent were police, there or anywhere? At the first international, against England at Twickenham on Saturday, December 20, the Times rugby correspondent UA Titley heard a policeman asked, what if demonstrators handcuffed themselves to a goalpost? "Sir," he replied, "we are well equipped with bone cutters." Police had a knack of finding humour; except it did not really answer the question. Police chiefs naturally spoke proudly of their men in public; 'the men of all ranks acted superbly', John Taylor said after Leicester. Ged Murray the student suggested the Leicester police acted with restraint and humour, while the bussed-in 'London commandos' - who had less fear of being caught? - were violent. An even more likely but invisible difference was the spectrum inside the policemen's heads; some welcomed, some avoided a fight, and those in the middle took what came with the job. In confrontations, who did what and where blame lay became too tangled for a court to truly judge. To take two Leicester University students among many in court for sitting in the road in Piccadilly after the Springboks' match at Manchester on November 26. The one who admitted a public order offence shouted 'get your hands off me, you bastards' when police carried him to the pavement. One who denied but was convicted of assaulting a policeman, said he was going to aid another demonstrator. Did the youths mean well, at least at first? Did the police cynically know that what they did would trigger a reaction, that would justify an arrest? If police were, as one Scottish newspaper described them at Aberdeen on December 2, a 'human shield', harm was inevitable. Could you blame anyone, if - as a Manchester policewoman, the husband of a policeman, wrote to her local paper – when kicked and pushed, he gave back 'as good as he gets'? A Yorkshire Post editorial in May 1970, recalling the rugby tour, showed sympathy for the police who, unlike protesters, 'had to abide by an established code of legal and social behaviour'. Except that with the police uniform (and pay) came responsibilities.

Two issues arose; was there 'police brutality' as alleged (for example) after the Scotland match at Murrayfield on December 6; and if so, was it excusable? Over the three-month tour, so many people gave the same sort of stories. Students at Murrayfield claimed police had their truncheons concealed up their sleeves; they pinned protesters' arms, forced their faces to the ground, and swore. One Scotsman reader after Murrayfield reckoned 'the police were not hitting them hard enough or often enough' and hoped that would be 'remedied'. The Scotsman did more than most newspapers; it featured several named victims. One 16-year-old lad, who 'had merely gone to watch the match', with his brother, was pushed by a policeman to the ground, 'where there was glass, although I had done nothing'. The Tory MP George Younger, newly returned from three weeks in South Africa, praised the Murrayfield police for 'a marvellous job under the usual deliberate provocation'. Maybe at some matches, in some parts of the ground, police and stewards came to a quick, informal understanding that their chiefs never knew about. John Gisby may have seen an example, in the second half of the Springboks' match at White City, Manchester. He wrote to the Manchester Evening News that he had lost respect for police. Stewards mingled among some demonstrators, 'and as soon as one opened his mouth he was grabbed and the area would become a mass of blue helmets'. Were Gisby's and others' tales of police fists and boots one-sided, however? The demonstrators, too, must have been on a spectrum of violence, from the anarchists at the front of the marches – even their 'smash racialism' banners were aggressive - to 'chaps who could not punch a paper bag themselves' punched by police at Swansea, according to John Morgan. There lay the worst unfairness, if big coppers picked on the smallest and meekest. Small but not meek was the Northern Irish civil rights campaigner and MP Bernadette Devlin. Though the most famous protester in the British Isles, she was not the most obvious marcher to Lansdowne Road in Dublin on Saturday, January 10, 1970. After the Ireland-Springboks match, when the Irish Times asked her to compare how the Royal Ulster Constabulary handled civil rights demos, with Irish Republic police and the anti-apartheid one, she had the wisdom of experience:

'As far as tactics are concerned, they are equally lacking in formal, effective training though as individuals they [Irish gardai] are more clever in their tactics ... they are more calculating in digging the boot in rather than immediately drawing their batons which draws attention to themselves. Nobody sees the elbows going.'

Like the hidden truncheons in Edinburgh, that television viewers would not see, police could be crafty. Devlin had seen how police ignored some crimes or provocations (rugby supporters throwing sandwiches and peel at marchers) and not others. When a man jumped on the Lansdowne Road wall to wave a 'Plough and Stars', the 'Connolly flag' of Irish socialism, 'they [gardai] immediately assumed that here was a trouble-maker who had to be removed'. And yet Devlin added that overall Dublin police behaviour was 'very good', while she intended to complain to the Garda commissioner. Perhaps she and other protest leaders could have such a split opinion of what police did, not only because the countless police-protester interactions defied a verdict (humanity's problem again of weighing qualities) but because the leaders had a mixed view of the social peace that police stood for. A Sheffield Morning Telegraph editorial of December 12 called the rugby tour a 'shambles'; the worse it got, the better it was for STST's cause. Their leaders were oddly emotional and cold at the same time. Militancy was, Hain wrote pitilessly in his memoir, 'necessary'.

★ ★ ★

The Ebbw Vale game was quieter, part of a pattern of less trouble in mid-week, more on Saturdays. In the House of Commons, Jim Callaghan batted off questions from MPs, flippantly agreeing it was better that police kept the peace, 'rather than have amateur assistants, no doubt of a very beefy character'. He did his business at the meeting with chief constables at the Home Office on November 24. Speaking notes, prepared for Callaghan by his officials, urged rugby clubs 'to recognise that they had a problem on their hands and to go out of their way to comply with police'. Again, those in authority showed how sensitive they were to publicity; the Swansea stewards' 'behaviour ... caused a great deal of public disquiet'. That seemed to matter more than the actual beatings.

The notes and Frank Williamson in his report to the meeting suggested a 'written notice' for policemen, as at Leicester. This would remind them what to do: people had the right to demonstrate peacefully; ejecting demonstrators from the rugby ground should be by police only, 'with the minimum of force' - a significant difference from 'reasonable force', let alone Swansea; and police should only arrest to preserve the peace. Police should brief stewards; appoint an officer to field complaints; and plan to handle dozens of arrests. Though Williamson and everyone inside the meeting were too polite to say so, as was Callaghan speaking to the press afterwards, they were learning from Swansea's mistakes. Details were fuzzy enough for police on the ground, whether on purpose or in the heat of getting the job done, to defy what rules London set. The meeting suggested stewards 'should be confined to general administrative duties', such as showing people to their seats; at Murrayfield, to name one big match, stewards were part of the police line. And did anyone tell Wilf Wooller?!

After Ebbw Vale came Twickenham again, in fact the Saturday before Callaghan's meeting. His notes, pointing to 'Maoists and International Socialists' and 'the uncooperative attitude' of demo organisers, expected 'a good deal of trouble' there. DAC Lawlor the Twickenham match commander reported afterwards a procession from

Twickenham railway station and in all 2000 demonstrating, compared with a crowd of at most 25,000 in a stadium of capacity 70,000. Then came Manchester; and Ulster, in Belfast, on Saturday, November 29. On the Tuesday before, Michael Stewart sent a telegram to the British embassy in Pretoria to explain delicately that 'the special situation in Northern Ireland' - more exactly, university students and Roman Catholic civil rights campaigners threatening a demo - caused the authorities in Belfast to call that match off that day. Harold Wilson on November 10 had asked Callaghan and the Defence Secretary Denis Healey to look into the match: "He [Wilson] thinks that this could spark off some serious trouble." The decision, then, while highly political, had security reasons; Met Police Commander John Gerrard flew to Belfast the day before the decision, to survey the Ravenhill rugby ground. And the cancelling came at short notice; as late as November 21, Sir Philip Allen was minuting on a report by Frank Williamson that Garda, police of the Irish Republic, were not allowed to come to see how the British policed the Springboks, ahead of the tour matches in the Republic, in another six weeks. While the cancelling in Belfast made newspaper front pages - like most news about apartheid tours - it was striking how casually rugby took the cancellation. It was part of a greater, decades-long indifference in mainland Britain to the near-war in Northern Ireland.

* * *

Cricket was an interested spectator. Around this time came MCC secretary Billy Griffith's third (at least) meeting with RA James of the Home Office who memoed that he would write to Griffith about the chief constables' meeting. Sir Philip Allen, as permanent under-secretary of state the most senior official at the Home Office, wrote to Griffith on December 8, presumably replying to a query from Lord's about a Times leading article on December 2. 'Demos and disorder' offered hope for English cricket. A club could hire police (usually football grounds, in case of hooligans, under the Police Act 1964). Clubs paid because they needed more officers than the police would normally provide. A demo and a probable breach of the peace were different; the expense for those police would not be charged to the club – 'nor should it be' said the Times. If Jim Callaghan had asked clubs, after Swansea, to leave ejecting trespassers to the police, and not club stewards, why should clubs pay? So the Times was asking. A Times leader was famously authoritative; could Lord's bank on it? Sir Philip Allen cast doubt; 'promoters should ... expect to pay for something beyond the normal', he wrote. And, going by the police at Springbok matches so far, cricket would need 'a considerable number'.

The Sussex county club, to name one, was evidently following the rugby. A sub-committee on December 1 submitted that the South Africa tour 'should not be permitted' due to probable damage to the ground 'and a crippling burden of finance'. Another on December 4 agreed to tell the TCCB meeting the week after that while Test grounds might be 'reasonably secure', county grounds like theirs were not, 'if the demonstrations are on the scale and as widespread' as rugby's. To back this, the county passed a letter from Sussex's chief constable to Lord's. Sussex had ideas – keep the tour to Test grounds only, and if SACA would not have it, invite the West Indies (which showed an eye for money; the Windies were the most popular team of the era). How can we explain that the TCCB meeting asked for a vote on South Africa touring the next summer and got 'a completely unanimous vote in favour with no dissenters or anyone expressing a dissenting opinion'? So one of the men there, Wilf Wooller for Glamorgan, told his committee men on December 16, the Tuesday evening after.

Even allowing for Wooller's prejudice, we can imagine that no-one had dared to be different; besides, the terms of the vote were deliberately narrow – not allowing debate or any of Sussex's choices (assuming that the Sussex man in the room had them in mind; one of the features of cricket's administration was that a county would send a chairman and secretary, men less likely to have a mind of their own than sub-committee men raising flaws). Wooller went on: "The TCCB chairman [Cecil Paris] then said it would now be necessary to examine the tour as a practical possibility in the light of the form the demonstrations against anti-apartheid had taken on the rugby tour." Counties duly gave 'widely different' estimates of policing. The counties generally thought it wasn't for them to pay for police (not the first or the last example of wishful thinking). The TCCB decided on a special committee to prepare for the tour, 'to discuss with the Home Secretary and appropriate officials the cost of police and to consider the possibility of opening a "Support the Tour" fund, which a great number of people had expressed a wish to support'. In other words, the English game had committed to a tour without a clue about its costs. It was going to appeal to well-wishers for charity – money that it already needed; earlier, that Glamorgan meeting heard earlier that the county had an 'income shortfall' of £4992 on record spending of £52,382 for the year (Championship-winning, to be fair). Even Wooller's own county had 'dissent' – a revealingly intolerant word, by the way; critics were only pointing out what they thought best.

When Glamorgan's finance committee heard of the TCCB meeting on January 9, one member, Jeff Cohen pointed out matches were 'easy to disrupt'. The chairman, Judge Rowe Harding, could do no better than say Glamorgan 'owed allegiance to the MCC'. The counties put their blind trust in the centre of power, that knew best, that had a mania for unanimity and hoarded secrets.

Interlude

Wilfred Wooller

He had a talent for falling out with people. In 1951 at Trent Bridge, Wooller was batting Glamorgan so slowly to a draw that Nottinghamshire captain Reg Simpson bowled an over by rolling the ball. Wooller called it bad taste and blamed the pitch. Tony Pawson used to look forward to playing Wooller's Glamorgan, that like Yorkshire 'never concealed their determination to win'. That could include unusual, because barely acceptable, behaviour in the field that in old age the Yorkshire batsman Bryan Stott recalled; knowing Stott would overhear, Wooller muttered to a fellow close fielder, asking who Stott was; trying to unsettle him.

Wilf Wooller; inspecting vandalism at a misty Cardiff.

John Woodcock recalled in old age: "He was iconic in Wales, of course," as a rugby player, "in that famous victory over the All-Blacks in 1935, and he was a formidable figure, massive figure in many ways, always alive, very difficult to argue with, very anti the antis. Very, very much so." Others, like Hain in his memoir, fell back on that vague word, 'colourful', when frankly Wooller was a loud-mouth. Wooller defies easy definition; Gerald Pawle in a pen-portrait in The Cricketer in 1972 chose as good a word as any; combative. "He speaks in a commanding and emphatic tone which endows all his pronouncements with a royal authority." He was right-wing: "He genuinely believes … in the importance of maintaining discipline and in the value of other virtues now considered old fashioned." It would be lazy psychology to say that years in Japanese captivity left

Wilf Wooller: the Welsh journalist JH Morgan in 1978 described him as 'a puzzling personality'; forthright, even aggressive, yet with a kind-hearted side and a well-informed love of the game.

their stamp on Wooller; except that he appeared to agree, telling Pawle that prison forged his 'strong and different views about post-war life'. He saw the world of the 1930s – when he began his amateur cricket career at Cambridge, and thrived – was ending, and disliked the new. Or, had he survived the camps, physically and psychologically, by shutting his eyes to all except what he had to confront, and wearing blinkers had become a habit? He was even less likely to see the student or protest point of view after his car at his suburban Cardiff home was the only private property vandalised on the 'night of the daubers' in January 1970.

* * *

At least English cricket was working towards something. Most churchmen in Britain and Ireland could only talk, and most talk was hostile to the anti-apartheid movement, certainly as it turned noisy. On the eve of the Springboks playing in Scotland, in a sermon at Glasgow Cathedral the Rev Dr William Morris likened protesters to 'witch hunters'. A house to house collection for the homeless or the starving was better than a march or sitting on a rugby pitch, he said. Having read that in the Glasgow Herald, John Morrow, chaplain to overseas students, replied that Dr Morris had recently taken part in a memorial service for Martin Luther King. Morrow wrote that non-violent demonstrations were a way of touching conscience (something else intangible and qualitative, that we keep coming across). Morrow touched on the biggest group of all, seldom met in this story; the non-demonstrators; the indifferent, who presumably were not likely to leave their television and go door to door for anyone.

How were churches, or any institution, or anyone, to adapt to the modern world – such as, to the extra leisure time so many were glibly predicting (besides well-paid work, they assumed)? They had to know what was around them and apply it. "We were learning with every protest," Peter Hain said of this time in his 1971 book – which was hardly surprising, as students at university were paid to supposedly learn. As early as Twickenham, the third of 12

Saturdays of the Springboks tour, 'we were really on the brink of stopping the match completely'. They did not know then what the book admitted; that was as close as they got; and only at Aberdeen, on December 2, did they come as close again. That was because police were learning too. STST were imaginative – Michael Denny wore a grey suit and was clean-shaven and so did not look like a typical student, when he chained himself to the steering wheel of the Springboks' coach at the Park Lane on Piccadilly on December 20, on the morning of the England match at Twickenham. The details, while entertaining, do not matter – Denny drove off, going beyond his plan, as the engine was running, only to hit a parked Post Office van down the road – so much as the police improvised. They borrowed pliers and bolt-cutters from nearby workmen, to cut Denny away and bring the coach back to the hotel so that the team left, in good time at 11.35am, 25 minutes after the hijack.

STST made it easy for newcomers to join in. Also on December 20, at Twickenham railway station you could pick leaflets telling you what slogans to shout; from the most obvious, such as 'apartheid out' and 'Springboks out', to the more complicated 'Smith, Vorster, [Enoch] Powell [who was not in power] out', and the aggressive and yet idealistic 'black and white, unite and fight'.

The only people not learning were the South Africans. On May 1, 1970, Special Branch overheard a threat to abduct Dr Luttig, the ambassador. Police took it seriously enough to approach him on his return from holiday in Portugal, on May 15. He intended to attend some of the South African cricket matches, by private car. Though demos had dogged Luttig for years, he was more worried for his daughter, who worked at a bank in Trafalgar Square, near the embassy. She went to work in the ambassadorial car; number plate, SA1. "It was agreed," said a police report, "that the car SA1 would attract attention and that it would be better if a private car could be used". The Met Police offered close protection to Dr Luttig, and two women detectives for his daughter.

Chapter Five

The stakes

We weren't playing cricket on the village green, like they did in 1926.
Arthur Scargill on the Saltley mass picket in 1972, in Richard Clutterbuck's Britain in Agony: The Growth of Political Violence, 1978

Around this time in one of his great works, Alexander Solzhenitsyn wrote of two kinds of people in the world; those that did the work of two people, and those that let them. Put another way, some people – whatever side they took – knew the stakes, and the indifferent rest left them to it, and at most talked in the pub over what they read in the papers or watched on television. Frank Williamson began his report on the Leicester match that it was public knowledge that the demonstrators were committed to preventing the Springboks match; the club was equally determined against. The game of rugby felt the same; so did the Springboks, for the tour was one of South Africa's 'few sporting links with the world', as the Evening Standard pointed out in a preview.

Across history, a demonstration, 'rally', or whatever you want to call it, has been a gathering of people, feeling powerless or otherwise frustrated, to voice themselves politically. It's striking how seldom the tactic works. Even large demos have either been crushed, like Wat Tyler's peasants outside London in 1381, then ignored; or counter-demo'd, as in May 1968 in Paris; or, for such is progress, merely ignored, like marches before the war in Iraq in 2003. Demonstrators, and above all their leaders, have to understand, that a demo is only a brief show of strength, to influence those in power to do something, unwillingly. Those demonstrating have to be at least as cunning and persevering as those in power. If demonstrators cannot agree what they want, those in power will hardly agree it for them. Hain and

'Stop The Seventy Tour', by good fortune or on purpose, had found a happy medium; their target was not too large and yet was large enough, and urgent, to inspire recruits nationwide. The larger Anti-Apartheid Movement (AAM), while meaning well, lacked STST's advantages. John Ennals, chairman of the AAM, speaking at a 'teach-in' at Edinburgh University in December 1969 before the Springboks played in the city, showed how naïve, or perhaps arrogant, he and his kind were. They assumed that South Africans would change once told they were stupid: "There must be very many sincere people there who have never thought that their way of life based on racialist principles may be wrong. The demonstrations will surely bring home to South Africa that the rest of the world has rejected their racialist regime and its oppressive policies." Even if apartheid were wrong – and only because it was a left-over from Europe's centuries-long imperial conquering of much of the world – the truth was that Britain and the western world had *not* rejected apartheid. Their navies docked at South African ports, shops stocked South African oranges, lords wintered there, electricians emigrated there. Ennals was one more wishful thinker, who had sat on stage at meetings and made speeches for years and changed nothing. Gestures satisfied such men. Outside the Springboks match in Dublin on January 10, 1970 before kick-off, someone burned two match tickets. Why did someone not use the tickets, to take the fight inside? If you wanted a symbol to cheer the crowd, why not burn pretend tickets? Bernadette Devlin, from an altogether harder school in Northern Ireland, was not easily pleased, and was unafraid to offend. Thousands marched in Dublin; yet it had been the quietest (for demo trouble) match of the tour. "If it had been properly organised today," Devlin said, "nobody would have got into the game and the match would not have taken place." It had become the fashion to mock those in blazers and ties who ran British rugby and cricket as amateurs – literally, because they did it for the love of the game, not money; and metaphorically, as old men set in their ways. Devlin saw that too many on the protest side were amateurs also.

* * *

Regardless of apartheid or any cause, sports stadiums moved with the times as they found it more demanding to keep spectators secure, and safe. Contrast the Wembley of the 1950s, when 250 policemen, 500 stewards, 400 uniformed commissioners and 100 car park attendants managed a generally good-natured crowd, with the Cup Final of April 1970, when 700 uniformed police and scores of plain clothes men faced 'skinheads' in braces and boots 'intent on causing trouble'.

The stakes for police were that the state gave them that task of control. Frank Williamson wrote to Sir Philip Allen at the Home Office on November 24, after the first Springbok international match, that as the 'guardian of law and order against all comers', police were 'pig in the middle'. That implied police could not please anyone, and explained why on the day of tour cancellation, a Birmingham Post editorial explicitly described police as 'the victims of violent demonstrations', though many more students went to hospital after demos (or nursed bruises privately) than police. In public, too, some police at least talked in terms of 'service', a significant difference from a 'police force'. The day before the Leicester match, chief constable John Taylor told the Mercury the police's role was 'to ensure that honest, law-abiding people can go about lawful pursuits in safety. The rugby match falls into that category; that is our primary objective.' Other, anonymous comments by the police suggested that in fact they were taking sides; if police 'failed', the tour could fold; if the anti-apartheid supporters won, it would be a 'victory for anarchy'. By framing the day in sporting terms – one side or the other winning – and damning the protest side as anarchists, police did not sound the neutral umpires they claimed to be; so Devlin would go on to argue. The police could have taken another stance. As Rowland Bowen pointed out after cancellation in his elegant journal The Cricket Quarterly, bear-baiting and cock-fighting became illegal after some campaigned against them as uncivilised. In other words, plenty of things (in a free country, after all) were debatable. Television, vastly more influential than Bowen, also disagreed with the police's self-image; according to Williamson, the BBC saw tour matches as 'a confrontation between demonstrators and police'; that is, in terms of news, or drama. Police could not help but see protesters as a challenge to their reputation, when only protesters caused a breach of the peace. The police's work for rugby and later cricket had its limits; when Thames Valley chief constable TCB Hodgson described policing Oxford University's ground as 'a very costly undertaking', he was using cost of the police 'service' as a threat to push the Springboks' match away from Oxford – and making it someone else's problem.

The equivalent threat by police to the side of protest was legal. Bristol AAM, careful to be in the right, wrote for and got permission 'to place a small table' in the middle of the city in 1966 'for the purpose of collecting signatures for a petition to the prime minister … provided that only one or two people are in attendance and that no demonstration takes place'. Demonstrators soon learned how to avoid arrest – or injury; leaflets by the National Council for Civil Liberties (NCCL) advised marchers at Leicester to get rid of anything that could be called a weapon, such as a pen-knife. As that implied, demonstrators could drift from innocence into a crime against public order, when ignorance, or not meaning to break the law, were no excuses. Police tried to inhibit protest by quoting dubious law at them, such as warning the Reading students at Heathrow for the arriving Springboks that waving placards and handing out leaflets was unlawful. Those police were only exploiting a genuine greyness. The injured batsman Colin Milburn, by April 1970 a columnist, like many claimed to have sympathy for 'demonstrators who behave peaceably', such as staying away from matches altogether or standing outside gates ('that's ok'). "On the other hand violence cannot be tolerated and I hope that offenders are dealt with severely in the law courts." Sitting on the pitch, hardly violent, counted as a common law breach of the peace; offenders could be bound over. If even after 'skirmishes' (as the police's operational order at Leicester in November 1969 set out) a demonstrator

Northamptonshire and England batsman Colin Milburn.

when asked was willing to move, or desist, the order was: 'no further action'. Outside, 'policy *must* be tolerance to a degree not normally exercised'. Police had to show 'great tolerance' to marchers; to allow, for example, sitting on the road. "Mere resistance to police is not a ground for arrest." Partly, tolerance was how the police were showing 'impartiality' – the 'key note of all police actions' according to the operational order of December 1969 before the Springboks' match at Bristol. Whoever provoked them, police had to be patient and firm (which was for police on the spot to calibrate). A demo experienced this as a cordon or line of police neither yielding nor offensive; an 'almost impenetrable barrier', so the Oxford Times called the police at the first, Twickenham match. The Bristol orders, too, told police to keep arrests 'to a minimum', even though police seldom had so many, hundreds, on duty in one place, prepared in advance. More often, when facing travelling football hooligans, police were outnumbered or simply not there in time. For instance, when rowdy Tottenham fans on their return from Derby on Saturday, September 20 were turned off their train at the Bedfordshire village of

Flitwick, and rioted, police made only one arrest, for theft of a lamp. A Home Office official called it 'lamentable'. Such hooliganism had been growing for years, partly because so few hooligans were punished. According to a Home Office report of November 1969, such hooligans searched and found with an offensive weapon had it confiscated, but were not always prosecuted; fans ejected from a stadium ought to go to court and be bound over, to deter others, the report urged. Most blatantly, when young Coventry fans on a train returning from a Friday night match at Wolverhampton in April 1970 rioted so badly that the driver refused to go beyond Walsall, police placed 58 in court the next day; only for the cases to be 'adjourned indefinitely'. Pinning offences on these hooligans was, to use a word new around 1970, too much 'bovver'. It spoke of police and courts without the equipment, or energy, frankly, to take on new sorts of crime, less obvious than bank robberies. Protesters exploited criminal justice weakness.

The anti-apartheid movement was only part of a wider protest that was testing legal boundaries. In June 1970, Bow Street magistrates gave a 28-year-old woman a three-month suspended prison sentence for throwing a tin of paint at Ted Heath as he went into 10 Downing Street after winning the general election. The tin (an 'offensive weapon') hit Heath but most of the paint went over a detective-bodyguard. A magistrate, Geraint Rees, told the woman: "This goes well beyond the limits of reasonable protest." Likewise after the Springboks' match at Murrayfield, the Glasgow Herald and Scotsman printed separate complaints that stewards and police went beyond reasonable force (kicking, punching, grabbing by the hair, harassing photographers). Who said what was reasonable? And if police constables were not showing their numbers, what was anyone going to do about it? Tony Smythe, the general secretary of the NCCL, wrote to Twickenham on Tuesday, November 18, 1969 – that is, soon after the 'self-appointed vigilantes' at the Swansea match – to ask for permission for 'observers' inside Twickenham at the next match, on the Saturday. The NCCL would in any case note anything outside. The 'liberties' that the NCCL stood for were as one-sided towards demos as the police could be towards apartheid sport. People other than police keeping order at events was nothing new - though the booming summer outdoor pop concerts were. Students could make their own stewards. For instance Tory MP Ronald Bell spoke at Leeds University Conservative Association in May 1970 behind a 'human barrier' of Conservatives, who could do nothing about the jeers, 'Sieg Heils' and so on, but did drag away a 'girl' who ran to the front and tried to climb onto the stage. Bell blamed the 'Stop The Seventy Tour syndrome'. In a country steadily more violent and threatening – or put another way, where more people were uncivil, intolerant, or politically activist (it depended on your view) – society had to decide where to set shifting social rules, which were not the same as the slower-moving law. If those aimed at by the protesters reacted violently, in words or deeds, society only became more uncivil. Thus in December 1969 a reader of the Saturday sports paper in Leeds, the Green Post, criticised Yorkshire captain Brian Close for saying: "If we do get a few demonstrators on the pitch when South Africa play Yorkshire, I hope that one or two of them come near me when I have a bat in my hand."

* * *

"The only logical answer to South Africa's stand is to quarantine that country until she changes her inhuman racist policy," wrote Ken Chapman in the Sunday Gleaner in Jamaica in March 1970. The British High Commission in Bridgetown dutifully forwarded the article to the Foreign Office. Why was Lord's – 'insulted' by South Africa over D'Oliveira, Chapman wrote – so obstinate, when it stood to lose so much, in tour profits, its good name? Years before, other sports, notably soccer, had expelled South Africa from international competition; in mid-May 1970, the Olympic movement finally did. Paradoxically, English cricket, which insisted on Stalinist conformity within, felt no need to conform with other sports. For reasons long forgotten, practical and emotional, selfish and high-minded, English cricket felt it stood to lose if it gave up white South Africa.

In one of his many books, Cricket Today, in 1961, Colin Cowdrey suggested that MCC's greatest contribution to cricket was that they had 'spread the gospel' to 'so many outposts of the Commonwealth'. Quite a few in English cricket were born in what had been the empire, such as Gubby Allen (Australia) and Cowdrey himself (India). Cowdrey's comment was as dubious as any idea that Churchill saved Britain in 1940, when in truth air force pilots and factory workers did. Australia and other countries managed to get the hang of cricket by themselves. At least Cowdrey – later a president of MCC – had set out a common view, adding the intriguing flavour of Christianity. Likewise Alan Smith, manager of the MCC party to the Far East in February and March 1970, described it in religious or imperialist terms as 'really a missionary tour with the basic arm of reviving cricket interest in places outside the first class cricketing countries'. Leaving aside whether Lord's meant it or not, and whether other countries felt like heathens in need of the 'gospel', MCC endured riots on its previous winter tours, of West Indies and Pakistan. Colin Milburn, a veteran of both tours, in an April 1970 column warned that as a result soon England's only opposition might be Australia (who had suffered riots in India only months before). New Zealand he appeared to forget.

Denis Howell at a January 1970 meeting with among others Jim Callaghan said '... many of the selectors and the cricket establishment generally had close business and personal links with South Africa'. Tellingly, the others in the room did not press for details. It was something taken for granted.

To show how widespread those links were could make examples tiresome. A few must do. Frank and George Mann, father and son, each met the woman they married when captaining MCC in South Africa. Vintcent van der Bijl, one of Wilfred Isaacs' team, was the son of an Oxford Blue who played for South Africa in the 1938-39 Tests; a series Denis Compton missed. The top scorer for Compton's eleven that played Wilfred Isaacs' team in July 1969 was Doug Insole, chairman of selectors during the D'Oliveira affair. Insole's only Tests abroad were in South Africa in 1956-

57. Oliver Leese - corps commander under Montgomery at El Alamein; 'an active director for several years' of Securicor, according to his biographer Rowland Ryder; president of the Warwickshire county club – met Vorster socially while holidaying in South Africa in January 1970. Also in South Africa, leading a party to watch Tests against Australia, Worcestershire county committee man Dick – the Honourable Richard – Lygon died suddenly in Johannesburg on February 24. 'He was having a drink prior to the start of the final day's play at the Test match', Worcestershire secretary Joe Lister wrote to his Sussex counterpart Arthur Dumbrell.

Likewise, a few words of praise will paint a picture of how men on MCC tours found South Africa: by Brigadier MA Green, manager of George Mann's 1948-49 tour ('homely') and Doug Insole in his 1960 autobiography ('I find it hard to imagine that there is a better'). Insole's tour in 1956-57 was John Woodcock's first there:

'... it was Peter May's tour [as captain] *and I remember on the boat out, we sailed out in those days, I remember some very well known South African political figure who gave us a talk on what to expect so it was very much on your mind then, but in fact I am ashamed to say, I suppose you could say I could be called apolitical as indeed were most of my colleagues including I should say Swanton.'*

Later Woodcock reported on 'rebel' 1980s tours. In old age he admitted he may have been naïve: "I had been a believer in the 'bridge', I thought it was the only way in which anything good might come of our contact with them ... we could have some beneficial effect." In fairness Woodcock was one of a crowd, and not only in cricket. In Pretoria in November 1969 the Conservative MP Eldon Griffiths argued in the Sunday Telegraph that precisely because white South Africa was still so close, Britain could do far more good by having relations. He trusted to the market, 'economic forces', 'to break down the walls of prejudice'. In the next issue, John Hatch, a former Durham RFC captain, accused Eldon Griffiths of 'repeating clichés of white South African propaganda'. Apartheid was not liberalising but oppressing more, he said. You can still argue who was right; perhaps both were. The vice-chancellor of Bristol University, Prof Alec Merrison, prodded by his local anti-apartheid movement, offered the principle that whatever happened, you had to keep 'channels of communication' open: 'silence as a weapon on personal or national level' was ineffective and dangerous, for instance in case of nuclear war (and Merrison was a nuclear physicist).

Powerful and clever men were applying their minds to apartheid as one of the most profound problems in world politics, on a par with planet-ending war, without an answer. JL Manning in the Evening Standard in mid-May 1970 questioned the calibre of men talking for English cricket. "I never did think that a private club which found the lbw law almost too much for them should be trusted with too many world problems. They are nice people and all that but they tend to get knotted."

A more penetrating comment to put to any dealer with apartheid was whether they had conflicts of interest. Did businessmen favour a 'bridge' as a cover for 'business as usual'? Did cricket come under business, or 'communication', neither or both? The trade in English and South African cricketers mirrored their countries' commerce, and in the late 1960s each was flourishing. One example, Chris Wilkins who landed in April 1970 to begin at Derbyshire, will show how the links worked, and suited everyone. The local press previewing Wilkins said 'Derbyshire will be only too happy to help him towards his ambition to play for the Springboks'. Just as informal scouts had begun to feed promising cricketers from the West Indies to English county cricket, Wilkins' three-year contract was 'all done through journalist Donald Woods, of the East London Daily Despatch. He had met Derbyshire people coaching in South Africa, such as George Pope and Fred Rumsey', the 1930s all-rounder and new county club public relations officer respectively. Coaches who placed talent with counties were doing a favour, and making themselves more worth hiring; counties were hiring glamorous, young, affordable players.

As that implies, money mattered. An undated document at Lord's estimated the 1970 tour finances. Takings for a normal tour would have been £242,000, except for security reasons spectators could not sit on the grass and would have to book in advance; Lord's anticipated only £140,000. In other words, thanks to the controversy, English cricket would take only 58 per cent, less than six-tenths, of what it might have. Add BBC's fee of £75,000 to televise, and income from the Post Office for the rights to run a 'dial-the-score' telephone service, and the 1970 tour would bring in £235,000. Costs were for putting on the Tests (£40,000), the tourists' expenses (£40,000), police protection (estimated £30,000), insurance (£35,000) and 'special equipment', presumably for securing grounds: total, £150,000. That gave a profit of £85,000. South Africa would have a tenth of that – usually, much more, but it could hardly argue. The five Test grounds got not much less than the other 12 counties; and the MCC gave itself nine per cent, £6390. This may have been an early, winter list because English cricket's insurer did not want to talk (a bad sign?) until after the Springboks tour. After the first Springbok match, Barry Newcombe reported for the Evening Standard that after police and transport costs, Twickenham had 'not much left'. Besides extra spending, rugby and then cricket had to reckon on less income. As an outdoor sport that stopped for rain, cricket's income from spectators was a guess at the best of times. At an emergency committee meeting at Lord's on February 25, 1970, two of the Test match-hosting county secretaries, Jack Nash and Ron Poulton at Headingley and Trent Bridge, warned that if tour matches were ticket-only in advance, as police asked, it would mean 'very substantial reduction in attendance'. The two men did not give up, as at a March 10 meeting at Lord's of county secretaries due to host the South Africans, they asked again if they could sell tickets on the day, only to be told 'tickets would be posted about two weeks before the match'.

After 285 county players voted 124-28 for the tour (many must have been away or chose not to vote), Jack Bannister of the Professional Cricketers' Association hinted in

January 1970 that some players voting against were thinking of money ('their careers') rather than principle: 'those employed by less affluent counties genuinely fear for their own livelihoods'. Like any number of occupations grumbling about their pay in this era – dockers, miners, teachers, even wrestlers – the employers (honestly or not) could claim poverty. On February 27, 1970 Wilf Wooller told the Glamorgan club AGM that some counties 'were very short of money indeed'. Derbyshire in 1970 had a mere 14 on the staff; one of the wealthiest counties, Surrey, for 1971 cut their staff by four to 17. Crawford White in The Cricketer in April 1979 spelt out what was usually too obvious to mention: "We all know that in every country Test match money is the key factor that keeps first-class cricket going. In England every county would be bankrupt without it." To be more precise, a few touring teams drew the crowds, usually England and Australia, and by the 1960s the West Indians. Having earned a reputation as dull, South Africa looked exciting thanks to the brothers Graeme and Peter Pollock, batsman and fast bowler; all-rounders Eddie Barlow and Mike Procter, and emerging batsman Barry Richards. In the South Africa winter of 1969-70, they thrashed Australia four Test matches to none. Tom Graveney, by calling cancellation 'terrible, just making things harder when they were trying to help South African cricket', genuinely spoke for English cricket. There was widespread relish to see if England could beat – and fund – 'without doubt the best team in the world', as Jim Parks called South Africa in late April 1970. Braced for trouble, he ended his newspaper article: "If only we cricketers could be allowed to get on with the game …. just as we did in the 'good old days'."

The inverted commas suggested that Parks, or at least the newspaper sub-editor, understood that the wish was wistful, even ironic. Except that plenty of other voices deplored the present and harked back to English cricket's past. Kenneth Gregory in the Illustrated London News in June 1969 sniffed that 'the primary aim of modern Tests seems to be the replenishment of county coffers', and argued that 'the only way for English cricket to emerge from its Never-Never-Land [itself a harking back to the Edwardian Peter Pan] is to put the clock back 40 years'. He wished for 'cunning slow bowlers' and the pre-1935 leg before wicket rule. He denounced sponsors. To him the John Player Sunday League new in 1969 and the one-day Gillette Cup competition were 'gimmicks'. Such an analysis seems incredible now; and even Gregory admitted the JPL and Gillette were popular. To such critics, cricket ought to do without money – or at least commercialism, which harmed the essence of the play. And yet lack of money was one reason why these same critics prophesised the decline of the game – or at least the writers of headlines for their articles did. 'Can cricket survive?' said the headline over Gregory's article. 'Is cricket dead?' asked the journalist Hugo Young in the Sunday Times in August 1970. Some closer observers of the game such as the Manchester Evening News' cricket correspondent John Kay warned in November 1969 that 'the future of first-class cricket is in the balance'. Lancashire had actually won the first Sunday League and as Kay acknowledged was 'attracting far bigger crowds' on Sundays. Cricket, then, had already found ways to become commercially viable; the problem lay in agreeing how to change. As Kay wrote, some counties 'wanted to reshape county cricket' after almost a century, and have more one-dayers; presumably, to bring in more money. For conservatives, any change was change for the worse; any personality proposing change was suspect. On and off the field affected each other; to carry on with Lancashire as an example, newcomers such as the 'enthusiastic' Cedric Rhoades as chairman had shaken up the committee, of 'old players and social big wigs'; and had been a pioneer of signing overseas players. That too divided opinion. Wilf Wooller in a 1972 interview believed that English cricket 'was going to suffer from the laxity of over-registration of players from abroad'. Wooller was a hypocrite; his county Glamorgan hired as many foreigners as any.

If conservatives felt under siege, at least English cricket was showing signs of life. How then to explain a reformer like

Rowland Bowen, who in his 1970 history of cricket saw 'no real future for highly organised cricket at Test match or first class level'. He concluded – pointing to the collapse in the crowd for the Eton-Harrow match and how England generally had 'started to grow up' – that by the year 2000 cricket would have neither money nor even adult players ('Wisden will long since have ceased publication'). We know now how eccentric Bowen's predictions were. What matters is that Bowen was no conservative; he was among those Hain thanked at the beginning of his 1971 book. The English game was deeply unsure of itself, on and off the field. Uninteresting play meant fewer watched, meaning less income, making players anxious for their living, playing cautiously; causing decline. Wilf Wooller in a 1972 interview praised the recently-retired Fred Trueman as 'a character who kept the game alive', implying that the 'economical and defensive' modern cricketer did not.

This crisis of confidence was nothing new. In November 1969 the Sunday Telegraph featured, from Michael Melford's book 'Pick of The Cricketer', an article by Arthur Gilligan, that ran: "Last year I heard a prominent man who had made his mark in pre-war days declare in the pavilion at Lord's that there would be no county cricket in ten years' time." The joke was that the article dated from 1937.

Likewise in the 21st century some were still grumbling that English cricket was going to the dogs – and they would keep on grumbling, because change is natural. The numbers in cricket, the runs and wickets and wins, are unarguable; the amount and pace of change, besides the quality of play on the field, are purely a matter of opinion. Denis Howell in interview in January 1970 claimed that cricketers were missing qualities of adventure, and 'a challenging spirit' - a 'frame of mind'. We are back with intangibles, that some people might not see, or care about. A seldom-admitted divide in any sport is between connoisseurs (or those who pose as connoisseurs) and the cheering masses, needed for their cash, but resented as ignorant. Debates always rage – in 1970, around the format of the game, and where the players came from - because two people can see the same things on the field of play, and say it's good or bad. While the controversy over apartheid found English cricket troubled, then, on and off the field, it was no more or less troubled than before or since, objectively; except, people who cared about cricket did not feel about it objectively. Nor did the amateurs who managed it; for them, administration was not a job but a way of serving the game. Perhaps Lord's, like Stalin, had reason for their mania for denying debate; if allowed, it would never end; there lay anarchy, wearing a suit and tie.

It did not help that the turn of a decade prompts a rash of stock-taking. In December 1969 in the Illustrated London News, David Miller named racialism and amateurism as sport's 'two burning issues'. He argued that sport, as a 'microcosm of life' could not pretend (as 'reactionaries'

Test and County Cricket Board (TCCB) delegates resume after lunch, December 11, 1969. While one smoked a pipe and another a cigar, while some wore different coloured handkerchiefs with their jacket, and some had more hair or were more comfortable having their photograph taken than others, the men were plainly socially alike.

did) it was apart from politics. Over South Africa, no doubt Lord's did not want to give in, Miller wrote; but 'discretion would have seemed to be in the circumstances infinitely the better part of valour'. Precisely because it was uneasy with itself, English cricket felt it had to stop the rot that the 'Stop The Tour' represented. Here English cricket had the comfort of a large body of opinion that feared STST as a political extreme: unpredictable, newsworthy, and always about to become uncontrollable. Protest against the Springboks developed 'almost a life of its own', Hain admitted in his 1971 book. The Daily Telegraph editorial on Wednesday, May 20, 1970, at the climax of the tour controversy, could stand for any number of conservative opinions: " .... the issue is not really about cricket at all but rather about civil liberty in our country, threatened as it is on the cricket field as in other fields by a fascist-minded anti-democratic minority". That implied sport, as English, stood for democracy. Surely sport and politics were mixing?! Leaving aside the hypocritical weakness in rugby and cricket's argument for apartheid tours, let us see the 'other fields' that the Telegraph mentioned.

A woman writing to the Scotsman in December 1969, about the campaign in Edinburgh, as in many places in this era, against fluoride in tap water, complained of 'rabble rousers' whereby 'the freedom of speech was trampled underfoot'. From the left wing came a related fear; one writer to the Scotsman after the Springboks' match at Murrayfield worried about 'the not-too-distant future when the Alf Garnetts of the New Right will be able to seize power by reason of popular reaction to these ineffectual demonstrators'. Some lumped together striking workers in Turin, May 1968 in Paris, Northern Ireland, and political meetings broken up on campus, and feared the mob. Some in politics used the unrest in general and cricket in particular to make a political case, and advance their own career (or try to). John Jackson, a lobby correspondent for a London evening newspaper, was a Conservative parliamentary candidate at the June 1970 election. Speaking in Leeds in mid-May 1970, Jackson accused the Labour Government of being 'a pushover for the rent-a-crowd thugs', and appeared to take seriously an anonymous letter sent to him, threatening to kidnap a leading cricketer for a £250,000 ransom. Some important players had been 'tailed' for some time, Jackson claimed. This was violent and irresponsible talk; had Jackson any evidence? Had he told police? In the Marylebone constituency, where Quintin Hogg was making much of 'law and order', the Labour candidate Keith Morrell defended Harold Wilson's 'reasoned statement' on the apartheid tour and condemned Hogg's 'hysterical outburst': "Many constituents are indignant at his treatment of a serious moral issue with such calculating contempt." Neither Jackson nor Morrell won. The Conservative Iain Sproat in Aberdeen did. In November 1969, taking aim at the sitting Labour MP Donald Dewar, who said the Springboks' match at Aberdeen should be cancelled, the future editor of an annual 'who's who' of cricketers said cancelling 'would encourage the extremists'.

Such Punch and Judy party politics added to a sense that the 1960s had gone wrong. In December 1969 the Evening Standard journalist John Grigg saw a 'growing malaise'; a sense that the welfare state and democratic socialism had come 'to the end of the road'. This was anticipating Thatcherism. Despite (or perhaps because of) so many people doing well materially, adults alienated from politics were showing 'widespread defiance of constituted authority'. Lord's could stand, with reason, as unpolitical, as part of what the Birmingham Post after cancellation called 'people in the middle who have the good sense to realise where the appeasement of arrogant militants can lead'. Norman Yardley, resentful after cancellation, wondered if 'fires so carefully induced can now be quenched'. He meant race relations, that some protesters raised in spring 1970. Here were the greatest stakes of all. David Steele, as a young Liberal MP the honorary president of the Anti-Apartheid Movement, told Leicester University students in December 1969 that a world war was more likely to arise from racial conflicts than atomic powers. Like others, he likened apartheid to Nazi Germany; just as, almost on the same night, did John Ennals, AAM chairman, at his Edinburgh 'teach-in', judging apartheid as 'just as dangerous to the world today as the system in Germany 30 years ago'. They meant the two regimes' racial basis; yet everyone knew the Nazis had caused world war in 1939. In Ireland, chairman of AAM, Conor Cruise O'Brien, in a 1967 lecture called South Africa 'in the deepest sense, a threat to world peace'; Aidan Crawley in his 1988 autobiography hinted at the fear that apartheid might lead to a racial nuclear war. Cricket was well out of its depth here. Paradoxically, while South Africa, and the related illegal regime in Rhodesia, took up so much space in newspapers and so much of the Wilson government's time, it was, as Conor Cruise O'Brien noted in Dublin, 'low priority' compared to all the western world's other political troubles. Why criticise a 'friendly nation' - as Geoffrey Rippon, Conservative defence spokesman, put it at a South Africa Club dinner in April 1970 - whose trade and security interests were 'so linked to Britain'?

* * *

The stakes for Wilson and Labour were high enough. As a rule, senior ministers such as Michael Stewart - the ones with most power to make decisions - stuck to the line that government would not decide on sporting tours to Rhodesia or South Africa, while junior ministers such as Hattersley and Howell, and MPs, without the power, did speak their minds, against. A clue to the disrespect MPs had for ministers - or for the unassertive Michael Stewart in particular - is in a letter of November 13, 1969 from Exeter MP Gwyneth Dunwoody. She asked for an 'urgent' (underlined three times) statement 'of what I can and cannot say about the South Africa rugby team which is visiting my constituency on December 27'.

WP Hartshorne of the Foreign Office spoke for (and in the manner of) all officials when he commented in September 1969 about the Women's Cricket Association's wish to visit both countries; Her Majesty's Government disapproved, 'but they will leave it to the good sense of the British sport authorities concerned to decide'. In a supposedly permissive age when in truth the state was ever more interfering – not only the 'welfare state', but 'compulsory mass medication' (fluoride in tap water), the first closed-circuit television, even double yellow lines – it looked as if over apartheid Labour was avoiding responsibility. The new nations of black Africa and the Caribbean, then and later, appeared more strongly anti-apartheid. For example in an April 1970 report on a possible 'African boycott' of the Commonwealth Games, Miss BJ Rogers of the FO noted their 'increasing frustration' at a 'lack of progress' at the United Nations and elsewhere. The truth was that those nations had not boycotted South Africa as Arab countries had boycotted Israel; because 'those countries most committed to bringing down South Africa,' her neighbours, were 'the ones who most depend on South African trading partners'. The politically embarrassing fact, then, that anti-apartheid Africa was stuck with apartheid economically made them more likely to seek the sop of a sports boycott.

* * *

As Britain gave up its empire and tried in vain to join the European 'Common Market', general historians of the 1960s have picked up what one, David Reynolds, termed 'a sense of decline – a word that was becoming a cliché'. Something becomes a cliché usually because it has a basis in fact; yet for all the anger of left- and right-wingers, many, including at Lord's, even the alienated, were getting on with their business. Just as two people can see the same sport or music and respond to it differently, so can we interpret Britain around 1970 differently. The workers striking for more pay were trying to keep up with others prospering. English cricketers, the only full-timers in the world, not in a union and thus unable to strike, wanted the same. Loss of jobs and whole industries would come later; so would, confounding assumptions of decline, big cars, and pay far beyond the average, for cricketers. An anonymous article in the Glasgow Herald in December 1969 identified the decade as 'the beginning of an era of decadence, modern society led by the trend-setting young'. The preface to Crockford's Clerical Directory for 1969-70 put the conflict between generations exquisitely: "There are times when we share the feelings of those who when they were young were told by their elders that they should be seen and not heard and who now they are older are told the same thing by their juniors: but we have to deal with the world as it is and one of the principal features of today's world is the revolution of the young." Assuming, once again, that most young people were setting trends, and not getting on with their lives, you could interpret 'the revolution' differently. While the intellectual CP Snow in 1968 wrote of a 'state of siege', he felt emotionally, not intellectually, hopeful; any hope lay in the educated young, who for one thing had 'thrown the prejudices of race away'. In June 1970 an education official addressing his fellows faced 'the unpleasant fact that many of the things against which the young are protesting are things about which we should all protest'. "I am a great believer in the young," Denis Howell told a school in his Birmingham constituency in May 1970. He too saw their idealism against prejudice; and their passion to change the world, whether (as at Oxbridge, and domestic science college students in Leicester in November 1969) for longer 'gate hours' so they had freedom to go out, or against apartheid.

Generations could clash over history; again, how you interpreted it, or whether it counted with you at all. In May 1970 at a Cambridge Union debate, the veteran pilot Douglas Bader said: "I had South African friends who died in the war so that you and I can stand in this chamber and argue with each other. It's time this was said. We are a different generation. You will feel the same about your generation as I did about mine and it is quite right that you should." Bader, while sounding strangely alienated for a man outwardly with so much – a heroic name, his name in newspapers, material comfort - had a point about the generation of '68 that knuckled under. The clash was partly, and obviously, in dress; the front page of the Daily Telegraph of May 23, reporting the cancellation, neatly printed pictures of Peter Hain (smiling, in polo neck) and Wilf Wooller (arriving at Lord's, wearing shirt and tie) so that it appeared Wooller was eyeing Hain. The Sunday Telegraph the next day ran a front page cartoon of a cricketer wearing whites and pads, with severely combed hair, arm in arm and carrying the same banner, 'Callaghan is a spoil-sport', as a stereotypical long-haired young protester, wearing kaftan and sandals. The Springboks tour, then, was a clash of culture; and personal hygiene. A December 1969 cartoon in the Glasgow Evening Times managed to mock protest, and women, and side with South Africa. While a long-haired, bearded man carried a banner, 'Go home Springboks' in the background, a dolled-up young woman said: 'Why send them hame? Ah wouldnae mind TAKIN' one hame.'

Chapter Six

Rugby: the last weeks

... foul ways are not always passable, nor to be used (especially in suspected and dangerous times) but where others fail.
   Herbert, Life and Reign of Henry VIII, 1649

The Springboks began their second month, December 1969, by landing in Aberdeen from Blackpool, and having a snowball fight on the airfield. The week before, Aberdeen Town Council voted 26-10 to allow the match. Councillors were giving themselves a say because they owned the ground; only, the local rugby union had booked Linksfield Stadium

Front page of the Aberdeen Press & Journal, reporting favourably on the police, even flippantly, after the demo against the Springboks ('Arrests 98 Complaints 0'). The main photo shows arrested protesters queuing to have their names taken.

in May 1968 'at an administrative level'. It was one more example of officials running things without the politicians noticing. On Tuesday afternoon, December 2, Aberdeen saw a quiet demo outside – about a thousand marching from the Market Stance in the city, then dispersing – and inside the most significant disrupting of play; whether because of good organising (by themselves, with little from STST at the centre) or because the crowd of 3264 and fairly small number of police, 360, left room for protesters. About 200 went in. About 60 or 70 ran onto the pitch, formed two circles in the centre, and linked arms. Two men climbed on a crossbar and only came down when asked, after police had cleared the protesters. Play stopped for seven minutes. Twenty ran on after half time and stopped play for about two minutes; later still two invaders hardly stopped play at all. The match, so far in the north, and against a lesser team – the North of Scotland lost 3-37 – was fairly unimportant. It did show police were thorough with those they arrested: 69 men and 29 women were photographed and charged with a breach of the peace. Police took another 30 away by bus and dropped them off towards the city. The demo got little sympathy. For the local Press & Journal, Peter Brown described how 'to a man we stood ... and applauded the South Africans off the pitch'. Another reporter wrote light-heartedly of how 'on-lookers were treated to some of the best tackling of the day' by 16 policemen in uniform, their ties off but their blue shirts buttoned to the top, and wearing football boots. Once anyone invaded, 'the chase was on'; then other police in regular uniform took over.

Protest was having an effect, for the Glasgow Herald could headline a story 'Quiet for Springboks' while they stayed at Peebles Hydro before their first international, against Scotland on the Saturday, December 6. Edinburgh was 'braced' for 'Springbok trouble'. The match was all-ticket – then unheard of - on sale through rugby clubs; however that never stopped people who wanted tickets. At a torch-lit procession along Princes Street on the Friday night, students were showing bundles. At the match, protesters failed to interrupt play, thanks to severe policing. Only

30,000 were watching, which lost the Scottish Rugby Union money although it said it was 'not out of pocket'. Behind the goals was banned to spectators. On the terraces opposite the stand, once the demonstrators made noise, police formed 'a second line of defence', as the Herald put it. The first attempt to invade came while the teams were in line for the national anthems; the few that broke through 'were quickly brought down with flying tackles and hustled from the ground'. The 'worst trouble' came after the match, when the demonstrators refused to leave; they threw beer cans, coins 'and other missiles' at the line of police and a line of stewards in front. Protest outside was peaceful, though about 150 youths jeered at the crowd as it left. Police ejected 65 and another 27 appeared in court on the Monday. One, it turned out, was a 24-year-old farmer and rugby club member who admitted a breach of the peace – throwing a beer can at a demonstrator. Did that reflect the ratio of demo-crowd violence? The press did not ask such searching questions and police, as after the crushing to death at Hillsborough in 1989, were careful to give their side of the story quickly. It worked: the Herald passed on how the police switchboard was 'jammed' on the Saturday evening with congratulations. Police did not have it all their own way, because some of those picked on had powerful people behind them. The Labour leader of Edinburgh Town Council, Jack Kane, wrote to the chief constable John Inch complaining that his 21-year-old son Denis, newly graduated from Edinburgh University, had been leaving Murrayfield on his own when 'he was pounced on from behind and frogmarched out, being struck in the back of a constable's knee' and thrown out of a gate. The Scotsman came out with 'allegations of police brutality', thanks to such witnesses as Sunday Times photographer Frank Herrmann (a 1968 veteran of Paris and the making of Sergeant Pepper) who saw 'a superintendent take a scarf off a student, put it behind his neck and then yank it. He was being held by three policemen which is a lot, for he was, as far as I could tell, not resisting'. Police threw Herrmann against a van and threatened him because he had not stuck to filming the match, as told to (itself suspicious; what had the police to hide?). A reporter for the Scotsman outside saw four held in a 'half nelson grip', 'so that their heads were pressed down almost to knee level as they walked'. This and grabbing of hair was either how thoughtless police made protesters comply, or sadism. Besides the protesters' human need to crowd together, what Norman Mair of the Scotsman identified as a 'heavily policed corral' was brutalising the experience of protest inside grounds. The protesters on the Murrayfield terracing faced five feet high steel barriers and 'a wall of police'. Protesters evidently knew what stewards were supposed to do, because they shouted at stewards to leave the police line; but police did nothing and some stewards 'laughed openly'. When the crowd parted to let a 'sobbing teenage girl' get on her feet, after a charge at the barrier, 'a steward leaned forward and mockingly shouted, "oh, what a pity"'. Protest had been contained; yet had made a mark. A diarist in the Scotsman who took the Springboks' side, Wilfred Taylor, admitted the objection to apartheid had been 'powerfully recorded'. Sports columnist (and future leader of the Liberal Democrats) Menzies Campbell called South Africa 'the greatest single issue in sport'.

Cricket was following the Springboks tour, to learn for when protest came to them. A demo, and any group within it, defied generalisation. Wilfred Taylor wrote ironically that two friends of his, 1939-45 war veterans in their sixties, had been steward 'thugs' at Murrayfield. George Miller, Scottish Cricket Union honorary secretary, wrote to Donald Carr at Lord's in mid-January 1970 that he had spoken to two chief constables about the Springboks, at the more recent Scotland-France match at Murrayfield. "Some of the stories were incredible but the one that takes the biscuit concerned a minister," leading the Edinburgh demo, who said it had to be over by 2.15pm "so that he could get home and watch the match on the television." Such relish of human shortcomings – could a man not protest and enjoy the rugby? - was only of a gentler sort than the steward who mocked the tearful girl. Miller's earlier letter to Carr, on December 24, was more meaningful: the Scots were 'apprehensive regarding their ability to pay for police protection particularly in view of last year's results which made a great hole in the funds'. While Miller had a point - Scotland's July 1969 match against the New Zealand tourists had barely made it to a third day – normally a touring team was the highlight of the Scottish (and Irish) cricket season. A sight of demos had been enough to make Scottish cricket falter.

* * *

Four matches later, the Springboks reached Exeter to play Devon and Cornwall on Saturday, December 27. The 1960s had made some inroads (although the motorway had yet to arrive) into what even its daily newspaper called 'hitherto Mother Grundy-ish ecclesiastical Exeter'. The county town had a university; students however were home for Christmas. Even here, precisely because protest was so extraordinary, STST could make a mark. Partly, because police by now could not take chances. In Exeter they were mounting their 'biggest operation ever', borrowing horses from Bristol and using 600 men, one-third of the merged counties' force. What the Express & Echo called an 'air of tension' all day was due to what might happen; not the little that did. It only took one man to telephone police and the newspaper office, to claim three bombs were inside the county ground and due to go off between 3pm (kick-off) and 3.30pm. About 300 marched, and 100 went inside. They sang 'We shall overcome' for half a minute before the match, the newspaper reported that night, 'but as the match began this was the only sign' of protest, drowned in the 15,000 crowd. Freelance protesters added uncertainty. A smartly-dressed man from London posing as a guest walked onto the second and third floors of the Rougemont Hotel in the city centre, where the tourists had their rooms. The intruder (later caught behind a toilet door) wrote such slogans as 'Springboks go home' on the walls in a felt-tipped pen; easily removed, the newspaper reported, so that none of the players saw it.

This was whimsical; childish. Victor Hart, one of the Exeter shopkeepers on Church Road on the way to the ground who had to shut for the day, wondered if the 'anti types would be quite so strong in their convictions if they were faced with the bill'. To him, as for so many, the demonstrators were only known from images on television of events elsewhere; that is to say, unknown. One of the Exeter marchers, Jack Priestley, gave an unusually vivid and unglamorously honest account of the Saturday. With 'collar up and hat down' – it was midwinter – he reached Princesshay, the arranged city centre rendez-vous, 'with trepidation'. "Ten minutes before the start and all we had were a dozen middle-aged women in anoraks, tweed skirts and woollen stockings, a group of hesitant youngsters from Torquay hiding behind an enormous banner, half a dozen clergy and about 200 policemen." Besides identifying the various 'anti types' – 'no long-haired yobs' – Priestley revealed the bashfulness of English people coming together; 'with a minute to go the other 352 arrived, all trying to be last'. Conscience, the need to 'stand up and be counted', overcame the dread of feeling self-conscious ('gawked at, perhaps jeered at').

A loudspeaker crackled, telling them to be 'silent and non-violent'. They walked downhill and over the Exe bridge; 'we shuffled past despondent reporters. What a job for the Christmas holidays – trying to get a BBC tape recorder to pick up a silent march!'. The absurdity continued. At their destination, lining the pavement on Cowick Street, by the ground, a man nudged Priestley and asked him to hold the end of a banner: "This lady's getting tired." Priestley asked what was on the banner. 'Boycott apartheid.' That's OK, Priestley thought, and the man nodded; the standing in silence went on. Priestley asked whose was the banner; when told it was the 'Young Blank' (Communists?), Priestley replied that he was a member of 'the other lot' (Labour?). The demo ended; police insisted on taking them back to Princesshay. Skinheads were still following the march – because they had nothing better to do on a Saturday afternoon in Exeter? Priestley recognised one he had once taught at Sunday school. From the light tone of Priestley's account, he was hinting that he and the march had not amounted to much. He summed up that he found the experience civilised: "Perhaps it could only happen in England. One thing is for sure. It could not have happened in South Africa."

* * *

Exeter and the next match, at Bristol on Wednesday, December 31, set a pattern. The week before, the Bristol Evening Post previewed the 'massive security exercise'. Police set up a marquee inside the ground and closed roads for a quarter of a mile around. Locals around the Horfield ground would have to identify themselves before police let them through a cordon. At barriers, police would only let ticket-holders through, and only cars with 'special stickers'

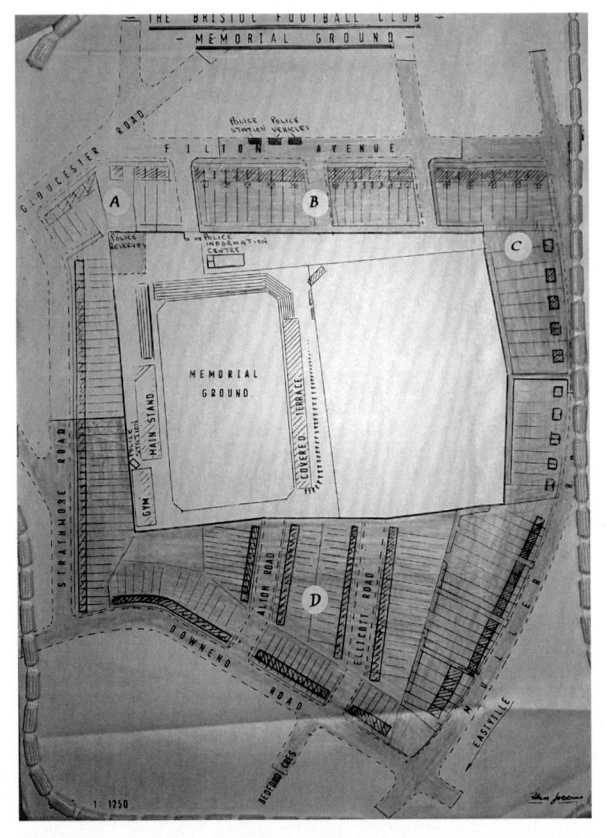

Police plan of operation to guard the Memorial Ground, the home of Bristol Rugby Club, zoned into four; and including two temporary police stations.

could go through to the club car park. Barry Newcombe after the tour recalled how, 'after bloody skirmishes' at Leicester and Swansea, grounds were turned into 'near fortresses'. At Murrayfield, the Scotsman's rugby reporter Norman Mair had seen that 'nothing short of a Grand National winner' could climb the barriers to the pitch. That was only the final layer of security; each layer sifted or deterred trouble. At Cardiff likewise in January, 'security men with dogs' patrolled outside the ground; four hours before kick-off, steel barriers sealed off the streets around Cardiff Arms Park. It left gaps in policing around the region; that afternoon, when Bristol Rovers played at home at Eastville, some complained of obscene chants. Policing the Springboks by now sounded much like policing football hooligans on a match day: the briefing of stewards at 1pm; the club taking police advice. At Horfield, the rugby club kept one end clear of spectators, so police could take anyone arrested through its entrance to the marquee, or another 'mobile police station', in the gym. Operational orders told a sergeant and two constables to examine the main stand thoroughly at 12.30pm, once police had secured the site; that is, to be sure that any bomb threats rung in later were hoaxes. Police had specialised tasks; if anyone eluded those lining the pitch, 'arresting squads' would catch them and eject them – not arrest them, for that would tie up officers when most needed. At the final whistle, police would 'form a corridor on the pitch for players and officials to pass along to the tunnel'; in other words, anything the crowd threw would hit police first. Communication, sparse by later standards – the whole operation had 15 radios – was enough to track the demo's main movements.

On December 31 police duly ignored an anonymous 999 call at 2.05pm that a bomb was under the north stand, due to go off at 3pm. 'Last night at Unicorn was just a rehearsal,' the caller said. Then police had caught two men – an Essex University student and a London lecturer – for a smoke bomb at the Springboks' city centre hotel. Post Office engineers traced the call to the 'Gloucester Road' area; hardly exact enough, and anyway too late for police

Rugby: the last weeks

Bristol police staff magazine cartoon. The joke takes some spotting. An inspector asks a sergeant 'where is 91'; the officer is out of sight, among the hippie protesters with their signs 'Stop the Boks; and the like, only holding one saying 'More pay Jim'; that is, the missing constable appealing to the Home Secretary for a police pay rise.

Memorial Ground gates, summer 2019; off Filton Avenue, between A and B on the police plan.

From the same police staff magazine, a drawing to show appreciation for hot drinks to keep officers going on a cold day of policing protest.

to check every callbox. At 2.45pm the Press Association told police that they too had had an anonymous call with the same threat. At most 200 demonstrators had met on Horfield Common; the low number suggested how the movement relied on students, now home for Christmas. The demo was marching around with a police escort, for show, and to keep themselves warm on a cold day. The police's only problem by half time was that their 'mobile reserve' was no longer mobile, because the civilian driver had gone. A constable tried to start the coach without the keys, and the club made a tannoy message during half time, asking the driver to return at once. Meanwhile the demo, having marched towards the city, was coming back along Gloucester Road and by 4.10pm was back in line at Filton Avenue, a stone's throw from the ground. By 4.48pm, the demonstrators were on their way to the Springboks' hotel; and police could begin to stand down. Police stopped a drunk man tampering with a car and took him home.

Churches still shied away from roughness around grounds. Thus while the Bishop of Bristol, Oliver Tomkins, said it had been wrong to invite the Springboks because 'the

South Africans bring the offence with them', the Rev Norman Moon, joint secretary of the Bristol Council of Christian Churches, would not sign a statement from Ron Press of the AAM, which included a meeting on Horfield Common. The churches proposed instead a 'teach-in' the night before. Days later the Archbishop of Wales, Dr Glyn Simon, in his diocesan letter warned that he would resign his membership of Glamorgan if the county played South Africa that summer. The gesture, that he urged others to copy, was moral only – Glamorgan had the archbishop's money. Wilf Wooller obliged newspapers with a typically aggressive reply, hoping that rugby and cricket players would 'retaliate by withdrawing their support from the church'. Churches and other anti-apartheid protesters were apart; or rather had never been together in the first place.

* * *

Gestures were easy and meant little; yet they meant something, and men in politics and commerce, beyond the men of morality, were starting to make them. Robert Lennox, the Lord Provost of Aberdeen, declined to write a message of welcome for the match programme. In Dublin, the Springboks' match day programme had only four pages instead of the usual 20 for an international; a steward admitted firms would not advertise. Paradoxically, the demos seemed to have the most effect, furthest from the scene; inside South Africa. In the review of 1969 by Britain's embassy in Pretoria, the charge d'affaires SJ Gross wrote that the demos 'did much to sour Anglo-South African relations'.

Those in charge of policing the Springboks matches by now had become skilled enough to react to protester moves. RB Matthews for example, reporting 'success' at the Coventry match on Tuesday, January 6, to Met Police Commander John Gerrard, told how 'we anticipated the main attack' on a 'long exposed flank'. Such metaphors came naturally to the police, a more military force than now; besides, Gerrard was a veteran of 1939-45 and had a Military Cross. Sure enough a 'show of strength' at the exposed end led 'some

400 to 500 very determined demonstrators' to charge the other end; a reinforced police cordon held, 'only just'. As at Swansea, demonstrators then went around the back of houses, and police on horses went 'at the gallop', which 'unnerved' the protesters. The 'battle then alternated' between the two places until half time, 'when I think they felt they had had their fun and they started to drift off home'. Matthews had feared 'tin tacks' - at Bristol, a teacher invading the pitch had dropped 366 upholstery nails and 249 drawing pins. This significant new tactic threatened to injure players who trod or fell on them. "You might like to know," Matthews reported, "that Research and Development have a machine rather like a garden roller which will pick up tacks or any other metal object from the ground." Next day the Springboks arrived in Ireland.

* * *

The cardinal question between Ireland and Britain for a thousand years has been; how alike are they? Physics and psychology were the same in each place; the higher a venue's walls, the harder it was to invade. After the international on Saturday, January 10, the Irish and Springboks swapped jerseys and that night after dining together laughed and joked at a demo outside; the same solidarity as Geoffrey Nicholson noted in The Observer after the Leicester match, when the two teams seemed to share 'a kind of blitz spirit'. Otherwise, Ireland offered more, and less, promise for demos than Britain. Police had no experience of large demos; nor did demonstrators. The Irish press followed British affairs including the demos far more closely than British newspapers covered Ireland. Ireland was notoriously under the thumb of the Catholic Church; what little its priests said or did publicly about the Springboks was in their favour. For instance, at Bray outside Dublin where the Springboks first stayed, the local priest the Rev Patrick Byrne at mass called on worshippers to welcome them outside their hotel, and thereby match the mainly Labour and Sinn Fein anti-apartheid protesters. That was an early episode of how the Springboks were an excuse for the politically minded in Ireland to take sides. In fairness, some in England were doing the same, whether the carriers of 'black power' or 'class war' banners, or the National Front fascists who tried to take them on. The two sides in southern Ireland were, to generalise, the familiar ones of the old and the new; those who stood by the traditions of state and church, and those seeking change; between the countryside and Dublin. The two sides seldom spoke; an exception was outside Thomond Park in Limerick, for the Springboks' second and final game in Ireland on Wednesday, January 14. Then the former Irish rugby international Marnie Cunningham, who had become a priest in Salford, stood beside demonstrators and 'exchanged greetings and gentle banter' with former teammates going to the match. Someone counted at least 25 priests going in.

The week showed how conservative Ireland was. Trade unions made noises yet as the Irish Times pointed out, trade unionists flew in the Springboks, housed and fed them, transported, televised and reported them. Again, this criticism was as true of trade unionists in England and, in 1971, Australia. Anthony Pratschke of the Limerick anti-apartheid committee admitted it was 'so hard to get people interested in social problems at home' that he hoped to develop social awareness through this problem from abroad. Complicating that was divided Ireland. The Saturday night protesters against the Springboks - presumably the most motivated - shouted 'B Special' and 'another RUC bastard' at police, seeking to insult them by comparing them to the sectarian police in Northern Ireland that Republicans hated. On the Saturday of the international match, the Irish Times ran a cartoon of men carrying banners, one about apartheid ('Ban the Boks', a catchy favourite in Britain), one ironic ('Ban everything') and most about Ireland - the GAA, the Gaelic sports body so bigoted that it did not allow members to even watch rugby; and the paramilitary IRA and UVF. If Northern Ireland Protestants - an odd minority, in power but embattled - did not identify with apartheid, Dennis Kennedy in the Irish Times on January 6 pointed it out for them. Having visited South Africa, he reported back that 'on religion the Afrikaner is very like the Ulster Protestants'.

As in Britain, some Irish politicians were exploiting sport, or any issue that boosted them and their cause. The Rev Ian Paisley was in London in mid-January, helping other Protestant clergy to protest against church unity talks by chaining themselves to the railings of Buckingham Palace, which the press dutifully photographed; the GAA condemned a threatened picket (which never happened) of the Springboks match by Unionists from the North as 'bigoted Orangeism'. It took a bigot to know a bigot.

The young could come up with bigotry of their own. The 200 Maoists on the march to Lansdowne Road chanting quotations from Mao's Little Red Book would have looked rum anywhere outside China. They outraged conservatives so easily offended that an editorial in the Irish Independent could deplore anti-apartheid slogans on walls as 'eyesores'. Besides, Ireland had its share of liberals like the future Taoiseach, Garrett Fitzgerald, who wrote to the Irish Independent that he was an opponent of apartheid (wasn't everyone?) but was for freedom of association and speech; thus he was against banning the Springboks' match. Outside the capital, in the small towns such as the 'rugby centre' of Limerick, people felt like Jack Priestley in Exeter; 'inhibited about parading in public', the chairman of the Limerick anti-apartheid committee, James Kemmy, admitted. Most of the hundreds of demonstrators that showed there came from Cork and Dublin. Only a dozen were waiting at the railway station as the Springboks arrived from Dublin, on the Sunday, January 11, compared with 100 applauding inside the station and 200 more supporters outside. When about to fly home three weeks later, Corrie Bornman the tour manager recalled Limerick as 'like a balm on our nerves'. Among friends, the Springboks shed the polite, sober 'composure' that had impressed Norman Mair of the Scotsman, among others, in Britain. Bornman called the Limerick protest the 'weakest reception yet' and said, gratefully or facetiously: "I felt like crying." Players blew the protesters kisses. An Irish Times reporter had spotted the thuggish side of rugby, so far well hidden, the night before in Dublin. At their dinner at the Royal Hibernian Hotel an

Rugby: the last weeks

"Stay where you are, man, from this angle I can't miss!"

Jak cartoons in the London Evening Standard of November 6 and December 20, 1969 playfully suggested a demonstrator might be thrown to a line-out and that a Springbok might kick the head of a protester, respectively. By letting slip their anger in Ireland, the players showed it was no laughing matter.

unnamed Irish player told a Springbok: "If this crowd of weird bastards touch us, I will tear them into pieces." The two walked out arm in arm as the crowd booed, screamed and chanted, and had the sense not to stand in the way of two big, fit men who presumably had been drinking and were spoiling for a fight. They had an excuse; one of the stones thrown at the Springboks' coach on the way there had broken a window. On the way back to their hotel, the Shelburne, only round the corner off St Stephen's Green, the Springboks shouted abuse in Afrikaans as demonstrators threw more stones, eggs and bottles. As a sign of how essentially anonymous besides uninformed the protest movement was, some Springboks who had not left by the

141

coach (a sign of lax security?) mingled unnoticed with the demo and walked. At the Shelburne, some Springboks went on the balcony and sang 'Go home you bums'.

If the Springboks had shown that they knew how to look after themselves, the Irish on all sides copied British tactics. The Lansdowne Road ground had new barbed wire; Irish rugby stewards wore red plastic armlets. Someone planted a fake ticking bomb (a clock and some wood) at the Shelburne; and a man with a 'northern accent' rang police and the railways to claim that the bolts on the track to Dun Laoghaire (which went past Lansdowne Road) were loose. Irish police were as brazen in denying wrong-doing as the British; the Garda commissioner lied that his men did not use their batons against the protesters outside the Royal Hibernian, when Irish Times reporters witnessed that they did; the newspaper's editorial weakly called the police chief 'not convincing'. Ireland, then, had much in common with Britain. Just as the Irish took so much culture from Britain (and gave, in fairness), so the Maoist and nationalist pickets outside the Springboks' Limerick hotel shouted 'Nazi collaborators' and 'Victory Heil' at each other, as if Ireland had fought the Second World War. Ireland's 1970 protesters, like Britain's, were far more numerous than on the Springboks' previous tour of 1965; up to 10,000 in Dublin (the Daily Telegraph in London said 5000), compared to 350 five years before. The Irish Times rightly called that 'impressive', for a city of about half a million; yet the numbers remained on the Springboks' side. At least 25,000 inside Lansdowne Road gave the teams a standing ovation. And as in Britain, those who took the affair most seriously – those pickets in the rain and wind outside the Springboks' hotel at Bunratty on a Tuesday night outside Limerick – could not help but act childishly, or as if on a stage. The Maoists snatched the nationalists' tricolour and broke the pole; the nationalists tore up a portrait of Mao and burned it, while the Springboks took photos.

* * *

The last five matches and two weeks of the tour saw the

working out of protest violence, and the policing defined to contain it. At least in newspaper reports, nothing had changed. For their match in Cardiff on Saturday, January 24, the Springboks in their hotel were 'besieged'; miners led a procession of a thousand to Cardiff Arms Park. Making the news more were the National Front, who at Cardiff came out to 'stand by South Africa', an echo of the Irish National Movement outside the Bunratty hotel, even down to what they shouted ('reds out'). The National Front's Oxford area organiser had taken to the Oxford Times in October 1969 to say his group would not take part in demos for the Springboks; why, he did not say (did he have any followers?). If the reason had been policy, it soon changed, to judge a London leaflet by the Front's organiser Martin Webster, in the hands of Special Branch by mid-November. Webster called the rugby 'our most important propaganda opportunity of the winter'. Behind the bluster ('hordes of leftists intend ... to try to stop the match and thus give the impression to the world's Press that the British people do not support the maintenance of white civilisation in South Africa') it showed the fascists were as much against things ('the fraudulent posturings of the left') as for anything. To encourage fascists to turn out, 'tickets for the match would be subsidised' or even free to some members (as they'd paid to join, they were only getting their own money back), and the Front was laying on coaches. A more obvious sign of the movement's weakness was that Webster cared so much about publicity. A 'comparatively small number of Leicester members' (so he admitted) had achieved what he claimed was 'massive local and considerable national Press' by counter-demonstrating on November 8.

If the National Front had had the numbers and the brains, they would have picked a target and done what STST was doing. A police memo days before the final match of the tour, against the Barbarians at Twickenham on Saturday, January 31, warned that protesters planned a 'sit in' inside the Park Lane Hotel, and to block the Springboks' coach. At the ground, STST hoped for 1000 demonstrators, some around the players' tunnel to throw dye, others to try to reach the pitch and sprinkle tacks, run around, link arms and go limp. The Met had police on duty in the hotel and in reserve in a coach. They plainly had spies inside STST, as the memo said it came 'from a delegate and reliable sources'. As an intriguing aside, on January 30 most of the Springboks visited Lord's, free of demonstrators.

The memo was right. STST planned to have someone inside the hotel ring when the Springboks set off; a car in front to stop their coach, and a car behind to box it in. Instead, the police brought the players out in pairs into taxis, to meet the coach. At the ground, smoke bombs and tin tacks duly happened; and magnets picked up the tacks. Police arrested 28 people, and threw another 46 out. Wilf Wooller reporting for the Sunday Telegraph saw 'vicious fighting for most of the match' and, yet more dangerous, 'surging crowds' where STST were trying to break onto the pitch. While the violent sort were never short of things to do, art students were dressed all in black, or all-white; a picket outside booed at those going in. A demo had something for everybody.

"How would you like to go, fast, medium, or slow off-spin?"

Jak in the Evening Standard tried to make a joke of the idea of stereotyped old cricketers pinning a hippie pitch vandaliser to a sightscreen and beating him with bats.

It was time to take stock; and take sides, as commentators had all along. The Western Mail in Cardiff, among others, looked ahead at once. Its editorial blamed 'reckless tactics' by a minority for 'a general feeling of antagonism towards violent protest, and the Conservative proposals to strengthen the law of trespass should they come to power may be a price that has to be paid for past lawlessness'. The MCC was, it warned, 'batting on a sticky wicket', by insisting on its tour. Peter Hain was already showing the politician's gift of a bad memory; re-writing the past, seeing only the good and looking to the future. Three months before, STST had spoken of stopping the Springboks' tour. Now Hain said: "We would have settled for a tenth of the impact. We could not have had a better springboard for the cricket tour, the reason for our committee. Because the rugby tour went the full stretch we now have groups committed to action in the summer throughout the country." Later, in his 1971 book, Hain said the campaign against the rugby tour had begun as a 'trial run' for the cricket: "It turned into a massive expression of anger and opposition ... one of the most successful and sustained protest movements seen in Britain." Hain was half right. It was sustained; in 15 matches, demonstrators reached the pitch. Rugby had succeeded; policing had cost it £50,000, about £2000 a match, and still left a 'substantial profit' according to rugby union treasurer Bill Ramsay. That was quantifiable. What of the intangibles?

Sport was a 'harmless release' of tension, according to a Sunday Telegraph editorial in May 1970. Protesters from the start, by their whistling, and rhythmic clapping, were making tension, denying those playing and watching the joy of passages of rugby, and, if the pitch invaders had their way, depriving everyone of the satisfaction of a climax and result. The protest went further. Whenever players stood for a line-out, arms raised, protesters made the straight-arm Nazi salute. At Cardiff for example, demonstrators gave the Nazi salute to rugby fans. Nazi symbols cropped up so often, it must have been deliberate. Among the banners at Exeter was one with a swastika, above the slogan 'Go home

Springboks'. On 'the night of the daubers', Monday, January 19, a swastika was among the painted slogans at Grace Road and Old Trafford, the Leicestershire and Lancashire cricket grounds. The Daily Telegraph printed three pictures of the first Springboks match at Twickenham; the largest was a close-up of mainly men, and some women, giving the Nazi salute. The caption noted that 'their chants of "Sieg Heil" were drowned by the applause of the spectators'. The Telegraph knew its mainly middle-aged readers would feel outrage. Most of them, like most rugby spectators, had lived through or even fought in the Second World War. There was no excuse. People had died by the million to prevent that salute.

While the rugby-watching and anti-apartheid sides alike at Springboks matches used noise to stamp their mark on territory, Nazi sounds and gestures were in the poorest taste; or, showed shocking ignorance of the recent past; or were done on purpose, as an insult. STST was no better than Hell's Angels who wore German Army helmets, and swastikas. They set out to upset, as did American students in London in May 1970 who left pigs' heads outside the offices of American companies and painted the doors with blood; as a protest against students shot dead in Ohio. They knew what they were doing and they wanted to rile the world. How else to explain the young man in Beatles-style haircut, clean-shaven, wearing a dark glove on his left hand, who, while on the march before the Springboks' Manchester match in November 1969, gave a 'black power' salute – while he stood, facing a press photographer?

They succeeded in riling some. In the Western Mail at the tour's end, JBG Thomas 'felt shame that young people have behaved so badly'. The novelist RF Delderfield in the first Devon Life magazine of 1970 deplored the marchers, on their way to Grosvenor Square 'to scream for Ho Chi Minh', for destroying wreaths at the Cenotaph on the way. Yet again, however, we cannot generalise. At Leicester, the day before Remembrance Sunday, a poppy seller, Joe McGarry, mingled among the rugby and demonstrating crowds ('the students bought them like hot cakes ... even those in the front lines were keen to buy them'). Once again, 'front line' sounded military. If some accused the protesters of the same as intolerance as the Nazis, perhaps the protesters felt they were fighting an undeclared third world war; or the never-ending war against injustices. At least basic respect was holding; for now.

* * *

After all, South Africa was STST's ultimate target. 'Vorster, we want you dead,' they chanted. On the field, the Springboks played 24, won 15, lost five and drew three. They drew with Ireland and Wales and lost to Scotland and England each by a narrow enough three points. The fact was that the Springboks did not win any of their four internationals and had the worst record of the six Springbok tours. What speaking in public the Springboks did was through their manager Corrie Bornman. He was hardly going to admit that the demos put the players off; and indeed he did his best to be light-hearted. At a dinner at Exeter he joked for example that the police nearly ruined the match, because without a demo, the Springboks were thrown out of their stride: "We had got used to it." Hain, bound to talk up STST, in his 1971 book called the tour 'an ordeal unprecedented in the history of international sport relations'. The Springboks were soon jumpy. In early December, Norman Mair of the Scotsman asked an official politely where the Springboks were practising: "Whereupon he turned his back." Mair learned that the man was only doing as the police had asked, telling no-one where the Springboks were going: "But it brought home to me the kind of atmosphere in which the Springboks have been operating." The South African public recognised it; a crowd estimated at 5,000 at Johannesburg Airport carried the returned players shoulder high, 'fired by the admiration', so the British embassy put it for the FO in February 1970, 'for the way in which they conducted themselves in the face of extreme provocation'. Again, it suggested that demos had most effect on those closest to them and farthest away; leaving those in between indifferent.

Cricket was watching. On January 30 and 31, in meetings with Cheetham and Coy of the SACA on a brief visit to London, Lord's told them 'that unless the climate of opinion on South Africa can be considerably improved in the mean time the touring players must be prepared to accept a hostile reception ... inevitably ... a great strain'. That was said in private. In public, previewing the season in April 1970, Jim Parks feared trouble: "It isn't possible to give 100 per cent under those conditions as the Springbok rugby team knew only too well ..." Barry Newcombe in his review for the Evening Standard spelled out what the Springboks had hated to go through: such as the 'telephone calls which warned them they would be blown up in their beds'. Although the Irish, let alone the British, press did not give the impression at the time – no doubt the Springboks did not want to let on – the Springboks said their four days in Dublin were the worst; they had more than 20 bomb scares, and loudspeakers taunting them at 3am on the day of the game. That spoke as much of slack policing as hardy demonstrators. If the Springboks had known what they faced, 'many of them would have thought twice about going', Newcombe reported.

Which side had won? A protest campaign was intangible, not like a sports match. Demonstrators had never numbered more than a tenth of spectators. The demos, while violating sport, had stayed within unspoken bounds. "It was all threats," Bornman reflected as the tourists were about to fly home. That said, the violent few had their photos taken and printed in the papers; they set the tone, not the hundreds who marched worthily, but not so newsworthily. It was not normal, as Geoff Clark the South African rugby journalist following the tour, admitted in The Times afterwards. The tour 'went the distance', as Newcombe put it, hinting at an inconclusive boxing bout; when the players and spectators had had to box. The last match at Twickenham had the gigantic total of 2000 police. The tour was over, Newcombe wrote, 'and it is a moot point whether there will be another'.

If the violent few had unnerved rugby, they had lost most other people. An Edinburgh reverend wrote ironically to the Scotsman in December 1969, after allegations of hair-pulling at Murrayfield: "A useful piece of advice for future would-be violent demonstrators would seem to be to get their hair cut." It helped that the tour, like others, ended with a fast, good-spirited game against the Barbarians that JA Bailey in the Sunday Telegraph called 'spanking' and 'a triumph for rugby football and for the Springboks in particular'. Just as praise for the Springboks as players – 'every man jack of them was a hero' wrote UA Titley in the Times – merged into a defiant identifying with South Africa, so praise of all the players – who showed 'admirable sang froid' when showered by 'cowardly' tin tacks, Titley wrote in Country Life magazine – identified rugby union in the British Isles with South Africa. "Goodbye Springboks!" wrote JBG Thomas in the Western Mail; warmly, not sarcastically. "Thanks for coming!" Such were the 'white busibodies of Toryism in sport', as Fareed S Jafri put it in the English-language Pakistan Times (dutifully sent back to the Foreign Office). He saw the tour as 'the first nail in the coffin of apartheid'. All these men were seeing what they wanted to. Few had been as detached, let alone as early as the Leicester match, as diarist Michael Williams in the Sunday Telegraph in November. Having been at the first tour match at Twickenham, Williams suspected cricket would be interrupted, and 'out of the question'. He did not like the 'minority fringe' for causing that – it was a 'shocking indictment', in fact; only, unlike so many others, he was realistic enough to see that sport behind barriers and police was 'a false triumph'.

Wilf Wooller, then, was far from alone when as a reporter at the Barbarians match he hailed the Springboks. What singled him out was how he delighted in the extremes of any position he took. At a Newport district meeting of the Glamorgan club in February 1970 he pointed out that the South Africans were due to visit in 1975. Was 1970 not enough of a hurdle?! Wooller was extraordinarily rude in public. On ITV on Thursday night, November 6, 1969, when Roy Hattersley said that his household did not buy any South African goods, Wooller replied: "This is the biggest load of hypocrisy I have heard in many a long day." At the Glamorgan AGM in February 1970, Wooller paid a telling tribute to their Championship-winning captain, Tony Lewis, who had 'now toughened'. Any threat to himself, or the Glamorgan club, Wooller made his own. He also had a way of royally speaking for Wales. On that ITV panel, when asked if the Springbok tour should go on, Wooller replied: "I hope that when they come to Wales they will be treated with the courtesy that they deserve and not that appalling situation we had at Twickenham from the Englishmen last Wednesday."

Wooller was no fool. He had cunning, or some internal compass that told him where to stand on any issue and disabled any sense of hypocrisy. In December 1970 a club committee praised his 'tenacious work' over 12 months, holding on to the money from the BBC for televising Glamorgan's Sunday League matches in Wales, rather than losing it in a general pool. This was the man who explained the decision to go on with the South African tour to that Newport meeting in February 1970 by saying it was by all the counties. This was doubly mischievous: all the other, English, counties shared their Sunday TV money, and any decision in English cricket was only formally by counties, which traditionally deferred to Lord's on international questions.

We would now call Wooller politically incorrect, or Trump-like. At a Glamorgan finance committee meeting on Tuesday evening, May 19, 1970 – two weeks before the South Africans landed, and nearly the very last moment it still looked likely – Wooller reported that Pakistan had just cancelled their under-25s tour; because of the South African tour, he said. Glamorgan would lose their match against the Pakistanis at Colwyn Bay, a profitable-looking one on the first weekend of August. Wooller shrugged: "One never can know what to expect from them."

Wooller, who gave his working life to Glamorgan cricket, only prospered so long because he was in like-minded company. John Stuart Weatling, a businessman and a Glamorgan committee member, was a founder of the 'Friends of the Springbok Association'. At one of Glamorgan's district meetings, at Bridgend in February 1970, the chairman Colonel BK Michaelson said that though the South African tour problems 'were great ... he felt democracy, law and order were at stake also'. Wooller could tell a committee that 'about six' members had resigned recently, presumably over South Africa, 'but against that ten new members and donations between £20 and £30 had been received as a mark of approval'. A Daily Express poll of 3000 people, published on June 1, the day the South Africans should have arrived, found 63pc were against apartheid, 10pc in favour. That made Wooller one of the one in ten; even more a minority than in South Africa, ironically, though sizeable enough to make Wooller no freak. "He genuinely believes ... in certain aspects of apartheid," wrote Gerald Pawle in a 1972 pen-portrait.

Wooller belonged to a streak in Britain that was more willing then than now to speak; perhaps it has merely become more careful. He did not act on any apartheid beliefs; Glamorgan hosted non-white touring teams, and hired the best West Indians or Pakistanis like other counties (except Yorkshire); you suspect that Wooller equally bore down on cricketers or clubmen of any colour. Wooller was a problem both for what he did, and what he represented. A gathering of 17 Glamorgan members in Swansea in February 1970 summed up the sheer undemocracy of English cricket. One of those 17, ST Isaac, began humbly ('he was an ordinary member of society and not Left in his views'). Then came a 'but': 'speaking as a realist', he was against the South African tour, for the expense, and harm to the game's reputation ('played behind barbed wire') and players. A committee man told him to shut up: "This was not a problem for the area meeting. Decisions had been made to play South Africa and there the matter should rest." A Communist Party meeting in Moscow or Shanghai could not have put it better; trust the people up the ladder who know better. In March, Bill Edwards told a Glamorgan finance committee meeting that he had attended two or three meetings at Lord's on details of the tour, 'and these were well in hand as far as Swansea were concerned, which was a ground not owned by the county' but the council. Glamorgan, in other words, could not build what protection it wanted; it had to rely on the St Helens sports club, which left things in disrepair. The same went at Cardiff – committee man Jim Pleass had raised protection of Sophia Gardens at an area meeting on Tuesday, February 17, only for the meeting to finally decide 'that this was really a matter for the Cardiff club'. Nothing was getting done.

That was a merely local hitch. The Yorkshire club AGM on January 31, 1970 revealed a basic flaw in the top-down decision-making in English cricket, when president Sir William Worsley told the meeting that the county club was awaiting the TCCB meeting on February 12: "We cannot make any decision at all until we know the result of that meeting." That counties looked to the centre for a lead was always an excuse to do nothing. Not that Yorkshire members were holding their committee to account about South Africa; instead, they asked why they were losing their best players. In fairness, what else was a county supposed to handle, except its own affairs? Wooller went beyond his job title. He clashed with Tony Lewis over the team selection committee, which was nothing to do with the secretary; as Wooller brazenly admitted at one of its meetings in June 1968 and as the finance committee in July 1968 confirmed. There Judge Rowe Harding said that 'over the years a great deal of criticism had been levelled at Mr Wooller'. As brazenly Wooller admitted the secretary's job was administration; 'in no other county was the secretary involved directly in the playing side'. Wooller could not give up the habit of speaking as if he were the club; and the elected committee weakly let him. At a Newport area meeting in February 1970, a committee man, GM Ashe, asked about 'a forthright letter sent by the secretary to a Mr Dennis Brutus'. This was the SAN-ROC appeal in writing (or as Wooller put it, an 'assault') for Glamorgan not to host the South Africans, that Wooller was about to lecture the finance committee on. Wooller replied to Ashe, according to the minutes: "The secretary said that with his background knowledge of the organisation he did not feel he had been blunt enough." In blue ink on the paperwork were the initials 'WW OK'. Wooller was marking his own homework.

He was only exploiting chronic weakness in the governance of English cricket. What else was a county secretary so sure of himself as Wooller to do? Yes-men left decisions to Lord's. Wooller – encouraged and given power of a sort by the press, radio and television, who always went back for a quote to someone reliably controversial – naturally stood up for his county; it was as natural for him to stand for South Africa, as in any case Lord's was doing. The paradox was that English cricket was not short of men who were used to giving orders. The MCC committee during this story included successful amateur county captains Brian Sellers, then Yorkshire chairman, and Freddie Brown; let alone the wartime air chief marshal, Lord Portal. Ironically, for those saying that politics did not belong in sport, the problem was classically political.

Any body of men have the choice of democracy, oligarchy or tyranny, for making decisions and (as important) checking them later. English cricket was in a democratic country with freedom of expression and a free press, that aired flaws and made Lord's look obstinate when it did as it pleased. That Insole never explained the D'Oliveira affair in public was understandable – the more selectors informed the public, the more everyone would make selection their business, and those talked about would feel offended (or would those not talked about be most offended?). Too many men in a selection or any committee, and nothing's ever decided. That pushed Lord's towards tyranny – which if well done, had merits. You needed a tyrant on the field of play; someone had to set the field. Tyranny, rightly, does have a bad name; even if tyrants mean well, they can turn corrupt; evil, or simply lazy. Better to take the middle way of oligarchy. It came naturally to the men of Lord's, their gentlemen's clubs in central London, the local association of the Conservative Party, and the charities their wives fronted; they put the time in for the love of it, as stewards, not for a quick business profit. An oligarchy, rule by a few men around a table, could give you all the good points of democracy and tyranny; or, all the bad.

Decisions took time to come out of an oligarchy. It took years for Lord's to agree to end amateurism, and to bring in sponsored one-day competitions. Likewise counties took their time to put up advertising boards around the field of play; without a tyrant making an order, it took that long to see if it worked for pioneers; to go over the pros and cons; to wear out the opposition, even. English cricket did not have time to spare over the tour; either it ran in the summer of 1970, or it did not, and deprived the game of crucial income. Above all STST was a test of how well cricket governed itself; which sounded less exciting than politics, which was why so few spoke of it.

An STST 'action sheet' as early as January 6 was telling supporters that 'as the rugby tour ends, planning and action for the cricket tour must begin'.

Chapter Seven

January and February 1970

The programme, then, for better or worse, is drawn up.
                    Lionel Salter, Going to a Concert, 1954

A new year briefly prompts longer perspectives. The February 1970 issue of The Cricketer magazine, surely one month late, asked various names their hopes for the 1970s. Only David Sheppard even mentioned South Africa; instead they wished for a better lbw rule; good wickets; or more amateurs; or the meaninglessly vague 'more tranquil era' (MCC president Maurice Allom). Christopher Hollis, The Spectator magazine's columnist on cricket, reviewed the scene on January 10. Wisely Hollis hinted that the MCC had already lost control of events; for they had 'put themselves in a position where they cannot cancel the tour without great loss of face for themselves'. Hollis foresaw bad all round; counties having to pay so much for police that they would go bankrupt; protesters, defying the law, might get their way anyway. Already cricket lovers – such as Hollis, who aged eight in 1910 gave a shilling to the Somerset CCC Shilling Fund - were looking ahead fatalistically, much as we look back on the outbreak of war in 1914; 'it is difficult to see how it [sabotage] will not happen'.

Lord's was approaching the authorities, trying to affect what it could. Billy Griffith visited Sir John Waldron the Met Police Commissioner on Wednesday, December 10. Griffith gave some news; that the tour might only run to five Test matches 'and a few other games', around England's six Test grounds. Griffith's timing was significant; he was visiting the day before the crucial TCCB meeting that confirmed the tour. That settled, Griffith met Waldron again on December 23, this time to tell him more detail; it was 'probable although still secret that the tour would be confined to 11 matches'. The price of police was plainly on Griffith's mind because Waldron noted that the MCC was 'perplexed about varying police chief constable attitudes, some saying matches could not take place and some suggested prohibitive charges'. An intriguing sign that Lord's sought a lead from the politicians was a draft letter from an official at the local government ministry, Sir John Lang. Lord's appeared to seek a ruling after South Africa, at the end of January, refused to allow an International Cavaliers team to tour, because it included non-whites. The draft said 'I expect that this would be a matter of concern to the Cricket Council. I shall be glad to learn as soon as possible what conclusion the Cricket Council have reached in the matter.' If Lord's was fishing for politicians to tell it to break with South Africa – to let politics into sport, which in public Lord's deplored – it failed. Lang's letter was unsent because even such bland remarks were judged 'rather too close to interference from the government'.

* * *

Newspapers put it on their front pages and called it the 'night of the daubers'. On Monday night, January 19, 1970, someone damaged 11 county cricket grounds. A Dorset vicar, John White, wrote to the Daily Telegraph that a BBC TV Panorama report that night on sport in South Africa had shocked him into wanting that country out of international sport. Then the next morning on the radio came the news that 'some fat-headed idiotic hooligans attacked cricket grounds'. The night's tactics, and the anger provoked, marked a new stage for STST, except that like so much else, it was not new. At Twickenham on Thursday, October 30, 1969, someone painted anti-apartheid slogans on a fence and the pitch. The local police Chief Supt RF Sterry viewed the attempt as 'amateurish', 'and indeed by the time we left the ground half an hour later the ground staff had successfully removed all traces of the daubing'. On Thursday night, November 27, police were patrolling the Aberdeen park due to host the Springboks when they saw a man crouching. When he ran off they set their dog on him. He was a bearded 20-year-old botany and zoology student, trying to spread 'no to apartheid' 25 feet across the grass. A court fined him £2. Around the new year someone had

The front page of the Brighton Evening Argus of Tuesday, January 20, 1970, reporting vandalism at Hove the night before.

painted likewise at Old Trafford. On Friday, January 16, Glamorgan's ground-keepers found damaged turf in the middle of the Cardiff ground; which they repaired. That day, MCC assistant secretary Jack Bailey warned the Sussex county club and police in Brighton after an anonymous letter to Lord's said Worcester had been 'done' (as it had) and a 'message' would be left at Sussex's Hove ground. Cricket knew something was coming.

The Monday night daubers wanted everyone to know. Students from the University of Sussex outside Brighton painted the slogans on the Hove scoreboard; so someone rang to tell the local Evening Argus. A 'youngish-sounding voice' told the Leicester Mercury that six ('of all ages') painted 'no race in sport' on gates, fences and refreshment bar windows. At Bristol someone poured weed-killer on the outfield and spelt out 'NO CRICKET TOUR', one letter to each window on the Jessop Tavern, until the last word, that had two letters to a pane, as if the dauber was in a hurry to finish. At the main grounds with high walls, such as Surrey's Oval, the daubers only painted on the outside; where they could, at Taunton, for instance, they painted on the inside. Also hit were Canterbury, Cardiff (again), Leeds, Southampton and Manchester (again). As John Vinicombe commented in the Brighton Argus, the damage at Hove could have been worse. There someone left a zig-zag trail of weed-killer, close to the square.

Such an 'action' had something in common with modern art; it amounted to little. What mattered was the meaning that people gave it. Whether the daubers were ignorant of cricket, chose not to do the worst they could, or found damaging a cricket field in the dark surprisingly difficult, they were plainly organised. As John Vinicombe said, it was a warning; that the protesters were 'in deadly earnest'. An editorial in the Manchester Evening News shrewdly suggested that the daubers' 'antics' might make cancellation less likely – cricket not wanting to give in to bad people - which made the night 'stupid and futile'. The chairman of the Young Liberals, Louis Eaks, told cricket 'to expect serious irregular assaults'. Clubs would have to start paying to protect grounds; itself a threat. As Gloucestershire county chairman Mike Jarrett admitted, protection was 'impossible'; the cost would be 'prohibitive'. Instead some counties did what came naturally; volunteers did it themselves. At Hove the chairman of the ground sub-committee, Jimmy Barker, an estate agent, proposed to be a 'one man vigilante' with a pigeon-shooting gun in the crook of his arm.

What about Lord's? Near midnight on January 19, a policeman was inside a van, watching the front of Lord's, when a car drove up. Two students, driven there by a 31-year-old housewife, walked to the main gate, carrying anti-tour posters. Waiting long enough for the crime to start (posting a bill without consent) the policeman arrested the two, who were fined £4 the next day. Had police elsewhere followed the news and been on guard, they could have caught the lot.

January and February 1970

A groundsman fills in the 'night of the daubers' damage at Cardiff; and paints over 'Racism out' graffiti on the scoreboard, January 1970.

January and February 1970

If the daubers were trying to intimidate, they had some effect. Two nights later Newcastle cricket club in north Staffordshire met, to decide whether to call off the Minor Counties match against South Africa, in July. Wilf Wooller in character made light of the damage to Cardiff – arguably the worst of the lot; turf cut from the square and tin tacks put in the hole. "It shows how little they know," he said. "We don't play the South Africans at Cardiff next summer, but at Swansea." Wooller seemed not to realise, or to ignore, the obvious fact that the daubers could come again. The daubers had revealed a difference that Griffiths had already in private disclosed; between larger Test grounds, easier to defend, and the other counties. Sussex revealed how they took peace for granted. At a usual match against a touring team, Hove hired two policemen, for £8. As for paying for more, Sussex committee vice-chairman FG White said the club did not have the money 'to throw away on a public responsibility of that nature'.

As with other protest, that broke the law or the unwritten laws of social conduct, the daubers angered newspaper opinion. To a Western Mail editorial it smacked of

Private security at Grace Road, February 1970; Alsatians and their handlers.

'terrorism'. Whether because editors saw STST as having gone beyond the pale, or because they had no time for anti-apartheid all along, they argued the tour was now about 'law and order'; which mattered above all. Michael Turner the Leicestershire secretary told the Mercury that 'these people who are fighting for civil rights are showing an odd lack of tolerance for other people's property', paid for by club members. Like the suffragettes of 1914 who set fire to post inside postboxes and even houses, STST turned to terror out of weakness; it was admitting it could not have its way by winning the argument. In a letter to the Daily Telegraph, the former High Court judge Sir Wintringham Stable called the digging of pitches a crime – a criminal conspiracy. He was 'mystified' why police did not act. Stable had set a trail that would lead to a conviction for Hain, in 1972, in a private prosecution, mainly on evidence in his 1971 book Don't Mess With Apartheid.

Daily Mail cartoon, January 21, 1970, reflecting how angry cricket lovers wanted to defend their grounds from protest. The reality was more ramshackle.

One reason why police got nowhere was that those who did it were hardly going to admit it, even if police knew which suspects to ask. Peter Hain 'disclaimed responsibility' as the Times put it, or as John Vinicombe commented in the Argus, 'piously deplored' it. Again, Hain showed more political sense than his fellow Young Liberals. Their chairman, Louis Eaks, said his members did it; the vice-chairman, Gordon Lishman, was even more helpful, telling various reporters that the idea had come from one of the executive; 'nearly 100 per cent of those involved were Young Liberals'; and they had asked in vain for help from what the Guardian termed 'other Left-wing groups'. Hain became gradually more candid. In his 1971 book he admitted the obvious that 'the raids came at just the right time' and it was 'understandable' to blame STST. In his 2012 memoir he was franker, yet still unable to admit what he was guilty of, including the deceit: "In truth it was indeed a covert operation by key STST activists executed from the centre with deadly efficiency and effect." The whole sentence rang oddly; an effective raid would have prevented cricket in the summer. Hain plainly was thinking only of the publicity gained; the menace (why else say 'deadly'?) to those places attacked. And what did 'executed from the centre' mean, when STST – as Hain and others lauded – was spontaneous, even more so than the Anti-Apartheid Movement, which did have an office? Hain answered in his memoir; reports of the raids 'poured in' to the Press Association, 'and to my home'. It can hardly have been a coincidence that the STST 'action sheet' of January 6 advertised briefings at Hain's home in Putney, the Friday before and after the 'daubings'.

In fairness to Hain, he was not making people do things. On February 13, someone painted 'Stop racist cricket' at the Edgbaston ground and a poster said 'you have been warned'. In case the Warwickshire club rubbed it out and kept quiet, an anonymous caller rang a local paper. Someone spread more weed-killer on the wicket at Bristol on the night of May 6. The digging up of the Headingley square in 1975 to ruin the last day of the Test match was one more example of a basic truth about sport; that as a sign of a civilised society, like the theatre, it needed everyone's permission.

* * *

Anyone taking the slightest interest in the Springboks tour did not need the 'night of the daubers' to tell them that the protesters against rugby might do the same to cricket. A Glamorgan finance committee meeting in Bridgend on January 9 heard that 'a special [Lord's] sub-committee was going into this in great detail, discussing every possible angle'. Just as in national politics after some catastrophe, the classic – sincere or cynical – way to defuse opposition is to agree to an 'inquiry', so that (if anyone is still paying attention) 'lessons can be learned', setting up a committee is a neat way to fob off critics. It says in effect: trust those in authority, and in the mean time - shut up! At a general committee meeting right after Glamorgan's AGM on February 27, Wooller showed how ferociously he made any doubters shut up. A club member, Dr Francis Jarman, 'had requested details about some club rules', without saying why (so what?). Wooller read the committee Jarman's letter and his reply. "It therefore came as a tremendous surprise that he had been attacked on BBC Wales and in a letter to the Western Mail for supposedly blocking a resolution by Dr Jarman on the subject of playing South Africa. This had further been taken up by the press", which took it 'as a misuse of the secretary's powers'. Who was Wooller to complain? Any club's secretary was supposed to serve members. A man forever in the papers and broadcasting, making money from journalism, was riled that someone took their grievance to the press?! The Glamorgan committee alas 'approved unanimously' Wooller, calling Jarman's 'innuendos an incorrect and unpleasant reflection' on them. In case Jarman did not get the message, Wooller was to give Jarman's letter and the newspaper clippings to the club solicitor, 'with a view to take whatever legal action was thought necessary'. For daring to air an opinion, his own club would threaten him with libel - an empty threat, yet serving to show Jarman who was the boss. Such bullying was the seldom-reported stuff of petty civic life - politics, if you like; teachers' unions would resort to it, for instance, if parents complained too hard against a teacher for hitting their child. Except that once enough people complained, they were beyond bullying. At their next meeting, on March 17, one general committee member, Roy Mullens, raised the question of 'members of the club who may feel disposed to be awkward' during the South Africa match, by then set for the end of July. The chairman, Ernie Billing, 'read out the appropriate part of the club rules which empowered the club to deal with members who may be acting against the best interests of the club, and it was considered this was adequate'. Again, here was a classic political question, a cause of the English Civil War; did committee men know what was best and have a divine right to rule? Intriguingly, the committee minutes record that the members then awarded themselves a crown of sorts: they 'should be issued with badges, and possibly a wallet container ... so that it could be clearly shown they were members of the committee'.

Not all county committees were as regal. At Worcester, the secretary Joe Lister wrote to Griffith at Lord's ('Dear Billy') on January 14 of his committee's 'anxiety expressed', after someone did damage with weed killer to 11 yards by three of county ground grass. Police wanted to discuss how to protect the club – more urgently than elsewhere, as traditionally Worcester hosted any tourists' first county match in early May. As Lister wrote, 'it is impossible to hold any meeting without some knowledge of the overall plans ... our ordinary members are also getting worried as to the effect a second incident would have on their cricket watching this summer and I am sure the sooner something is made known the better.' Lister was politely asking Lord's to do their job. As early as Griffith's meeting with Sir John Waldron on December 23, using an appropriately sporting metaphor, Waldron reported, 'the ball is firmly in the MCC court to make the decision; Griffith appreciates this'. One of the many flaws in the running of English cricket was that decisions leaked to the well-informed. Wooller was evidently closer to Lord's than Lister, because on January 9 he had told a Glamorgan committee the MCC was shortening the tour. Or, Wooller knew and not Lister because Worcester's would be among the matches cut; they had no need to worry. Lord's would tell them, and everyone, in good time; after the TCCB met on February 12.

* * *

Lord's travelled at committee speed. On December 29, Griffith reported on his meetings with Waldron to the emergency committee set up after the TCCB meeting of December 11 and 12. Waldron urged Lord's to protect the tour with stewards ('as many as we could lay our hands

February 12 meeting of the Cricket Council at Lord's. A few concessions to modernity: name plates (a symbolic change from everyone chummily knowing everyone else) and a woman in the room.

on') and to erect 'some sort of wire fence, about five feet or six feet high around the whole playing area'. Here was the first sight of what became the notorious and defining image of this story. Sensibly enough, because Waldron was a busy man, he recommended that Lord's consult Andrew Way, a retired Met assistant chief constable. Previewing the TCCB meeting of February 12, John Kay was plainly in the know about the shorter tour. He drew out the obvious news; this would be 'cricket behind barbed wire barricades'. In April, in his weekly column Colin Milburn was 'rather sad' about the fewer matches ('I would like to have seen the MCC stick their neck out and attempt to stage the tour as planned'). The cut had at least given Milburn a job to do. As promotions manager of the International Cavaliers, that would play counties to fill the blanks in the tour, he would arrive in town a couple of days before ('obviously this will necessitate me making a comprehensive tour of the local pubs and clubs'). Milburn then, like others in February, fretted that Lord's had given STST half a victory – at least half, because the tour would be 12 matches instead of 29, and last only from 12 weeks from early June, instead of the usual 19 from the end of April to early September. Hain was warlike, promising a 'sustained and militant campaign'. In his 1971 book he mocked 'the almost farcical lengths' Lord's would go to, to protect their 'precious matches'. In truth, Lord's was circling the wagons closer, like settlers on the prairie before the natives attacked. The 'abridged' dates and venues that Lord's sent to SACA next day were:

Monday, June 1: arrive (Heathrow)

Saturday, June 6: Southern Counties, Lord's

June 10, Northern Counties, Trent Bridge

June 13, Yorkshire, Sheffield

June 18: First Test, Lord's

June 27, Warwickshire, Edgbaston

July 2, Second Test, Trent Bridge

July 11, Surrey, the Oval

July 16, Third Test, Edgbaston

July 25, Glamorgan, Swansea

July 30, Fourth Test, Headingley

August 8, Lancashire, Old Trafford

August 13: Fifth Test, the Oval.

If anybody was guilty of anything, English cricket receiving that itinerary was complacent. The week before, at a Newport area meeting of the Glamorgan club when Wooller hinted at 'revised' fixtures, only 11 members turned up, and asked about car parking at the Cardiff ground rather than the tour. Around this time at the Yorkshire AGM, members voted 69-42 to keep their South Africa match. One year later, ten times as many voted over the sacking of their captain, Brian Close. In the Wisden Almanack in April, editor Norman Preston congratulated himself on printing the updated tour, and blithely added 'I suppose there is a chance of the Counties putting on some extra games'. Most crassly of all, Wooller at the Glamorgan AGM in late February spoke of the county's 'privilege' of playing South Africa, as three-day champions; likewise Lancashire earned their fixture as the first Sunday League winners, and Yorkshire as Gillette Cup winners in 1969.

EW Swanton, as editor of The Cricketer, in its March issue called the shortening a 'golden chance that has been missed'. He meant a chance to postpone, until South Africa reformed; equally, some were 'furious' that the shorter tour gave in to violence. In pure sporting terms, as Wooller told his AGM, 'every county wanted a crack at the South Africans'.

At least thanks to Lord's everyone could now plan. Some plans were more newsworthy than realistic. The English press lapped up 'speculation' from South Africa that some South African 'sportsmen' would accompany the tour, to 'put a stop' to Hain. Wilf Wooller, ever willing to give a quote, said he had no objection to 'a friendly wall to shield the players' from demonstrators. Even Wooller understood that he might offend by welcoming apartheid-white vigilantes to do the job of police in Britain: "But there are times when the police cannot intervene for the simple reason that they are not there." As British diplomats in Cape Town reported to the Foreign Office, the vigilantes' 'very presence would be provocative'. At the other political extreme, almost with relish, the Pakistan Times correspondent Fareed Jafri warned that cities such as Birmingham, the home of a Test match and right-winger Enoch Powell's constituency nearby, 'could explode' racially. The Cricketer in its February issue got round to printing at length the debate at the Cambridge Union of November. Less dramatically, Lord's got down to details. The tour matches would have a matting pitch on a hard base, agreed with SACA, in case protesters ruined the usual turf pitch. Thomas Cook, the South Africans' travel agent, reported 'considerable difficulty in obtaining the services of any coach or car hire firm' to carry the tourists. Lord's acknowledged that they might have to offer to pay for any damage from demos.

Most importantly, Lord's moved to look after itself. Lord's told SACA it would 'completely revise' the financial deal, 'in view of the many imponderables'. The TCCB would guarantee South African expenses up to £40,000; offer up to ten per cent of profits; and in the 'very unlikely' event of the tour being called off before the tourists set off (as in fact happened), the TCCB would not give any refunds. South Africa could take it or leave it. A later sign of Lord's covering itself was a letter to SACA president Jack Cheetham from Griffith, 'purely privately' (a sure signal of something dubious and deniable). Griffith asked Cheetham for an idea of his board's contracts with players in case of the tour 'having to be abandoned after the team arrives in this country'. As Griffith wrote, they had discussed it, briefly, when Cheetham was in Britain. Griffith had the 'impression' that SACA would have to pay the players for a full tour, even if they were only a few days in Britain (without bringing any income in). Lord's in short wanted to know its 'possible financial commitments'. Like one man asking another beside a swimming pool what the water was like, Lord's was now ready to jump: "... we are now determined to do everything possible to ensure that the tour will be a success and I am sure you appreciate that we would greatly welcome any help you can give to improve the climate of public opinion in this country." That harked back to Raman Subba Row wishing for some good PR. He would have a wait. Even in the 2010s, a generation after apartheid fell, South Africa still did not look like correcting the racial make-up of its cricket team to reflect the country.

* * *

A few – only a few – cricketers were taking a stand. In early February, Lancashire's fast bowler Peter Lever made the front page of the Manchester Evening News, as the first player on 'a matter of conscience and principle' to 'request' not to play the South Africans. If the club said he had to play, 'then I would have to give more serious thought to the situation', he said. Lever did admit he played against South Africa in 1965, for the Minor Counties, and Lancashire: "I was weak about it then. I didn't stick to my principles." Just as someone has to be the first to poke their head out of the pavilion, after a shower of rain, STST was giving the likes of Lever the freedom to be brave – and denying authority the freedom to punish. Cedric Rhoades, the Lancashire chairman, agreed it was a matter of conscience: "If he doesn't want to play, that's all right."

Lancashire and England fast bowler Peter Lever bowls Gary Sobers for 79 in the final Test of the Rest of the World series, Saturday, August 15, 1970.

The MEN was inaccurate. Already in January, Bryan Davis, Glamorgan's new batsman from Port-of-Spain, had told the Western Mail he would not play South Africa. Of Glamorgan's other foreigners (more foreign than the English, that is) Majid Khan, studying at Cambridge, said defensively he had not made up his mind; and Tony Cordle, from Barbados, wintering in Cardiff, was as cagey. Wooller – are we surprised by now? – was shifty. Davis, he said, had mentioned it 'informally ... but I have never been told officially'. This was some cheek as Wooller was about to hound a member for going to the press. Wooller added, as insincerely: "This would be a matter for the selection committee, of which I am not a member." When it suited him, Wooller hid behind committees. To a question at an area meeting for members, Wooller stuck to the fiction that Davis' stand was not 'official', in writing, though Wooller had already acted sinisterly on the other sort of writing –

'certain press statements' by Davis. Wooller had written to Davis, 'to inquire how they had come to be in the paper'. The last word, for the time being, came from Glamorgan captain Tony Lewis, who when asked about the shortened tour neatly denied it was anything to do with him ('my brief is simply as a cricketer'), reminded everyone who were the champions, and why ('the wonderful team spirit we have built up in the Glamorgan dressing room') and let everyone know that he was on the players' side ('Glamorgan would never impose heavy-handed treatment or in any way victimise a player whose conscience would not allow him to play the tourists').

The cricket world was watching. A British diplomat in Port-of-Spain reported (for what it was worth) to the Foreign Office on February 24 that most in Trinidad thought the tour would be harassed into failure. Officially, the West Indies was saying nothing against England; unofficially, West Indians were urging those playing county cricket (such as Bryan Davis) to boycott South Africa's matches.

* * *

Whether players made a stand or stayed with the herd did not matter, in a way; or perhaps at all, if the clubs, above all the police, could not keep grounds safe. In Northamptonshire for example, one of the counties cut from the tour, Chief Supt Tom Nicholson called that 'very sensible': "From the cricket point of view I would like to see the South Africans here; from the police point of view guarding the county ground would be very difficult."

Looking back, Hain in his 1971 book reckoned that STST could not really lose, as long as the campaign continued, and got publicity; by the later Springbok matches, 'all pretence of a normal game was forgotten', thanks to barbed wire. It looked bad and made bad PR. John Thicknesse in the Evening Standard saw 'concentration camp overtones'; the Pakistani writer Omar Kureishi in the Guardian mocked a likeness to 'Fort Zinderneuf in Beau Geste'. In the Birmingham Post, the former Labour MP Jim Simmons asked the obvious spectator's question: 'who can really enjoy cricket behind barbed wire'?

More to the point; would the wire do the job? The Leeds Green Un, reporting an early county match between Yorkshire and Surrey at the Oval, reckoned it 'did not look much of a deterrent'. The Fleet Street journalist Ted Corbett reminisced that an unnamed cricket correspondent (himself?) found himself locked into Lord's after a late press conference. Aided by two MCC officials, the reporter climbed over the barbed wire on top of the Grace Gates. The man didn't scratch his suit and no-one challenged him. The two 'MCC types' made him promise not to tell. That said, in mid-May 1970 police did arrest two 'coloured youths' who tried to climb the gates.

The wire gave a charming insight into two-class Britain. As a Lord's report put it, wire was 'unnecessary' in front of the pavilion, partly because 'known and trusted members of MCC should be invited to occupy the front seats of the ground floor of the pavilion'. If not young and mobile enough to tackle invaders, at least they might be in the way. The Oval did the same; wire ringed the boundary in front of the public seats, not in front of the members' stand. As Surrey member Michael Loosley complained in the county's 1971 yearbook: "It was presumably felt that no Gentleman

The pavilion, Kensington Oval.

or Lady member of the Club ... would run on to the pitch and disturb play, whereas an ordinary member of the public was more likely to do so."

Where could you get barbed wire – on the cheap, ideally? The Army, obviously. In April the Conservative MP for Edgbaston, Jill Knight, wrote to the defence minister Dennis Healey, asking why Warwickshire CCC's request to 'borrow' coils of barbed wire was taking the Ministry of Defence so long. Yorkshire already had theirs; and Trent Bridge was expecting theirs. The case came to the junior minister Roy Hattersley, who ruled that Warwickshire should not have any, on the 'principle that the Services should not be involved in matters concerning the South African tour'. Why had the Army given Headingley 200 coils in February, then?! Hattersley asked the chief of staff at Northern Command (who admitted his 'error') to ask for the wire back. And Nottinghamshire would not get any. This minor misuse of

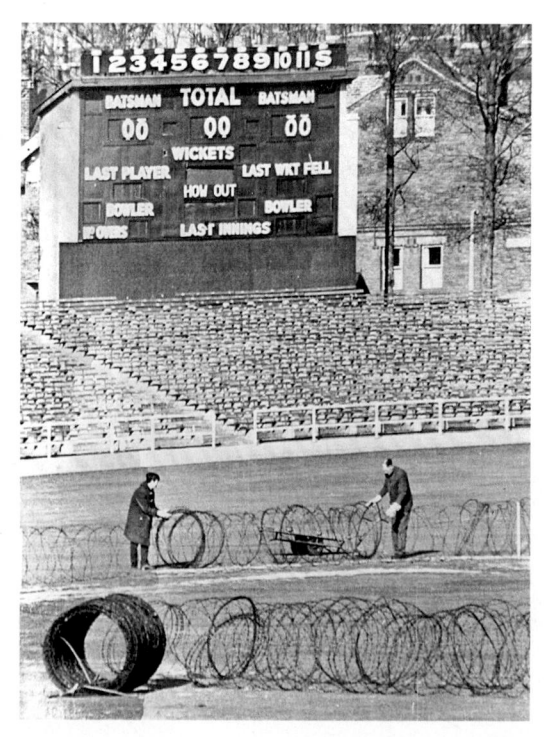

March 1970: barbed wire laid around the square at Headingley.

public property was important enough for Hattersley to send a letter about it to Harold Wilson in April.

* * *

A sports stadium is not a castle, or prison; it is made to let people in, and out, by the thousands, in minutes. It must also screen the play, so that people outside cannot watch for free; or, better still, get in without paying and have a better view. Football had a tradition of supporters trying their luck; for example, thousands of Liverpool fans scaled ten-foot walls, broke iron chains on gates, and poured through turnstiles, for an FA Cup replay at Port Vale in January 1964. Those were the 'vulnerable spots in the perimeter' an unnamed policeman talked about before Leeds' FA Cup match at Sutton in January 1970: "We shall keep a close watch on them." For safety and security, then, sites were gradually raising fences; around this time cattle strayed onto East Midlands Airport, for example. As so often, the greater threat was human. The Love Affair, a 'teeny bopper band', playing at a Bristol club in July 1969, needed bodyguards to reach the stage. Once there, the guards linked arms; protecting against a 'mob' whose only crime was that it felt too much.

Cricket, part of this changing world, gave the impression it was happier stuck in the past. Glamorgan, for instance, in March 1969 admitted that it needed another 150 yards of boundary rope for Sophia Gardens in Cardiff; and in a riverside corner, the railings were 'of little value'. Ernie Billing suggested 'non-members were inclined to get in over the wall'. In July 1968 Wooller reported that at St Helens, Swansea, the gardens of private houses were a problem; as indeed they proved for the Springboks match. Glamorgan posted a steward there for a busy Sunday match. The club was amateurish in all senses of the word; a handful of paid officials and stewards did the routine work, committee men and other well-wishers helped when they could. In 1968, Wooller was asking British Railways in vain if they had any seats to sell; instead through a local businessman the county came by seats from Pontypridd magistrates court.

County cricket, used to patching and buying second hand, was not well used to suddenly paying for the best security; or anything. Griffith chaired a meeting of secretaries of the tour match-playing grounds to discuss ground security on Tuesday afternoon, February 10. Their adviser Andrew Way came up against the make-do-and-mend philosophy of county cricket. As gently as he could, Way told them that police would give more help to those who helped themselves. Volunteers? Glamorgan asked. Way agreed they could work, if briefed by police, and 'carefully instructed in their duties'. Way suggested such basics as insurance cover, and offered the wishful idea of using police 'keen on cricket' as stewards; except that surely police would want every man they had.

Ron Poulton reported that Trent Bridge had four infra-red 'beams'; if one broke, an alarm went off in the local police station. Way replied unhelpfully that the Metropolitan Police were opposed on principle; and anyway, police might not respond in time to an alarm. The product did not come cheap - £500 to fit, about half a player's annual wage - and birds or even pieces of litter might set it off; which was why the false alarms put the Met off. Sure enough, by April 29 Poulton was writing to Griffith that the beam was 'not entirely satisfactory', as wind could set it off. In fairness, such early electronic security was faulty anywhere (and would be for decades). That left the more traditional night watch. Griffith had done some homework; about 30 companies could supply security officers and dogs. Securicor and Group 4 were 'thought the most reliable'. A week of 24-hour cover by two men and a dog would cost £180 or more; about half what police would cost. The local police for Lord's had suggested flood-lights. Leslie Deakins from Edgbaston said Warwickshire had added lights to the tops of stands, that had 'proved most effective'. The drawback; lights might keep neighbours awake.

Nearer the time, Lord's hired Securicor. An undated memo included other possible ways to secure a field of play; a ditch (less visible than a line of police); or even an electric fence. Lord's was weighing up ideas – such as tinned beer and plastic mugs only at bars - that would take decades to develop as private security in general and event stewarding in particular boomed. Lord's took care over the words on tour tickets, as it would form a contract between the club and buyer. A ticket – the same today, if you look at the small print - had to say that police could eject trespassers, and give the name of who the contract was with.

The TCCB emergency committee meeting on February 25 reviewed security so far. Leeds and Manchester too had gone for flood-lights. Costs ranged from Wooller's 'nil' at Swansea (either aggressively wishful, or he had won over his local police) to Edgbaston's £120 a week for patrolling guards plus £300 for installing the lights. John Nash at Leeds had asked local police to provide a 'man and a dog', only for police to tell him to hire a security firm. Sir Philip Allen of the Home Office, Waldron and the other chief constables with tour matches, meeting on March 5, heard that cricket generally had considered Securicor, but found it 'too expensive'. Already in February John Thicknesse was calling the arranging for the tour 'a weird mixture of prudence and thoughtlessness'; on the one hand, barbed wire; on the other, no insurance.

* * *

Would the time come when *not* paying for security would prove the more expensive choice? It might, so a strange and unpublicised episode one weekend at Lord's suggested. In the early hours of Saturday, March 7, someone must have left a cider flagon, with about two pints of petrol inside, and a gallon-size beer can with water inside, near the Warner Stand. Inside the stand was another cider flagon. A night watchman on his rounds at 5am found the flagon and beer can in the open, and placed them out of sight, thinking they belonged to a workman. As he was going off duty, he mentioned it to the clerk of works. Meanwhile the Evening Standard rang the local St Johns Wood police station, that an anonymous caller had said a Lord's stand was on fire. That night, when the watchman came on duty, he heard the story, put one and one together, and told the ground superintendent Richard Gaby; who on the Sunday morning found the second flagon and a cigarette lighter. Local police wondered if the intruders had really wanted to start a fire, and the watchman had put them off; or, what the police leaned towards, whoever it was merely wanted to plant the idea of what they could do. The details went to Special Branch.

* * *

Like the odd mix of methods Thicknesse had spotted, it was hard to make sense of a contradiction in what Wilf Wooller told a Glamorgan area meeting on February 3. Besides the dubious claims (such as, the tour was in the best interests of even non-white South African cricketers), Wooller argued English cricket was on the side of society, which might face the same violence if cricket gave in to demos – indeed, Wooller said cricket was 'the thin end of the wedge': yet Wooller said that the game 'had been driven into a corner' by agitators. If that were so, Wooller had helped to make that; for a reason. He wanted to force cricket to unite, against an enemy.

The Sunday Telegraph of January 25 trailed a 'Save the Seventy Tour' fund. The newspaper quoted Wooller, who as its rugby writer had plainly tipped it off. Money would 'flow in' from supporters and vigilantes would defend grounds, said Wooller. Hypocritically he was using the press the same (and at the same time!) as Bryan Davis. To Wooller, players were not supposed to have opinions, let alone air them.

Others meanwhile were airing options. David Solomons of the Bristol Evening Post had been talking to some west country cricketers who had recently voted against the tour in the poll of players. On January 31, he suggested a multi-racial touring team. Lord's was ahead of him; it had been thinking of such an alternative (or maybe inviting Pakistan or India) since at least November 1969. An undated paper on such a 'world eleven' set a player's fee of £120 and noted 'if a fully representative side was available' – the doubt came because counties would have to release most of the 'world' men – 'the financial results might be nearly as good as for a

South African tour'. The TCCB meeting of February 12 duly agreed that in the event of 'substitute Tests' counties would release any men; or rather, if a county refused, it would not get any profits. As a sign of how narrow-minded counties were, or careful to defend who they paid for, the TCCB's May 27 meeting had a 'long discussion' about whether counties could have their World XI men on Sundays – that is, the rest day of the 'Test'. Was it fair to have those men playing a Test on the Saturday, driving perhaps hours to play a 40-over county match, and driving again, to return to a Test? Lieut Colonel GCG Gray of Somerset proposed to release for Sundays, seconded by Lancashire secretary Jack Wood, who stood to gain as two of his men, Clive Lloyd and Farokh Engineer, duly featured in the Rest of the World series. That vote was lost 6-11. The world's best players could have a day of rest like England's.

* * *

Between January 22 and March 10, South Africa thrashed Australia in four Tests. Brian Johnston the BBC's cricket correspondent took up an invite from Charles Fortune to do radio commentary; understandably. Who would prefer an English midwinter?! Johnston did however put himself in the pay of the apartheid equivalent of the BBC.

English newspapers sent men to report. "I don't think I looked forward to a series more," said Michael Melford in an undated letter on Sunday Telegraph notepaper, probably in early January 1970. He was asking Cheetham of SACA ('Dear Jack') for an interview. "[Jack] Bailey as you know has been laid low with flu for a week but I talked to Donald [Carr, copied in] and he thought it might be a good idea if of course you hadn't arrived over here." Cheetham in fact was due in Britain after the First Test. Melford suggested half a dozen questions, 'which you can answer or not as you wish'. "I like to think," he went on, trying to sell what he wanted to Cheetham, "that a carefully presented interview might be helpful to all our causes and it would be very nice to see you anyway." Melford asked Cheetham to leave a message at a hotel in Johannesburg, or via Lord's. This rum letter went beyond a journalist buttering up someone to get an interview. Melford was neither neutral in what he wrote ('our causes' presumably included the tour going ahead) nor how he went about his business (using Lord's as a postbox). It made him sound as much a cricket PR or an agent for Lord's as a newspaper man.

Brian Johnston reminisced that he had 'many opportunities' to talk to the new South African captain Ali Bacher, and his deputy Eddie Barlow. "John Woodcock, Michael Melford and I used to rehearse Bacher and Barlow in TV technique, in preparation for the hostile interviews they would undoubtedly be faced with in England." By doing a good turn, those three journalists could expect favours in return. However, this too was rum. Were the three as helpful to the anti-apartheid side? A chatty letter of March 28 from Melford to Carr suggested not. Melford and Woodcock had evidently interviewed Hassan Howa, president of the non-white South African Cricket Board of Control. Howa had, so Melford wrote, 'told us such a lot of lies and half-truths that nothing he said can be taken as gospel'.

Any journalist runs the risk of appearing to approve of who he's reporting on, simply by writing about them fairly. Having interviewed Ali Bacher for the Guardian after the series in March, Henry Blofeld called him fascinating, reasonable and unusually pleasant. Melford went beyond; he wore blinkers. Melford – and, we can imply, Carr at Lord's – saw good in South African whites and bad in non-whites.

* * *

There's no law against wearing blinkers. It becomes unsafe when you're crossing a road in traffic. The men, English and South African, meeting at Lord's at the end of January showed signs of putting on blinkers, of looking only towards the tour beginning in about three months. 'Worse to cancel now', said Raman Subba Row. At least that suggested some sort of weighing of options. When Arthur Coy asked if the safety of players were guaranteed, Lord's could not say so; outside the grounds was the police's responsibility, Lord's said. It would 'make representations' to the Home

Office. Gubby Allen said away from grounds it would be 'an unhappy time'.

In mid-December Jack Cheetham had made a statement, to much publicity across the cricket-playing world, that South Africa's teams would be selected on merit alone. He spoiled it the next day by correcting himself; he said he had not said when the change would start. That was at best clumsy and bad PR; at worst, it showed the white South African equivalent of Lord's was without the willpower to do what Cheetham ('an honest man' said the always judicial John Arlott) said it would. Even if Cheetham wanted to go beyond his words, would his government let him? Commenting from the British embassy, Paul Killick pointed to Vorster's new year message. South Africa could not be dictated to in how it ran its own affairs, Vorster said. If anything, Killick told the Foreign Office, the apartheid government was taking separate development in sport 'to its logical but nonsensical extreme'. Hassan Howa the non-white South African cricket administrator, could say, as he did in April, that he had sympathy for Cheetham, but mixed trials were the only way to select a truly South African side. If SACA had wanted to, it could have picked a couple of 'coloured' South Africans good enough to play professionally in Lancashire leagues, such as Cec Abrahams (father of 1980s Lancashire captain John) and Dik Abed, to name two in the 1969 Wisden. More provocatively, Rowland Bowen in a letter in the Guardian challenged South Africa to ask Basil D'Oliveira to play. As an aside, a little-known but endearing side to Lord's in this era was how it politely replied to letters no matter how crackpot; in October 1969 for instance, a man wrote from a hospital bed in Kuala Lumpur asking why England did not pick D'Oliveira and Sobers. Carr wrote back that Sobers was not eligible.

Cheetham's hollow December words were enough to please those who wanted to think well of white South Africa, such as Billy Griffith at Lord's ('a great step forward'). The Glasgow Herald commented that Cheetham at least 'tacitly acknowledged ... concerns outside South Africa'. The editorial claimed that contacts, whether in trade or sport, could 'only have a liberalising effect' on South Africa. This was dangerously naive. It ignored the risk that unless you were careful, when you metaphorically shook hands with apartheid, whatever was on its hand could stick to yours.

As always, actions spoke louder than words. The Lord's emergency committee for the tour noted days after Coy and Cheetham's visit that 'much of the value created by Mr Cheetham's statement had been destroyed by the BBC television programme Sportsnight with Coleman'. A cartoon in the Guardian on January 30 summed up the latest neatly: a portly gentleman in pads and wearing a cap marked MCC was saying 'only a few bumps' as he pushed a roller along a cricket pitch, flattening two people whose shirts said 'Ashe visa' and 'D'Oliveira' and a third man holding a placard 'No Cavaliers tour'.

Apartheid was starting to pick on the wrong people. The International Cavaliers' impeccable membership included famous cricketers old and new – such as Colin Cowdrey and Ted Dexter, and Denis Compton as president. The presenter of Sportsnight, David Coleman, was one of the founders. He broke the news of the cancellation of a Cavaliers tour of South Africa on the Thursday night, January 29. The sports agent Bagenal Harvey, the Cavaliers chairman, wrote with the story to Sir John Lang – one sign of Harvey's contacts – in a letter of February 3. The Cavaliers had written to SACA in November, hoping for a tour for charity in January 1971, to include the likes of Gary Sobers and the Nawab of Pataudi; that is, the captains of West Indies and India, the world's two most senior non-white cricketers. SACA acknowledged the letter and said they had written to the South African department of sport, for their 'official attitude'. That said it all about how South African cricket dared not cross its government. SACA duly ruled on January 23 that its government would not allow the tour, and SACA would not support it. David Coleman knew Harvey had written to South Africa and, no doubt sniffing a story, 'insisted on knowing the outcome'. Coleman was a bright enough journalist to ring SACA's secretary Syd Martin, 'and his full confirmation is on tape'. That mattered because

Cheetham claimed SACA had been 'misinterpreted'. As Harvey told the Press Association – and if anyone in British sport knew how to use the press, it was him – if (as was SACA's excuse) they wouldn't support a private tour, why had they not told the Cavaliers that? As Lang noted to his political master, Denis Howell, it was 'significant' that SACA rejected a tour on the grounds of colour. The Cavaliers had rumbled SACA's dodge of leaving nasty decisions to their government. As for South Africa refusing a visa to the leading American tennis player, the 'coloured' Arthur Ashe, it led (eventually) to South Africa's ban from the Davis Cup. In the Guardian, Omar Kureishi asked if South Africa found some 'masochistic pleasure in committing suicide in the world of international sport'.

The Cavaliers publicised their story to the full to give English cricket a reason, or at least an excuse, to postpone or cancel the tour. Far from debating it, a February 4 memo by Raman Subba Row and Jack Bailey for the Lord's committee arranging the tour said blithely that SACA was 'making every possible effort to further the cause of multi-racial cricket'. At most the memo admitted that the Ashe decision, and 'our inability to persuade the SACA to appear on television with a firm rebuttal of the Cavaliers allegation did not help'. That was what wearing blinkers did to the men at Lord's; given the choice, they believed SACA that the BBC was making an 'allegation'.

* * *

In fairness, Lord's was not the only one to say something that – cynically or in ignorance – had little to do with reality. Michael Stewart the Foreign Secretary told the British High Commission in Kingston, Jamaica on February 12 that 'ministers regard the decision to invite the South African cricketers as entirely one for the cricket bodies in this country'. Stewart was asking his diplomats not to 'make any specific inquiries which might be construed as cutting across that assurance'. In truth others in the Labour government, once politics got going again after the midwinter holiday, were trying to take the fight to Lord's;

partly because Lord's was taking the fight to Labour.

We might explain Stewart's message by a question from Graham Angel of the Home Office to the Foreign Office on February 9. Would West Indies, India or Pakistan refuse to tour Britain, or accept MCC tours? The Home Office 'understood' that the Foreign Office was against influencing other countries (surely the job of diplomats?!). "It would however be helpful to have an assessment of whether it would be possible to exercise any such influence effectively either overtly or covertly." Taken together, it looked as if the Home Office and the Foreign Office, Jim Callaghan and Michael Stewart, were trying to thwart each other.

Callaghan was due to meet a deputation from the Cricket Council, including the Conservative home affairs spokesman, Quintin Hogg, on Thursday, January 29. Callaghan prepared two days before, by seeing Denis Howell, the junior Home Office minister Elystan Morgan, Sir Philip Allen and five other Home Office officials. Howell thought it 'likely that they [Lord's and Hogg] would wish to draw the maximum political advantage' from the meeting. Callaghan made the shrewd and crucial point that 'the Cricket Council would be relieved if the tour were cancelled but would prefer a solution in which they could claim that the government had compelled them to cancel it. The latter situation should be avoided.'

As the meeting heard, police could not offer either side a 'solution' – chief constables had 'widely differing views' about how many police it would take to protect a tour match, and the cost; and few chiefs wanted to be the one to cancel a match. Even more practically, against 'determined opposition', no number of police could keep a cricket match going; and even if police could, it would be 'wholly unreasonable' given their other duties. As for the law on charging for police services, someone quoted the 'Glassbrook Colliery case of 1925' when police had put in a bill for extra policemen during a strike. The legal argument – which had gone to the House of Lords and found for the police - hardly made for clear politics. Likewise it was 'very difficult' for the government to apply 'direct pressure' on Lord's; but 'it might be possible for the FCO [Foreign and Commonwealth Office] to mobilise opinion', such as in the West Indies – a further sign that Stewart's message to Kingston was his way of blocking the Home Office.

Callaghan summed up, speaking freely among his own people. Understandably as a politician he spoke of public opinion, 'at present inclined to the view that the matches should go on and that it would be the duty of police to allow them'. Public opinion was the prize; and for a politician, the only worthwhile gauge would be an election, which Labour might well call that year.

When Quintin Hogg had met Gubby Allen and Jack Bannister around this time, Hogg had suggested a delegation to Callaghan, that he would accompany as their local MP, 'to get the Home Secretary to come to some basis'. Callaghan, seeing his political opponent on the other side of the table, would be sure to guess that Lord's was taking political sides – as indeed they were. Hogg told Lord's that if the Callaghan meeting brought no 'satisfaction', Hogg 'might pursue in House'; that is, take the case up in parliament. Gubby Allen proposed attacking on another front; the press. He said Sir Max Aitken, owner of the Express newspapers, was due to return to London, and Lord's agreed to make an 'approach to Sir Max'. Lord's might launch an appeal for funds through the newspaper. Allen was one of many supposedly uncommercial amateur cricketers who in truth had made money and connections in the City of London, as a stockbroker. Allen knew his man. Lord's would ask Aitken if 'the principles connected with the tour were those with which his newspaper group would wish to be associated'. In plainer English, would the Labour-hating Express bat for the South African tour? On the principle of (so Allen told Hogg at their meeting) 'question of right of individual – must not give in to mob rule'. Here Allen was inviting sport and politics to mix. You could hardly make up a cause more Conservative. It was for something; on the cover of the '1970 Cricket Fund' brochure was an evocative photo of a sea of heads facing the square at Lord's, 'the scene we must protect'. The cause was also against something - scruffs with placards. And as Callaghan admitted, privately, public opinion was on cricket's side.

* * *

Callaghan duly met Hogg, the MCC staffers Griffith and Bailey; the administrators Maurice Allom, Gubby Allen, Cecil Paris, Raman Subba Row and Freddie Brown, and the cricketers' trade unionist Jack Bannister. Callaghan was an able politician. He opened the January 29 meeting with costs of police at football matches the previous weekend, no doubt wanting to unsettle the visitors. In return Lord's gave away as little as they could – they were 'thinking' of a shorter tour – and put on a brave face. While tour matches would 'undoubtedly' have 'more interference than usual', this was 'not unknown in the West Indies or in Australia at the time of the Bodyline controversy'. Lord's was forecasting that the tour would be one of the rowdiest of all time, and appeared not to mind. It was 'reasonably confident' that any 'interference' would not prevent play. The main concern of Lord's – here subtly throwing some responsibility onto Callaghan – was damage to property. The Cricket Council did its best to pose as 'encouraging the liberal elements in South Africa, and to this extent their objectives were the same as those of the demonstrators. It was unfortunate that they disagreed about the best methods of achieving them.' The cricketers were taking the mickey. A Foreign Office report to its man Killick in South Africa the same day passed on what the Home Office made of it: "The MCC were apparently rather unforthcoming ... nor was the discussion particularly wide-ranging."

Callaghan tried to make the deputation understand the task they were setting themselves. Some demonstrators 'no doubt' would make trouble, 'but many would be acting from a deep conviction. Police would need to exercise special skill in those circumstances and would have some hard judgements to make'. He left unsaid that Lord's would have to explain if police or stewards cracked heads or had their heads cracked. Except that, as the Foreign Office told

Killick, trouble at tour matches would lay the government 'open to the charge of not being able to maintain law and order ... and the Opposition can be expected to make the most of that point'.

Facing political enemies, Callaghan had been posing too; as the man in charge of public order, not giving away whether he shared the 'deep conviction' of anti-apartheid, or indeed any conviction.

* * *

The Labour Government and cricket were talking, if only so one could not blame the other later as unhelpful. Paradoxically, neither side wanted the public to know; they agreed on January 29 'to limit any comment to the press'. Both sides by habit did their business discreetly; undemocratically, you could say.

County clubs did have annual general meetings, as the place for members to have their say, except those running the club made sure it was hardly easy. You had the unspoken weight of conformity. Critics had to overcome the feeling that all was in order – or did you not have trust in authority? Who in a club or even a democratic country wants to raise their hand and risk being on the smaller, losing side? At the Lancashire county club AGM, on February 5, Cedric Rhoades the chairman had no time for members who wanted to un-invite the South Africans. The county committee was 'unanimous', he said; maintaining 'contact' with South Africa was the best way to 'fight' apartheid (which the committee detested, naturally). The committee won a vote, just as it had its way on a higher subscription the next year, to do something about the club's extraordinarily high £12,000 loss.

This was the season for county AGMs. Nottinghamshire cut its short on January 28 when fund-raising stalwart Eddie Marshall, talking about how hard it was for the club to make ends meet, collapsed and died. At a committee meeting on February 9, the club 'generally favoured the tour', 'providing that complete indemnity could be obtained against any extraordinary expense or damage'. This was pure wishful thinking; wouldn't we all like to do things, and not have to pay if they go wrong?!

It was time also to prepare for the tour in the usual detail. On February 13, the TCCB wrote to club secretaries due to hold tour matches to meet at Lord's on February 25. After lunch in the pavilion, they would decide on the 'various ramifications' of matches being all-ticket. They would face the same dilemma as the ancient Trojans did, letting in the wooden horse; demonstrators could buy a ticket, the same as genuine cricket-watchers. In case of forged tickets, which police had come across at Springboks matches, police were already telling Lord's not to post tickets to buyers 'until the last possible moment'. The warning was sound; in May, Birmingham University students, to name one STST committee, knowing that Edgbaston was limiting ticket sales to four each, asked friends to buy several, for the committee to re-sell.

At a meeting with the consultant Andrew Way at Lord's on March 11, Griffith, Carr and Richard Gaby agreed to 'no pass outs' – in other words, to prevent a genuine supporter entering, leaving with a 'pass out' ticket at lunch, and handing it to a demonstrator. The application form for tickets would have to say so. Time was short for everything to fall into place. On February 20, Griffith wrote to South Africa, asking if they needed a scorer, probably paid £5 a day, and a masseur or physiotherapist: "We had better start looking in the very near future." Syd Martin replied on February 25 – good going, in the age of airmail – that their former Test player Atholl McKinnon would be baggage-master and scorer; and South Africa would be 'grateful for assistance' to find a masseur.

A paradox was that the government, cricket and police were working to contain STST; yet when the movement appeared in public after the Springbok matches, it looked laughably weak. On the last day of February, three men held an STST meeting on Lewisham High Street in south London. The local press afterwards said that a crowd did not collect;

'and the passing Saturday morning shoppers appeared to be completely indifferent'.

* * *

A further paradox was that at AGMs and in private, those behind the tour believed, like Callaghan, that public opinion mattered. In the words of the February 4 memo by Subba Row and Bailey, 'the majority of people would be disappointed if the tour did not take place'. Yet English cricket would not keep its friends, even club members, informed. In a 'confidential' letter of November 21, 1969 Griffith urged county secretaries to say nothing in public about police protection: "It is important that no encouragement should be given to those whose avowed intention is to stop the 1970 tour ... any statement highlighting our difficulties or showing any wavering in our resolve should be avoided at all costs." Cricket made much of its stand on principles, perhaps partly because it was so uneasy about the practical 'difficulties', and certainly because principles sounded grander. Thus Subba Row and Bailey's memo said 'no blackmail', meaning; South Africa were 'our traditional opponents', and the tour was 'in the interest of world cricket'; the game would not give that up for a few demonstrators. However, as the memo admitted, 'it would be difficult to reconcile our constantly stated intention with any change of heart'. Newspapers faced the same dilemma. They had only gradually awoken to apartheid, like everyone else; if they changed their mind about the tour, to be in the right, might readers ask if the newspaper got it wrong before? Thus the Birmingham Post was an exception on February 10 when its editorial said for the first time that the tour should be called off, 'because of the force of a moral case which should have been heeded long ago'.

One of the most famous names in British sport did not have to justify any change in belief because, as he put it (or as a journalist put it for him) in his column in the Sun newspaper on February 17, usually he steered clear of politics, religion 'and the like':

Live and let live, that's my motto. But there is something I want to get off my chest because I feel so deeply about it. I think it is an absolute disgrace that we are allowing the South Africa cricketers to tour this country in the summer. I think the tour should have been called off and the South Africans left to stew in their own juice. All that nonsense about cricket building bridges for a better understanding between the two countries cuts no ice with me at all. We have been playing them for years but they have done nothing about their scandalous apartheid policies. As you know I used to live in Belfast and there is plenty of bigotry and intolerance there. The only difference was that it was religious not racial. But I have seen the bitterness that exists between Catholic and Protestant and I want no part of it.

So said George Best.

SPRINGBOK SPORTS TOURS – — WHY ALL THE FUSS?

1. **WHAT'S APARTHEID GOT TO DO WITH SPORT?**
   With South African sport, everything! Apartheid decides, on the basis of race, what sport every South African is permitted to play, where he may play it, and with whom he may play it. All sport is rigidly segregated and non-whites are excluded from representative South African sides

2. **BUT WHAT'S APARTHEID GOT TO DO WITH SPORT HERE?**
   Where contacts with South African sport are concerned, a great deal. South African touring teams are 'whites only'. It's no use assuring everybody that "of course we don't agree with apartheid", and then going ahead and playing against apartheid teams. If we genuinely reject racialism in sport, then we ought to show that we do, and the only obvious and effective way of doing so is by refusing to play against racially selected teams

3. **BUT SHOULDN'T WE RATHER "KEEP THE BRIDGES OPEN"?**
   The 'bridges' have no effect upon sports apartheid. During the past 20 years that we have been playing Apartheid teams, racial discrimination in South Africa has got worse, not better. We kept 'the bridges open' when the Nazis excluded Germans of Jewish descent from German teams, and it didn't help then either. Will we never learn that you can't compromise with racialism?

4. **BUT AREN'T DEMONSTRATIONS UNFAIR TO WHITE SOUTH AFRICAN SPORTSMEN, WHO MAY NOT EVEN APPROVE OF APARTHEID?**
   If they don't approve of it, why don't they say so? Each member of the Springbok Rugby team was invited to say that he disagrees with racialism in sport—none has done so

5. **BUT ARE ANY SOUTH AFRICAN NON-WHITES UP TO INTERNATIONAL STANDARD?**
   Surprisingly, in view of the poor facilities and opportunities, many are. Basil D'Oliveira is one; Humphrey Khosi the ¼ miler, Papwa Sewgolum the golfer and Precious McKenzie the weightlifter are others. And there are many more like them. Over 5,000 non-whites play Rugby in the Cape Province alone, and there are over 20,000 non-white cricketers in South Africa

6. **BUT WILL REFUSING TO PLAY WHITE SOUTH AFRICAN TEAMS MAKE ANY DIFFERENCE TO SPORTS APARTHEID?**
   Certainly. Sport is one of the few spheres in which white South Africans are still accepted internationally. It is therefore vital to them to be able to send teams abroad, and important to them that these teams should win. They are sports fanatics. So opposition to their tours troubles them deeply. The only concessions they have ever made have been a result of strong opposition to sports apartheid; they have never reacted to gentle persuasion.
   Above all, real opposition to sports apartheid is a tonic to the morale of the 13 million non-white South Africans

CONVINCED?
Then stop supporting racialist sport; stop going to watch the Springboks; stop making excuses for white South African sportsmen; STOP THE SEVENTY TOUR!
For further information, contact the 'Stop The Seventy Tour' Committee, 21a Gwendolen Avenue, London, S.W.15

_{Printed by Denny Bros., Bury St. Edmunds.}

STST leaflet stating the case against 'bridges' with sporting apartheid: 'they have never reacted to gentle persuasion'.

Chapter Eight

March

It is not knowledge we lack. What is missing is the courage to understand what we know and draw conclusions.
Sven Lindquist, final words of Exterminate All The Brutes

March generally, as in this story, can be a quiet month, of preparing for a busier summer. STST held a national conference on Saturday, March 7 at Hampstead Town Hall, to agree in outline its work; a mass demo at Lord's on Saturday, June 6, the first day of the tour; and 'direct action' demos at indoor events, such as an international badminton tournament at Wembley in mid-March; against chess, even. Hain told the press confidently afterwards: "We are on the crest of a wave. We intend to sweep over all other sports." Branching out made sense, if it kept enthusiasts busy and gave them experience; STST would have to work out details.

In his 1971 book Hain recalled Mike Brearley spoke at Hampstead, and remarked on 'a courageous step for someone still intending to play first class cricket and who while opposing the tour did not agree with direct action tactics'. While Brearley had stuck his neck out, it's wrong to project his 21st century status as an Ashes winner and author of On Captaincy onto 1970. He was never your typical professional cricketer. By 1970 he was hardly one at all. After a 'bitterly disappointing' (so said Wisden 1966) tour of South Africa in 1964-65, Brearley averaged 20 for his county in the 1965 season and in the next five seasons

Mike Brearley.

played at most half a season. Only on becoming Middlesex captain in 1971 did he set out on the road to the England captaincy.

On that Saturday evening, anti-apartheid protesters interrupted a singles tennis final at the Albert Hall, four miles from Hampstead. The demo marked a significant change; neither player was South African. The target was Rothmans the sponsor, for doing business with South Africa; and the Lawn Tennis Association, in case it did not support a ban on South Africa in the Davis Cup. Any protest movement faced this dilemma; where did you stop? You could protest against friends and suppliers of your main target, and their connections, until almost anyone could be your target. Would that simply turn everyone against you? The Albert Hall crowd booed until police took the protesters away.

* * *

On Wednesday morning, March 11, 1970, at Lord's, four men - Griffith and Carr, Gaby the ground superintendent and Way the retired policeman - inspected defences. Dannert wire - coils of barbed wire, like a concertina - was laid out in front of the Mound stand. The men agreed on chain link fencing in front of it, all around the ground. The front three rows of seats in each stand would have to go, and the tickets for those in the fourth rows would have to warn that they would have a view through wire.

In case spectators jumped from the grandstand balcony, Lord's would lay three coils of barbed wire inside the fence, on the grass. They would buy three flood-lights, for £301. In general, the record of their meeting agreed, 'dogs were the best means of protecting the ground'. Lord's had not heard back from Scotland Yard, about the Met Police using Lord's as a 'training centre' for their dogs; and indeed had not heard from police about any of their arrangements. Over the Easter weekend at the end of March, Lord's would hire two men and a dog from Securicor.

How did it come to wire and dogs? Taking a military turn

came naturally to these men. Griffith was a glider pilot at Arnhem; Donald Carr, though just too young to serve in the 1939-45 war, was born in Germany in 1926, son of an officer serving in the British Army occupying the Rhineland. Football had shown the way. Once hooligans turned malicious in the mid-1960s, clubs put up physical security, such as barriers behind the goals. Sheer physics meant that a single line of stewards could not contain perhaps scores of people, at speed, aiming at the field of play. Most stadiums did not have the room for a second line, and even Lord's could not hope to draft the many hundreds of men that would give a deep enough defence. Griffith could only plan for 'some badge or armband' for official stewards, and wish for 'a useful reserve of potential stewards …. through local cricket or rugby clubs'.

The authorities were likewise trying to cover themselves legally. At a meeting of the TCCB on Tuesday morning, March 10, the chairman CGA Paris - after reminding everyone that everything was confidential - admitted that getting insurance in case of tour cancellation was 'proceeding quite slowly'. The first TCCB meeting after cancellation heard (when Mike Turner of Leicestershire asked) that the game never did get that insurance.

On legal advice, the TCCB had to pass a resolution giving Paris or the secretary Donald Carr the authority to take legal action 'against persons threatening or attempting to disrupt matches'. An impeccable former amateur county captain, Stuart Surridge for Surrey, proposed it, and another, Bunty Longrigg for Somerset, seconded it. The meeting agreed that counties hosting South Africa should pass similar resolutions. An early sign that English cricket had lost freedom - to its insurer, ironically, not any demo - came when Brian Sellers reported that his Headingley was 'very reluctant to allow an artificial pitch' in the middle of the square. If a pitch were damaged, why not repair and level it, and then lay a mat? Donald Carr replied that their insurance cover required an artificial pitch where the South Africans played.

The TCCB decisions duly filtered down to counties from those who were there. A week later, Wilf Wooller told Glamorgan's finance committee that its tour match would be all-ticket; and no tickets sold on the day. Although Griffith had told county secretaries a good 15 weeks before that matches would be all-ticket, only now did Glamorgan have in front of it a recommended form of words to go on the ticket, to tell the customer that if police or anyone in club authority judged them 'to interfere with the normal course of play or the enjoyment of other spectators', they would have to leave. The committee, needless to say, passed it unanimously. According to what Griffith told the press around this time, clubs might ask spectators for more; a signature to a 'good behaviour clause'.

Wooller had crowed in January that 'daubers' went after the wrong ground. From a general committee meeting of March 17, it sounded as though Swansea, the ground due to host the tourists, was damaged enough by neglect. Bill Edwards reported that one pitch cover, badly damaged in a storm, needed repairing; so did seating against the wall near the scorebox; and the roof section where the committee and members sat. As for doing anything to prepare for the South Africans, Edwards suggested it was 'best left for the time being', 'to see how other grounds fared'. In keeping with the mania for secrecy and herd-thinking, Edwards thought 'it in the interest of the county that as little as possible be said', and the committee agreed (unanimously, of course) to their fellow committee's words for the tickets. As a clue to how urgently Glamorgan was readying the Swansea ground, in May Glamorgan's finance committee heard that St Helens seats had been sand-papered smooth 'and a new process put on them to avoid snagging stockings'. Wooller wrote to Griffith on April 23 that the local council, owners of St Helens, 'are very concerned indeed'. Everyone agreed it was best not to draw attention to the tour. Wooller boasted:

I have already had a splash in the local paper saying that any damage is to be charged against the rates and not against Glamorgan. This might cause the militant student element to hold their hand for the time being anyway. That is why

I think it is a pity to have to lay a hard wicket because the moment we start doing that it is bound to be splashed across the papers and invite the intentions of the demonstrators.

Wooller seemed not to notice the contradiction that he had chosen to publicise that Swansea taxpayers would have to pay for ground repairs – which would hardly please the mass of people who never watched sport, nor interest students – while everyone else in authority in Swansea plainly hoped by keeping quiet the problem might go away. Evidence that Wooller was a national, not merely a local menace, was in a memo by the Met Commissioner Sir John Waldron to Sir Philip Allen at the Home Office, after Waldron visited Griffith at Lord's on March 19. "I asked him what he could do to make Wilfred Wooller fall into line," Sir John wrote, ".... Wooller is something of a law unto himself."

Wooller was only the loudest-mouthed example of those in charge of the game who were evidently annoying senior police such as Waldron. He noted that the MCC was expecting to be called to the Home Office again. He asked that Callaghan tell them 'that they must face facts and accept the responsibility of the tour. This means they should not haggle over police costs provided they were not unreasonable. There is the danger now ... that the old and die-hard members of the MCC committee will try and put the squeeze on the police'. As every ground and match was different, the price of police was always, as Edinburgh chief constable John Inch had put it after the Springboks' match at Murrayfield, 'negotiated'. Facing an unpleasant and demanding, summer-long, and above all avoidable round of STST demos, police from Sir John Waldron down were evidently on the side of Callaghan, their employer.

* * *

Abroad saw nothing of this. On March 25, Reg Taylor – a 1930s Essex player now chairman of Wanderers cricket club in Johannesburg – wrote to Lord's asking for tour match tickets. For four weeks in February and March, the Duke of Norfolk took a team of mainly county players on a tour of the West Indies, captained by Colin Cowdrey. EW Swanton went as treasurer. Mike Griffith, Sussex captain and son of MCC secretary Billy, was wicket-keeper; at Port-of-Spain they played Trinidad including Bryan Davis; cricket was a small world. Last stop was Bridgetown in Barbados. On March 18, John Bennett of the British High Commission there reported to London that he had discussed the South African tour with Peter Short, the Barbadian cricket organiser, and Swanton. In England meanwhile, John Arlott stood in for Swanton as editor of the April issue of The Cricketer. Arlott's editorial was blunt: "It seems that the best to be hoped for is a series of Tests completed at vast expense for protection, before meagre crowds of screened spectators in an abrasive atmosphere and at a financial loss which the game has never been worse prepared to shoulder."

John Arlott

Chapter Nine

April to mid-May

Jim [Callaghan] has this terrible problem of the South African cricket tour, where the Cricket Council have so far absolutely declined to change their attitude.
Tony Benn diary, after May 17 Cabinet meeting

"This is the time of year," wrote Jack Arlidge, in April 1970, "with cricket about to start again, when we think ahead to pleasant summer days and the joy of reclining and relaxing on a lovely ground in the peace and quiet of the beautiful game with the beautiful name." As a Brighton sports journalist, Arlidge was too sound to stick to clichés for long. "Peace and quiet!" he went on in Sussex Life magazine. "Rarely in the whole history of sport has there been such chaos and confusion ..." He had watched the recent South Africa-Australia Tests and could see only worse trouble ahead. "There has got to be a complete change of heart in sunny South Africa. Their top sportsmen want it. The world

Cartoon in Morning Star, neatly (if optimistically) showing English cricket under bombardment from churches, unions, students, protests, MPs and a TV-ban.

expects it. The thought of county grounds being carved up, of riots inside and outside the grounds, and of possible injury to players and spectators is alarming to anyone with the real interest of the game at heart .... It will benefit cricket in the long run if they don't come."

Brian Sellers, the Yorkshire club chairman, told his players to leave any South African trouble to the authorities. He predicted cricket was 'in for a troubled season'. The Yorkshire captain after Sellers, Norman Yardley, in a newspaper column in early May felt able to preview 'a splendid series in prospect'. The 'problems to solve' according to him were purely in team selection; the tourists' weak spin bowling and England's middle order batsmen; 'but a tremendous contest is certain', he summed up.

The artificial pitches as laid by mid-April at grounds hosting the tour were a symbol of upset to come. Billy Griffith had written in March that there was nothing in the laws to stop counties playing on such pitches, if captains agreed; they could even change from turf during a match. SACA had accepted – how could they not? – in February. Lord's had Astro turf, indoors, since spring 1967. At Edgbaston, where groundsman Bernard Flack laid a man-made strip, Warwickshire bowlers Bill Blenkiron and Norman McVicker told WG Wanklyn of the local Sports Argus they were happy to bowl on it. England selector Don Kenyon, watching, asked what if a bowler had to run from the mat onto wet turf. As Wanklyn commented: "No-one knows that answer yet."

The same unknown went for the whole tour. 'This obviously cannot be a real cricket tour,' Clifford Makins, sports editor of the Observer, wrote on Sunday, April 12. He was defending how he proposed to cover the matches, 'while remaining alert to the wider implications'. Besides the politics, to go on the front pages, he had in mind the practicalities of filling his own pages; if reporters refused to cover South Africa, he would use reports from agencies. Those organising the tour had their own practical tasks. On April 15, the South African embassy thanked Donald Carr by letter for a list of possible invites for a cocktail party.

A Bolton Methodist church invited the South African team to read the lesson on Sunday, August 9, while they were in Manchester to play Lancashire. Jack Plimsoll, the tour manager, accepted dates for speaking at the Wombwell and Northern cricket societies in Yorkshire. He wrote to Griffith ('Dear Billy') asking to meet 'one of your leading umpires' to discuss the new lbw rule, which was new to South Africa.

Grounds were ready. Nottingham had barbed wire on the outside wall, lights from dusk to dawn, and a policeman and dog patrolling every half an hour. For their matches, the second and sixth of the tour, police in plain clothes would stand at entrances and sit in the stands, besides uniformed men; and 80 to 100 would sleep there at night. Edgbaston had two security guards; one patrolled with an Alsatian while the other swivelled a searchlight. "He also has at hand a button which activates the public address system and if anyone is seen they are warned with pre-recorded message to stand still, otherwise the dog will be released." Perhaps because it sounded so Colditz-like, Edgbaston was keeping such security 'strictly private'.

As in every mid-April, the new Wisden Almanack came out, to record the news of the year before and to itself make news thanks to the editor Norman Preston's notes. John Arlott in the Guardian quoted Preston on the tour at length and praised his 'objective view, worthy of the Almanack'. Arlott was hardly the man to give an objective view of Wisden, as its book reviewer; such have always been the conflicts of interest over Wisden. If anyone writes about cricket, they either write for it or wish they could. That explains the forever uncritical praise of Wisden as 'the Cricketers' Bible' (to quote an arrogant 1970 advert; was the Bible the Christians' Wisden?!). In truth Preston's notes, as so often, fell dismally short. Preston stated the issues well enough only to ask unrealistically for 'an authentic Championship' in 1970, without Test matches, ignoring that the game had tours every summer for a reason; it needed the money. Arlott noted without comment an article by Michael Melford on 'Ups and Downs of the Springboks' that in 2000 words said nothing of apartheid except for a

More Apartheid problems

A Daily Mail cartoon of April 28, 1970 tries to link 'apartheid problems' with the ostracised Chinese Communist leader Chairman Mao, who's just launched a satellite. He and other world leaders such as umpire United States President Richard Nixon wear cricket whites.

hint at the end about 'other influences'. At least Rowland Bowen acknowledged in his pages of 'Notable events in South African cricket history' that whites were not the only people in the country. Whether because Wisden had to balance writers as politically different as Melford or Bowen, or because it was yet another institution compromised by its history of ignoring apartheid, Wisden gave no lead to its readership.

* * *

On Monday, April 20, a van pulled up at the Grace Gates of Lord's. One man showed an MCC membership card, another a squash racket. They said they were going to play squash. Bill Leonard the gateman was suspicious. How many MCC members drove vans?

What was in the back, behind the curtain? he asked. Nothing, the men said. "Let's have a look then," said Leonard, one of generations of white-coated men who enforced the school or prison-like rules: don't park there; no women in the pavilion, no entry without a tie. Inside the van were men, including four coloured, wearing whites, who had planned to play cricket at Lord's. They set up stumps on St John's Wood Road instead. "An ITN camera team appeared from nowhere," reported Malcolm Dean in the Guardian, who himself was suspiciously on the spot. Reports differed about how long these dozen STST demonstrators stopped the traffic; five, eight or ten minutes. Strikingly, while reactions differed – some drinkers at the Tavern next door came out and cheered, an 'irate bus passenger' urged a bread van driver to run over the stumps – no-one appeared to think about apartheid. How could they? It was all a stunt. The demonstrators sat in the road, then let the traffic go and went in the Tavern. Police arrived without arresting anyone. The audience of average English men and women – seldom seen in this story – had begrudged giving five minutes of their day to STST, although the street theatre amused some and the prospect of being 'on the telly' pleased others. Media-savvy STST had given trusted journalists the exclusive, novel, visually striking story beforehand. That protesters and media alike were willing to hold up traffic for the sake of a story, showing their contempt for others, went unsaid. In an ever more televisual society, argument was no longer everything; just being on TV counted ...

* * *

... as Harold Wilson understood. At 9.30pm on Thursday, April 16, on ITV's This Week current affairs show, he answered at length the question; would he be going to watch any South African tour matches? "Certainly not, good heavens no," he replied:

No, I had some questions about this in Parliament today. I think the decision to invite them, to have them coming, was a very ill-judged decision. It isn't the first time I have said that if the South Africans behave as they do with apartheid in the matter of sport then they really have put themselves outside the pale of civilised cricket and civilised everything else .... I think it was a mistake.

Wilson called a general election for June 18 on Monday,

Harold Wilson.

May 18. At the time he said he settled on the date five or six weeks before; meaning he had just decided, when he was giving that ITV interview. That made his comments with hindsight even more significant:

I don't believe they [tour matches] *should be disturbed by digging up pitches or violence. I believe that everyone should be free to demonstrate against apartheid. I hope people will feel free to demonstrate against apartheid, I hope people will feel free to do that but not by violent methods and not by nasty, sneaky little things like sort of mirrors, to deflect the sunshine into batsmen's eyes, and so on. That's a bit of a cheap way out. Let's all express our detestation of apartheid in any peaceful way, let the matches continue. I think the MCC have made a big mistake.*

For days leading Conservatives such as Quintin Hogg condemned Wilson, claiming he was inciting people to break the law. Even if he were, it suited Wilson to pick such a fight. The Observer's political columnist Nora Beloff among others spotted that such a punchy statement - by

Wilson's or any politician's low standards – was 'intended to stimulate the party faithful'. Wilson was never going to be the MCC's friend; why not use them?

The MCC was foolishly willing to be used. As early as November, Geoff Clark in the Times had noted that television debates over the Springbok tour were 'utterly predictable'; the antis were more intellectual, skilled debaters; those on sport's side came out less well. So it was on BBC TV Panorama between 8pm and 8.50pm on Monday, April 27 (after Star Trek and before the news and Frankie Howerd in Up Pompeii; such were the good old days of British TV). Speaking for cricket were Maurice Allom, Wilf Wooller, Cedric Rhoades; MJK Smith, of Warwickshire, MCC captain on their last tour of South Africa; and the Tory MP and shadow cabinet law spokesman Sir Peter Rawlinson. Against were David Sheppard, Arlott, Hain, Dennis Brutus and the Labour MP Brian Walden. 'We are not likely to have fuller or fairer consideration of the rights and wrongs,' the Lancashire Evening Post's critic said the next day. The presenter Robin Day let the debate run, leaving no time for a report on the Vietnam War.

In a memo the next day William Watson of the Foreign Office wrote that 'the Cricket Council team made a pretty poor showing'. In the Sheffield Morning Telegraph, Pat Roberts judged that 'the anti-tour people on the level of debate alone won hands down! Not one of their many relevant, cogent and logically argued points had been taken.' That Allom said the ten in the studio were on the same side was 'beyond belief'. Rawlinson was so naïve 'as to be laughable'. Wooller said we were not at war with South Africa; there was no reason not to play them. So badly did cricket authority come across, the antis confronted them, like boxers moving in, sensing a knock-out. 'Mr Wooller seems unable to take the actual point,' Brian Walden said. Sheppard asked: 'Do you understand?' Arlott spoke as he already had in public; the tour mattered beyond cricket. Had the officials taken expert advice on community relations? he asked. "Eventually they answered they had not," Roberts reported. "They threw in so many red herrings it was hard to keep pace." One remark by Allom made cricket look particularly dim, even dangerously like apartheid South Africa: the thousands of non-whites near the Oval in south London never went to watch matches, except when the West Indies were playing, he said. Roberts added: "Has he counted how many whites don't go too, I wonder."

Had cricket put up the right men? Where was the PR-savvy Subba Row? All ten were used to speaking in public. The pro-tour side, for all Rawlinson's talk of principles of law and order, placed themselves at a disadvantage simply by going on a current affairs, not a sport, show; they were admitting the tour was political. They looked like what they were: middle-aged or old men, not used to facing questions – or to be exact, motivated questioners - in life generally, let alone on radio and television. Wooller alone was, except that usually his interviews lasted only a few minutes, all that broadcast news bulletins wanted. He could not keep his bluster going for longer.

By contrast, Peter Hain had a letter published in the Times and Guardian on the Thursday, April 30, that was assertive ('Lord's is in the dock now'), confident ('massive public opposition grows') and party-political (calling the tour 'a Conservative Party showpiece'), while closing with a graceful offer: if the Cricket Council were to cancel, it would show 'a dignity worthy of the game itself'. A letter to Wilson dated that day from David Sibeko, head of mission for the Pan Africanist Congress, made the uncomfortable point that 'apartheid in South Africa is not sustained by overseas sports tours; it is sustained by overseas economic investment. Under your leadership Britain has maintained and even increased her investment in South Africa.' That morning, the tour reached the Cabinet for the first time. Signficantly, the agenda item named not the tour, but the 'threatened African boycott' of the Commonwealth Games, due to run in Edinburgh in July.

A memo from Callaghan to Wilson later that day showed how right Cabinet member and diarist Richard Crossman was to note that 'Harold and Jim Callaghan are taking enormous time and trouble over this'. Callaghan was either well-informed about Lord's or had intuition. Some of the Cricket Council 'would die in the last ditch rather than call the tour off'. Others wanted to 'get off the hook – especially if the Government could be made the scapegoat'. Callaghan was as sharp in his aims; 'to intensify the pressure by all the unofficial means we can find in the hope that the nerve of the Cricket Council will crack'. Wilson had raised in Cabinet 'the role of Securicor dogs and stewards'. The Cabinet minutes, in their dry style stated 'there should be no question of their [police] being supplanted ... by private agencies'. The left wing of British politics generally was suspicious of the likes of Securicor as a 'private army' in the pay of industry and the rich. Police, too, saw private security as a rival. Wilson had spotted a useful possible way to keep the police on Labour's side against Lord's. A note from Callaghan showed another idea – finding some legal way of keeping the tourists out in the name of public order – could not work.

Wilson plainly felt he had an issue he could take further; he went on David Coleman's Sportsnight show that night. He was able to pose as reasonable ('we all say no politics in sport, I agree with that') and against apartheid ('they wouldn't have D'Oliveira, they have got their segregation') and put pressure on Lord's. He agreed with Coleman that policing a cricket match would be more difficult than a shorter rugby match. Wilson raised the possible boycott by non-white nations of the Commonwealth Games that summer in Edinburgh ('a tragedy for Scotland'). Wilson stood by young and idealistic demonstrators (and possible voters). "I know that has been misunderstood, but this is a free country and I hope no-one is saying that there should be a law that nobody can ever demonstrate." Wilson presented himself at once as a man of conviction and a moderate: for freedom, against its misuse.

Previewing the actual cricket season, Jim Parks admitted to 'considerable apprehension' and could not resist wishing he was back in the early 1950s, before 'one-day knock-abouts', when 'the South African tourists were welcomed with open

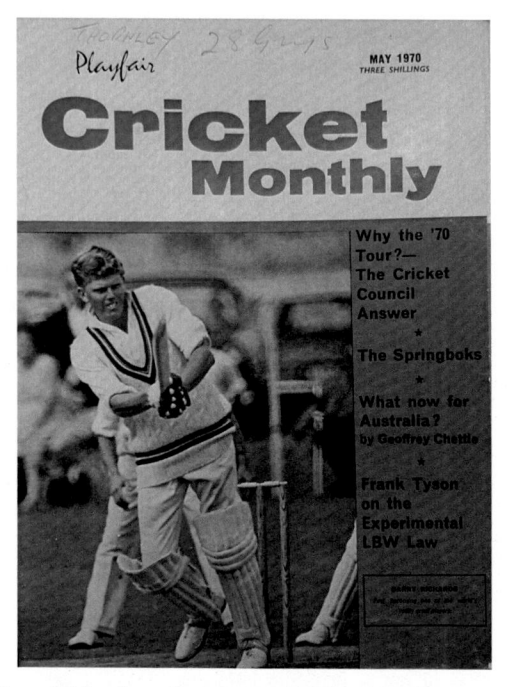

By putting Barry Richards on the cover and profiling the South African tourists, Playfair Cricket Monthly like most of English cricket showed itself for the tour.

arms'; when, he might have added, he was in his early 20s, not of an age to retire. EW Swanton, in his editorial for the May issue of The Cricket, was more composed than most. He admitted 'almost every traditional institution' was 'under attack' but urged readers not to suppose 'that our beloved world is going utterly to the dogs'.

Saturday, May 2, brought the first round of Championship matches; and demos. A handful stood outside Bradford Park Avenue; a dozen students picketed Trent Bridge. Whether because handing out leaflets did not appeal, or the South Africans' first match was five weeks away - or because county cricket was so unpopular, even to protest against - STST turn-out at Lord's and the Oval was likewise 'very poor', according to Special Branch's fourth report on STST, dated May 11. Police reckoned Hain, Hugh Geach the STST secretary and London organiser Simon Hebditch were 'fast losing control' because they could not organise better;

April to mid-May

England captain Ray Illingworth bowls Rest of the World captain Gary Sobers for 80 in the first innings of the Third Test, Saturday, July 18, 1970. Alan Knott is behind the stumps and Colin Cowdrey at slip.

Communists were 'offering' to help. The handful at the Oval demo, where Nottinghamshire captained by Sobers were visiting, waved some unsavoury banners, such as 'One way ticket for Sobers to Bantuland' and 'Send the Uncle Toms to the reserves'. This insult to the world's premier playing cricketer implied that he was guilty of accepting apartheid. Meanwhile a letter went from West Indian campaigner Jeff Crawford to 18 West Indian and 11 coloured players such as D'Oliveira (starting 'Dear Brother'). It gave them until May 15 to say they would not play against the tourists. After cancellation, Raymond Illingworth complained that he, 'and I suppose all connected with cricket have been cheesed off hearing the demands and taunts of these demonstrators'.

Illingworth, since the previous summer captain of Leicestershire and England, was in truth wounded by finding suddenly that what he loved to do for a living made others angry. The protesters anticipated worse to come. In early May Nottingham STST organisers wrote to the city council asking that 'cricket loving' local magistrates not hear cases of protesters. Paradoxically, in these last weeks before the tour, cricket grounds were the least important places: parliament, television studios, and wherever men of power met, mattered more.

Wilson, like so many who were for the tour, said 'no politics in sport'. Then, and even now, when we ask whether sport (done for pleasure, in leisure hours) and politics mix, we imply that sport is pure, and wicked politicians are itching to dirty it. We would do better to ask: why sport in politics? A politician as skilled as Wilson only reached the top in politics, and stayed there, by giving himself to it. Signficantly, some spoke of 'the game of politics'; that is, politics was not always, or even mostly, about passing laws and making speeches, but about gossip; about who was rising and falling, and the ambitions of you and others. Politicians had no need to mix with sport; they had their own. MCC placed sport in politics as soon as a politician, Quintin Hogg, spoke for them. Who paid for police; violence in public; how we treated foreign countries; all were political. Wilson only turned to sport when he felt he had to. Perhaps we feel unease that the two mix because sport is in public – professionals playing without an audience is somehow unnatural, even sinister – and so much politics is done, like office-politics, in private; in corridors, over a drink. So it was with Wilson and his government's work to stop the tour.

* * *

On April 30 Lord's made a press statement: "It is surely the Prime Minister's responsibility to decide whether this country is being blackmailed." While unfriendly – Lord's was following the Tory line that a few protesters were blackmailing the country – Lord's was at least admitting the tour was Wilson's business; that sport was in politics. The Cabinet heard of an inter-departmental committee, under

Dennis Howell, that was to consider ways of 'applying indirect pressure to the Cricket Council with a view to persuading them to re-consider the South African tour'. In another sign that these politicians actually preferred not to interfere in sport – they had enough on their plate – the Cabinet minutes noted that a mainly white Commonwealth Games 'raised implications which went beyond the sphere of sport'; presumably foreign relations generally. Wilson could wonder aloud to the Cabinet whether to deny entry to the tourists at the airport – neat, if legal – thanks to a memo from Dennis Howell dated April 28. In theory, Howell told Wilson, the government could amend instructions to immigration officers; only, any change would have to go through the Commons, and 'would be a matter of fierce controversy'. Could you claim the tourists would cause a breach of the peace, or the Commonwealth Games boycott? No; because others, not the cricketers, would do the violence and the boycott, and in any case, if the tourists had a father born in Britain, they had an absolute right to enter. That Wilson had Callaghan give him a similar report after Cabinet suggests that part of Wilson's power lay in getting second opinions, even if it made extra work for ministers. In other words, Wilson did not trust Callaghan.

"I am all things to all men..."

An unfriendly cartoon of Harold Wilson in the Sunday Telegraph of May 3, showing him wearing various sports' clothing, to paint him as 'all things to all men'.

The first weekend in May was a traditional time for Labour to rally. On Sunday, May 3, Wilson spoke at Colston Hall in Bristol. He sought to pin on the 'disorganised Tories' the badge of apartheid in a long set of rather lame sporting puns about the 'football' of party politics: "First it's cricket. One day they are playing away with Rhodesia, the next they are at home with South Africans." Meanwhile in Trafalgar Square a crowd of Conservative Monday Club anti-Communists (variously estimated at 500, or 2000) had a shouting match with left-wing marchers passing South Africa House.

Howell's committee had been meeting since late April. On Monday afternoon, May 4, Howell told his fellow junior ministers – Maurice Foley (Foreign Office), Merlyn Rees (Home Office) and Bruce Millan (Scottish Office) – that Wilson had gone as far as he could, on television on April 30. Howell passed on, accurately, Wilson's recent thinking: the prime minister could send for the Cricket Council and ask them to cancel, but what if they said no ('an intolerable situation', according to Howell)? The committee loyally believed Wilson's interview with David Coleman had 'improved the posture of the government' as any blame for 'disturbances' in the summer would 'rest squarely on the Cricket Council'. Indeed, if the government did anything else, it would provoke protest from someone. The government had to keep doing nothing; or, as the committee put it, 'watch developments'. Of those who gave a thought to a boycotted, all-white Commonwealth Games - 'appalling', Cabinet minister Anthony Greenwood called it in a minute to Wilson - most were only thinking of their own interests; curiously few felt for the 40-year-old Games apart from the Edinburgh organisers. One was the Birmingham Post athletics writer Randall Northam who found it sad if the Games were to crumble 'because of the head in the sand attitude of the Cricket Council'.

Otherwise, everything about the affair was coming to the boil. Thanks to the Commonwealth Games, the stakes had become higher than cricket. Anthony Greenwood agreed 'we are in a critical situation', and suggested sounding out 'selected High Commissioners in London' such as India, Barbados and Jamaica, 'about the possibility of their governments saying that if the Cricket Council goes ahead, it means the end of Test Match Cricket'. Britain's ambassador in South Africa, Sir Arthur Snelling, wrote to Sir John Johnston ('Dear Jack') at the Foreign Office on May 5 that 'nothing that is being said by anyone in Britain' – by Peter Hain and Bishop Trevor Huddleston on the anti-apartheid side, Quintin Hogg on the other – 'passes unnoticed'. In Britain, commentators were picking up that Wilson was deciding whether to go to the polls in June, or wait. In the Western Daily Press, Gary Hicks noted that besides the economy – always the basic issue – violence on cricket fields 'could easily rebound on Labour, now that the Tories have made law and order a major election issue'.

* * *

Protest was radicalising thanks to STST. As early as November 1969, Special Branch had noted anti-apartheid as 'a unifying factor among the various factions of the extreme left'. It appealed more emotionally than Zimbabwe, Palestine and Cuba (one of the few places the left approved of, compared with the bewilderingly many countries it found fault with). Opposing the Vietnam War was losing its appeal, since the United States plainly (and naturally) took no notice. Pardoxically, the very fact that STST was popular and unifying threatened to split it, if the extreme few would not keep the peace at public demos. Early on STST organisers had seen they were powerless. Before the Springboks arrived in Exeter, city councillor Keith Taylor said: "If we do get a small fringe going on the pitch, there is not much we can do about it." Special Branch in its May 11, 1970 report noted slogans painted on the pavilion of Blackheath cricket club in Kent; and threats against Peter Hain, the South African ambassador, and the MCC secretary. In other words, those feeling strongly for the tour were going to extremes also. Mainly, they were only talking; John Jackson, in the name of 'Support The Seventy Tour', said for example that calling off the tour would be 'a total surrender to anarchy'. Violent words or acts always provoked at least as bad a reaction; after the Springboks match of November 22 at Twickenham, hundreds marched on the police station, broke a window and tried to force the doors, to free 15 arrested protesters. Seven more were arrested.

Special Branch in April noted threatening telephone calls and letters to 'cricket personalities', 'particularly D'Oliveira'. Both sides could abuse D'Oliveira, for not supporting them. At least during the Springboks tour, such threats were against the actual players. By April and May, some threats were against people who had no say over the cricket tour. For example, police called on the Stockport home of retired Lancashire bowler Brian Statham after a call to a Manchester newspaper threatening the kidnap of his wife Audrey, if Lancashire played South Africa. The kidnap threat against Nottinghamshire chairman Jack Baddiley only prompted him to say 'I am going to do my utmost to see this tour through'. A caller had rung BBC radio in Nottingham, Trent Bridge secretary Ron Poulton, and two Nottingham newspapers; one of them reported the man had 'an educated voice'.

Newspapers were irresponsible to give these threats the time of day, let alone print Baddiley's farm address, as one Nottingham newspaper did. Some threat-makers plainly followed the news. On Friday, May 15, for instance, Brian Close launched the 'Support The Seventy Tour' in Leeds, pictured alongside John Jackson, the Yorkshire committee man and England selector Billy Sutcliffe, and Yorkshire

Brian Close; 'genuinely a hard man', Brian Rose recalled in his 2019 autobiography.

club secretary John Nash. Close spoke in character: "I have had to fight many times on the cricket field, but this year we are going to have a new experience in having to fight to play cricket." All Yorkshire's players wanted to play South Africa, he went on, and 'a lot of coloured players in this country' who were however 'put under pressure by their own countries' not to. The next day, as Close related later, 'three CID men turned up at Middlesbrough', where Yorkshire were playing Glamorgan, 'and said they had been tipped off that protesters were going to make a kidnap threat'. As Close told Bill Bowes for the Leeds Green Un: "If anyone tries to stop me …. well, it would take four or five of them."

Who was making these threats? Did Leeds, Manchester and Nottingham each have someone angry and cowardly enough to ring, or was someone at the centre of STST directing? The news was enough to give people ideas. The very first act in July 1969, against the Davis Cup in Bristol, had included an anonymous 'phone call, traced to a kiosk in the Kingswood part of the city, warning of a bomb at the tennis club. Police searched without finding anything. Police took seriously a threat to kidnap the eight-year-old son of Princess Margaret, Lord Linley, at his prep school in April 1970, for a ransom and release of serious criminals.

Making threats was all the rage. In May 1970, detectives escorted the prime minister's son Giles, a student in Brighton, after a letter sent to a newspaper said the IRA planned a kidnap. If the tour had to stop, or else you were going to shoot the Queen at Heathrow Airport, because you had a high velocity rifle with telescopic sights – as someone rang the Press Association to say on May 18 – why did you not shoot someone first, to show the world you were serious? Because to be a crank was easy. Police used to call it 'ten pence terrorism'. For the price of whatever coin you had to put into the 'phonebox, or a stamp on an envelope, you could get away with anything: like the caller in Oxfordshire in November 1969 who rang 999 to report hoax accidents; or the letters in January 1970 pretending to be from the Race Relations Board telling companies to raise

'Tell me, David, if the tour DOES take place, what are your feelings about praying for rain?'

Daily Mail cartoon of May 4, 1970 has David Sheppard carrying a 'Stop the Boks' banner and a harassed-looking Harold Wilson asking him, 'if the tour does take place, what are your feelings about praying for rain?'

their quota of 'coloured immigrant workers' to four per cent in the next ten days, or else. On a par were potty ideas like David Wilton-Godberford's. The London University biology student proposed to breed thousands of locusts and release them at cricket grounds. Not before much publicity, authorities pointed out that without heat, locusts would just squat; and how would the student transport them, anyway? Even more quoted was the joke by the Bishop of Gloucester, Basil Guy, that Christians should pray for rain, to wash out the tour. The Guardian printed a long 'sermon' by the Bishop of St Andrews, Michael Hare Duke, mocking the tour ('false Sheppards .... have nearly had us out with a new rule of Love before Wicket'). Precisely because this was no time for whimsy, some people clutched at it.

* * *

STST, on the other hand, had no time for whimsy because they had no time. Hain was overworked, a Special Branch report of May 19 gossiped, and Ruth and Michael Craft (professional protesters from CND days) 'almost by default' were 'becoming more significant'. Ruth Craft and Hain were preparing a 'commando group' of young Liberals, Communists and Socialists, 'to dash to any part of London at a moment's notice, either for direct action .... or to form the basis of a demonstration'. Hain, if only he knew it, had the honour of a mention in Cabinet on April 30. Callaghan reported he had a letter from Hain 'asking for assurance that the police would not adopt discriminatory methods' against demonstrators. Callaghan proposed to return a 'form reply'. Both sides knew by now which levers to pull or how best to stop the other side pulling their own. On May 5, Hain called on countries to withdraw from the Commonwealth Games, claiming a link between the Games and the tour; cricket's invitation allegedly reflected on British sport as a whole. If the Labour Government avoided English cricket, it felt even less like 'getting entangled' with Commonwealth countries, 'if at all possible', as Howell's committee put it on April 24, after the president of the Supreme Council for Sport in Africa, Abraham Ordia, a Nigerian, decided on a Games boycott.

Conference at Marlborough House in London, January 1969, host Harold Wilson with fellow Commonwealth heads of government. The Commonwealth had some political and diplomatic importance.

* * *

When meeting as early as April 1969, Howell left Griffith 'in no doubt about his own personal view', against the tour. Significantly, and perhaps fatally, Howell did not mention the threatened African boycott of the Commonwealth Games, although his briefing notes did. Presumably, MCC felt the Games were nothing to do with them, and Howell let them think that. Even if Howell had raised the Games, Lord's had enough to think about; such as insurance, and money. The Birmingham Post reported in that the Cricket Council had insured the tour for the enormous sum of £250,000 - many millions in 21st century money; except that to earn it the tourists had to finish at least three matches, or SACA or governments had to call the tour off. At the April 30 Cabinet, Callaghan told ministers that 100 police hired for £11 or £12 a day each would be a 'strain' on the MCC and other county clubs, 'which might induce them to reconsider'. Lord's evidently felt it needed more money from beyond its usual sources. Wilf Wooller as ever was in the know, and let others know; in mid-March he told Glamorgan committee men of a proposed national fund. Lord's duly launched it on April 23. The list of patrons and committee members was an intriguing who's who of English cricket, and of well-wishers towards the game; from a painfully narrow and pukka band of men (and Rachel Heyhoe). The most obviously cricketing names included Allom, and past and present county captains Derrick Robins, Brian Sellers, Brian Close, Colin Cowdrey and Tony Lewis; and even a couple of common players, Alec Bedser and Jack Bannister, and a football manager, Joe Mercer. Otherwise the social standing was impeccable. From the aristocracy came the Duke of Beaufort and the Duke of Norfolk. Plenty of men had had a good war: Lord Portal, Douglas Bader; and the chairman, Charles Newman VC, hero of the commando raid on St Nazaire. Two were bishops: Bath and Wells, and Leicester. More tantalising was a list at Lord's dated March 13 of other possible patrons: the broadcaster David Frost, singer Harry Secombe, and from football Sir Matt Busby ('or Joe Mercer') and Bobby Charlton, besides another aristocrat, the Yorkshire president Sir William Worsley.

Six men had said no; one was Field Marshal Bernard Montgomery. In the next Sunday Telegraph - usually as sure a friend as English cricket could hope for – Peregrine Worsthorne blazed that the Cricket Council had taken over governing of the game from the 'politically inept MCC' yet had 'learned little about the handling of public affairs since the blunders of the D'Oliveira affair'. Montgomery with his legendary bluntness told the Sunday Telegraph: "I object and I have always objected to putting my name to round robins to newspapers and in any case I haven't any money to spare. What I do have to spare I give to Hampshire. They can support the fund if they like." By May 1 EW Swanton in the Telegraph was reporting that the Fund had a 'steady if not exactly spectacular start', standing at £15,000. Donations ranged from shillings to £250 a time, mainly from individuals. Lord's had asked for £200,000. Besides paying for dearer insurance, the fund itself was insurance; except that how much Lord's needed would depend on STST, and the minds of spectators. By mid-May grounds hosting the tour admitted bookings were well below average; CG Howard at Surrey called it 'disappointing'; Yorkshire had taken £3000 instead of the usual £10,000. Swanton suspected that 'many normal patrons are intending to watch from the safety of their TV screens'.

What would happen at Lord's, as the supposed home of cricket, the most obvious target? The local rector, the Rev Noel Perry-Gore, was planning a 'vigil of prayer for race relations' in St John's Wood Church. Perry-Gore said he was not taking sides; likewise the curate, the Rev Robert Reiss said: "People seem to be dividing more and more into camps over this issue." He worried about trouble outside the ground. No wonder, judging by the local MP Quintin Hogg. At Exeter in late April he said Wilson and Callaghan would be partly to blame if anyone got hurt in demos. "I cannot tell what will happen in the ground," Hogg said. "I fear for what may happen to constituents of mine who may not wish at all to be drawn into this childish and despicable affair," that he had done his best to fuel. Having suffered at Swansea from what Hain called a 'private army of rugby thugs', protesters were ready to complain in advance. Cricket however did not seem to have as many lusty, right-wing young men to call on.

On May 5 Billy Griffith signed an appeal to 13,000 MCC members: "The police have indicated that it would be very helpful to them if honorary stewards were available to assist them .... Volunteers will be fully briefed as to their duties by a senior police officer." Here was the great British tradition of public-spirited work on the cheap: the Home Guard and civil defence in the war (and after), first aid and parish councils, and indeed playing for your county at cricket or rugger as an amateur. The sheer boredom of protecting a field in the spring dark put off most. Sussex's ground sub-committee heard on April 27 that Hove had lighting, but had dispensed with watchers, 'due to the lack of volunteers'. The tour fund would pay counties for ground protection, at the end of the season, the committee heard.

At Old Trafford, police had asked Lancashire for 120 stewards each match day, club secretary Jack Wood wrote to Billy Griffith on April 23, 'and we are shortly to have a meeting with League representatives in Lancashire in the hope that they can provide able-bodied men'. Wood detailed the ground security. Two floodlights lit the pavilion and another two the square. Police looked around the ground every half hour from 7pm to 7am. From Headingley, John Nash wrote similarly; Yorkshire were seeking 150 to 200 stewards. Wilf Wooller, who by his public posturing had set Glamorgan up as a target, could only report 'a certain amount of casual stewarding'. John Nash had promised the Leeds launch of 'Support The Seventy Tour' that the rate-payers would have to pay for police. Tory councillors in Birmingham voted down an amendment that Edgbaston should pay extra for police. The city's parks department likewise made life harder for protesters by not allowing them to gather in Calthorpe Park, over the road from the Warwickshire ground. Any demonstration would have to form in the city centre, which would give the police more work and might cause trouble; but further from the cricket. Blinded by their selfishness, glad of donations from anywhere – Newman said that Lord's would not take money from South Africa, yet how could they tell? – English cricket muddled on.

* * *

Cricket could muddle on partly because whatever it did not want to hear, it could dismiss, as coming from enemies. What David Sheppard launched on Sunday, May 3, was harder to ignore. Its vice-chairmen (one senior Tory former minister, Sir Edward Boyle; one Labour, Reg Prentice); its aims (for a 'passive, massive' demo outside Lord's on June 20, the Saturday of the first Test match) and even its name (the Fair Cricket Campaign) were carefully moderate. Sheppard had created something potentially crucial: a go-between. After Sheppard and Boyle met the Cricket Council for three hours on May 5, they saw Howell, and with the blessing of Lord's or not, gave the Labour Government what it was badly short of: insight into cricket's decision-makers. "They said that the hard-liners on the Cricket Council are led by Aidan Crawley," Howell noted afterwards. He did not have to remind colleagues that Crawley had

"*I know who you're against, but who are you for — Peter Hain, the Bishop of Woolwich, Harold Wilson or Edward Boyle?*"

A Daily Telegraph cartoon of May 4 cleverly identified that the 'Stop the Tour' protest movement was fragmenting.

Aidan Crawley.

entered the Commons in 1945 as a Labour MP, only to turn Conservative. That was the worst possible news; it made the affair personal. Lord's evidently was thinking of the Commonwealth Games by now, as Sheppard passed on the Lord's view that Kenya would 'hold firm', that is, attend Edinburgh, 'and that will determine the matter'. In a memo Howell argued, 'based on nothing very positive', that while the Cricket Council was refusing to alter its plan, and some members were 'obstinate', others would – here Howell was echoing Callaghan – 'welcome any development to get them off the hook'.

Like the Americans and the Soviets in the Cold War, or indeed the Boers and the black majority (eventually), Labour needed to pass private messages to Lord's, to do any political business with it. That Labour struggled to find even the weakest personal or social link showed how Labour did not belong in what Anthony Sampson, the author of the 1960s best-seller Anatomy of Britain, had called 'the solid substructure' of Britain; put more catchily, the Establishment, or ruling class, that Lord's was a part of. Howell's April 28 memo to Wilson had suggested asking the (Conservative) Lord Beatty of the English Association for the Commonwealth Games to approach Lord's; and wondered if the Duke of Edinburgh 'might bring his influence to bear on the Cricket Council'. In green ink Wilson commented: "Peaceful pressure as [Howell] suggests on Cricket Council is the right course. I would not seek to enlist the Duke I think."

Wilson hoped that a 79-year-old former Labour minister, Arthur Woodburn, would put 'pressure' on Alec Douglas-Home; they made as different a pair as you could imagine, but were both Scottish Privy Councillors. When the junior ministers met on May 4, Maurice Foley gave the Foreign

The Queen and Prince Philip with Harold Wilson.

Office view that Jomo Kenyatta, the Kenyan president, was reportedly for the Games; as was Kenneth Kaunda, the president of Zambia. Bruce Millan passed on Douglas-Home's opinion; the Cricket Council would only respond to a direct Government request. In his memo of May 5 Howell suggested that Arnold Smith, the Commonwealth Secretary-General, should approach 'one or two African leaders who are thought to be lukewarm' about the boycott; that is, to urge them to keep with the Games. Labour had little to show for a week of looking for levers to pull. Wilson's remark about Prince Philip was intriguing; did Wilson refuse that possible royal channel because it was not done for any politician to ask the Queen's husband for a favour; or, because Wilson suspected Philip would not take Labour's side? Royals have long stayed out of politics – at least in public; we may have a clue to their thinking from a meeting of the South African Society in London at the end of May to mark the centenary of Jan Smuts. A message from the Queen Mother read: "I am indeed proud to pay my tribute to a personal friend and a fine South African." Hardly the ingredients for an attack on apartheid.

At the next Cabinet meeting, on Thursday morning, May 7, Howell came in to report 'several helpful private initiatives were in hand'. Correctly he singled out David Sheppard for

Queen Elizabeth the Queen Mother and Harold Wilson.

raising 'race relations' with the Cricket Council; which Lord's had not heard or asked about. Race (also called community) relations was a tellingly vague phrase, that as significantly has lately gone out of fashion. Then it amounted to politely wishing that Britain's cities would not burn in race riots like America's. Race relations, then, could be a powerful tool against Lord's – but for that very reason, dangerous if out of control.

* * *

On Saturday, May 9 at Lord's – the tour would open there, four weeks to the day – Billy Griffith wrote to grounds hosting the South Africans. It was time counties told players 'to avoid all contact with the demonstrators whatsoever'; except that Griffith would let players use 'restraint' on anyone damaging the pitch. Then cricketers had to 'use the minimum possible force' and 'must at all costs avoid becoming involved in any strong physical contact'. Griffith did not say how a cricketer – sticking out as a target, wearing white – could avoid 'contact' when invaders ran at him. Instead Griffith went on: "It would be a greater mistake for the players to get involved in a free fight and successfully protect the pitch than it would be for them to stand back and let it be damaged." Griffith seemed to accept that England players might throw punches – either because they wanted nothing better than to clout protesters, or in sheer self-defence – on the televised field of a Test match at the home of cricket.

In the News of the World the next day, the sports editor Frank Butler wrote that the tour hadn't 'a cat in hell's chance of moderate success and should be called off now .... common sense must now prevail. For heaven's sake call the tour off now before the blood flows'. As people on all sides were facing such prospects – if only as a few pages away in their diary – the TCCB felt it had to send a letter dated May 11 to counties, assuring them there was 'absolutely no foundation' to any 'weakening towards the 1970 tour'. In Nottingham, Nottinghamshire committee man Michael Dennis reported on a meeting with two senior county policemen and Jack Bailey, MCC assistant secretary. Police were 'anxious to do all they possibly could to help the club'. Reg Simpson, at least according to the county club minutes, was only interested in selection of the Northern Counties team that would face the South Africans at Trent Bridge. He hoped for a 'firm policy'. Nottinghamshire duly agreed to tell the TCCB by letter that Sobers as the county's contracted man should not play. Instead they suggested making the match a 'Test trial'. In other words, possibly the most riotous event in Trent Bridge's history was 30 days away, and the club only cared about the fitness of their overseas player.

News of the World sports editor Frank Butler.

* * *

Those for the tours, in rugby or cricket, reckoned that sport was a force for good. Anthony Sampson, reporting on the South African election in the spring of 1970 for the Observer, revealed that as a lie. In the ten years since he had last been there, the apartheid state had broken black politics and set up secret police. Sport had become 'a kind of metaphor for broader politics' precisely because the rest of the country was so repressive. More proof of the lie was arguably the most disgraceful part of this story. Whether several counties each had the same idea, or did as Lord's told them, the English game planned its own apartheid by keeping non-whites away from the South Africans. On May 12 Peter Wight, the former Somerset batsman from Guyana, then living in Bath, told the local Bristol Evening Post that he was not standing as an umpire in any South Africa matches. "I am pretty sure no Commonwealth umpires have been asked to stand in their matches. But if I had been I would have accepted. I think they are a fine side and I would have enjoyed being present at one or more of their matches." Wight was hardly a trouble-maker; he said he was 'obviously' opposed to apartheid, but like D'Oliveira felt 'contact' was better. Did Lord's not pick Wight on purpose? If selectors of players are notoriously secretive, the selecting of umpires is even less likely to leave a trace. The facts are that Wight was one of 24 first-class umpires in 1970, and as the South Africans had 12 matches, it might have seemed obvious to use all 24 once. Wight stood for the Australian tourists in 1968, the West Indians in 1969, the Indians in 1971 and the Australians again in 1972.

The same went for players. On May 20, Les Ames as secretary of Kent replied to a Griffith letter of the day before; Kent were not playing when the Southern Counties were due to play the South Africans first, making Kent players obvious choices for some of the combined team, 'but obviously it would be prudent not to include John Shepherd and Asif Iqbal', the West Indian and Pakistani. In fairness, the Indian board sent a telegram to Lord's on May 4 saying they were 'not in favour of Indian players playing against visiting SA team in conformity with its stand on apartheid'. Likewise the Indian authorities told Lancashire not to pick Engineer. At Old Trafford, Cedric Rhoades said nothing of that; only that the club and Engineer and Clive Lloyd had 'mutually agreed' that the overseas men would be 'excused duty', although neither player had asked. They had received anonymous threatening letters and telephone calls. Warwickshire did the same around the same time for their three; the West Indians Lance Gibbs and Rohan Kanhai, and the Pakistani Billy Ibadulla. Club chairman Edmund King spun it as if Warwickshire were doing the players a favour ('it was becoming an unfair burden .... all three were relieved .... will be greatly missed'). King claimed to be 'staggered' that anti-apartheid supporters said they would take that decision to the West Midlands Race Relations Board; that is, as discriminatory. In a letter to the Birmingham Post, Hugh McGrath of Edgbaston said of the three: "I am mystified as a black man that these chaps should chicken out in this undignified way. I would expect them to take a stand on principle."

From a letter by Warwickshire secretary Leslie Deakins on May 12 to Jack Bailey, it sounded as if Lord's had complained about not being consulted. That implied that Lord's wanted to set a common policy about picking non-white players; or was yet another example of the official mania for unanimity; or maybe Lord's did not want to be seen to give in to threats. Deakins said letters from the public to the three had asked for their co-operation, and did not threaten: ".... it was therefore strictly correct to say that at this stage the players were more embarrassed than anything else although they might have had natural concern with regards to their families .... indeed had we felt a common policy was desirable in this matter I am afraid we would rather have assumed we should have been advised accordingly for there has been a great deal of Press publicity over several months on the score of approaches to overseas cricketers", by protesters.

This was a rare and therefore revealing, albeit private, rebuke to Lord's; was Deakins feeling the strain? As he did admit, the result would be 'all-white' games. Apartheid was corrupting the English game before the South Africans had even arrived.

Also on Tuesday, May 12, Griffith and Bailey of the MCC and Geoffrey Howard of Surrey met John Gerrard of the Met Police. Lord's was offering to pay at most £400 a day for police, pleading poverty because of 'few bookings so far'. Mr Gerrard called £400 'totally unacceptable' and suggested £750 a day. Three weeks to the day would be the South Africans' first full day in the country, and Lord's was haggling about protection.

The next day, Griffith met some supporters of the Fair Cricket Campaign for an hour: Sir Edward Boyle; Mark Bonham Carter, the Liberal chairman of the Race Relations Board; and a Conservative London councillor, Lena Townsend. Meanwhile, thanks to another MP about to retire like Sir Edward, Philip Noel-Baker – former Olympic athlete, and Nobel Peace Prize winner – the House of Commons agreed to an emergency debate on the tour, the next day, Thursday, May 14. As Sir Edward said after he left Lord's: "Clearly a decision will have to be taken pretty soon."

* * *

The Commons was not the place to look for a decision. Philip Noel-Baker opened what one of the speakers, the Tory Sir Derek Walker-Smith, called 'a short debate' at 4pm and it ended on the dot at 7pm with talk of cranks, birdbrains 'and the self-important sanctimonious prigs', by the party-less Desmond Donnelly, who may have had in mind some MPs he was facing. The paradox was that members of parliament spoke more than 20,000 words, an average of two every second, without any vote at the end. Later that night they debated hare coursing for another three hours or more, in vain because the election came before they could pass any law; and they agreed such business as sending a chair to Swaziland's assembly. Why did they bother?

The Times' digest next day of 2700 words covered three columns. This was politics as theatre; regular outbursts of Opposition or Labour cheers or cries of 'no'. The Times left out much of the sheer rowdiness – 'listen to the Tories jeering', said Michael Foot – that the Hansard record included without giving a sense of how it was a game to these men – 'a dirty political game', said Marcus Lipton, Labour MP for Brixton, 'next to the Oval', and 'many thousands of coloured British citizens'. Needless to say, to Lipton it was a game only the Tories were playing. The MPs could only urge the Cricket Council, as some did, either to think again or go on. Few speakers gave a sign of expecting anyone to change their minds, as a result of hearing them, let alone of changing their own mind. That was not the point of the 'brief' speeches that the Speaker asked for because he had 30 names who wanted to speak. Mostly the men – only men spoke, except for interventions by Anne Kerr, a Labour protester against the Springboks – were politicians of weight, such as the former Tory minister John Boyd-Carpenter, Heath's deputy Reginald Maudling, and men already in this story: Howell, Prentice, Boyle, and at the end Callaghan, to assure MPs that police could handle 'the usual crowd of ruffians'. Such a debate appealed to the sort of men who liked the sound of their own voices. They mistook words in the chamber for real power; or knew the difference and went ahead anyway. Besides their own enjoyment they were thinking of the publicity; besides in the Times, local headlines to help them at the next election, likely soon; as Boyle and fellow Tory Sir Charles Mott-Radclyffe noted, they were probably making their last speeches in the Commons.

The arguments had something tribal about them; Tory and Labour each stood for a philosophy. That the philosophies clashed made the debate popular for another reason; each side could show their supporters how they differed from the other lot. It called into question the idea since of a 'Butskellite' consensus in that era, ended by Thatcherism in 1979. The idea has some merit – why else did people say it? – because both sides said they were for democracy. The Tories stood for tradition, for freedom under the law; the basic principle (as Maudling put it) that 'any man is entitled to do what is lawful and to expect that the state will protect him from unlawful interference'. Commons politics as something shared helped in that deeper consensus, just as lords and MPs 'thoroughly enjoyed' playing cricket against each other, as Mott-Radclyffe mentioned. Labour had arguments as idealistic: the tour would kill the Commonwealth Games and cause 'racial tension' (Noel-Baker); or 'social disorder' (Frank Judd). To say that the cases for and against the tour were fully put is another way of saying that the newspapers had said it all already. Denis Howell did have one piece of news; that morning he had chaired an 'emergency meeting' of the Sports Council of Great Britain. It had decided that governing bodies had three responsibilities: first to their own sport; then to all sport and 'the community as a whole'. Howell read out the Sports Council's resolution, urging cricket to withdraw the invitation to SACA, because 'the longer-term interests of multi-racial sport in the Commonwealth' mattered more. Democracy, freedom, liberty; all those words of principle had limits, according to the Sports Council (set up by Labour and handily saying what it wanted). One sport, in other words, had to give up something – possibly the finest summer's cricket of the century – for the 'team', and in return worse things, such as 'the potential danger to race relations' as Reg Prentice put it, would not happen. Cricket had the worst of the deal; it lost something, in return for things that would happen anyway (the Commonwealth Games) or an absence of bad (disorder). The conclusions that each side drew were as much at odds as the arguments they came from. For the tour to go ahead would be 'an endorsement of racial prejudice' (Frank Judd). A cancelled tour would be a victory for 'mob rule', said the Tory Sir Derek Walker-Smith, halfway through, quoting a Times leader of May 2 – cleverly making it more likely that the Times would quote him, as it duly did.

If the cricket tour were as Noel-Baker said at the start a 'burning topic', surprisingly few people asked what the tour would do for cricket, for good or bad. Howell did say bluntly that 'international cricket must be multi-racial or die' because, so he hinted, other Commonwealth countries would no longer 'find it possible' to play England. Yet for every Labour, or Tory, argument, the other side could counter. Sir Charles Mott-Radyclffe claimed that to cancel would be 'the beginning of the end of international cricket', because other countries would find a political reason to cancel; such as India and West Indies, over Britain's policy of 'controlled immigration'.

The exceptions to the party-political lines were telling. Sir Edward Boyle was careful when he broke the Tory norm of supporting the tour. He said he did it 'reluctantly' and set out his cricketing credentials; he was a member of MCC and recalled how he had first watched South Africa in the Lord's Test of 1935. He did not add – it was after all a short debate – that he was then aged 11 and went on to become the first eleven scorer while at Eton. He sat down to Labour cheers and a tribute from the habitual Labour speaker Willie Hamilton. Others, to their credit, did admit that the issue was not simple enough for one side to make all the sense, and for the other side to be insincere. Howell for instance spoke from six years of experience that the relationship between government and sport was 'very delicate indeed'. Boyle was glaringly one of few to seek to answer good points from the other side, rather than press his own; Callaghan to his credit spoke of a 'conflict of rights'. Perhaps it was no coincidence that Boyle was leaving politics, if he no longer fitted into a more aggressive Tory Party or politics generally. Or perhaps the House of Commons had something else in common with sports; men were ruthless in judging you by what you attained, whether a batting or bowling average or ministerial position.

The Times only printed Conservative and Labour speakers. David Steele spoke about the Commonwealth Games, as a Scottish MP and 'Liberal spokesman for Commonwealth affairs'. He admitted that the Games organisers had been 'slow to recognise the dangers' and their plea to the Cricket Council 'belated'. Perhaps because he was equally free of Labour and Tory tribal positions, he aired 'the basic hypocrisy' by sports and the public alike that you could have multi-racial athletics in Edinburgh while an apartheid team was in England. Like Willie Hamilton (another Scot) before he spoke and Frank Judd after, Steele did not believe Cricket Council members were stupid – a typical politician's trick of denying something while planting the word in your head. More insightfully Steele claimed the men of cricket were 'frightened and worried'; afraid to change their mind. Callaghan in his few minutes' speech made sure to have a dig likewise at the men he had already faced and would have to face again if they did not cancel the tour by themselves. Callgham spoke of a 'lurking belief that I detected in the Cricket Council .... that it was a lonely band of heroes standing against the darkening tide of lawlessness'. He added sarcastically: "I can relieve the Council of that burden." With the centrist touch that would stand him in good stead as the next Labour prime minister, Callaghan trusted, however blandly, in 'the good sense and the long traditions of the British people'.

The debate would always end on an abrupt and thus odd note, and the final speaker, Desmond Donnelly, made it more so. He urged cricket 'not to surrender to mob rule, to hooliganism' and to the cranks and so on. Donnelly had resigned from Labour and was then expelled from the tribe. The Labour MP Andrew Faulds taunted Donnelly with his 'impending political extinction'. Donnelly indeed lost the 1970 election as an independent and within four years was himself extinct. A pity; because his speech that evening was as informed and heartfelt as any. He had spotted a fellow Anglo-Indian, Raman Subba Row, in the visitors' gallery. Donnelly had had a good war – as those who haven't been to war put it – in the air force, and recalled serving in the desert with a South African squadron. If South Africans were good enough for fight with, 'they are good enough to play cricket against us, or life has no meaning'. Some, far from all, had identified with cricket, such as Mott-Radyclffe ('a fan all my life'). Donnelly alone hinted at some greater meaning in cricket; or did he have a glimpse of lost meaning in his own life, and his own suicide? At least as one of the founders of the British Empire eleven in 1940, he earned an obituary in Wisden. In death that may be the most that any of us can hope for.

* * *

That Labour and Tory were so tribal raised a problem.

Donnelly was an exception, a (former) Labour man with a rural seat, Pembrokeshire. Sir Edward Boyle was a rare Tory in a city constituency, Handsworth in Birmingham, with many immigrants. Otherwise the Labour speakers stood for urban areas – Reg Prentice in East Ham, Howell in Birmingham, Frank Judd in Portsmouth – that took immigrants first. By contrast Tory MPs came from suburban and rural places that hardly saw a non-white face and thus saw no need for 'race relations': Maudling at Barnet, Boyd-Carpenter in Kingston upon Thames, Mott-Radclyffe upstream at Windsor.

At least among themselves MPs behaved. A teacher from the London School of Economics, Jonathan Rosenhead, at 6.51pm threw leaflets onto the floor of the Commons from the gallery. A door-keeper handed Rosenhead to the police, who escorted him from Parliament at 2.30am, after its sitting, chair for Swaziland and all, ended at 1.53am. The previous Friday, Michael Stewart the Foreign Secretary had had his ordeal at the Oxford Union, pelted by paper balls, and jostled as he left. Most in that debating hall were not demonstrating; yet about 100 shouted so loud, for two hours, that they drowned the debate. Could 100, let alone more, spoil Lord's, four weeks and a day later?

Politics was not all, or even mostly, about public speaking. On Thursday, May 14, the businessman Cecil King had gone to Ted Heath's flat for lunch, 'the only other guest being Cowdrey, the Kent cricketer'. It was a tantalising sight of Cowdrey as a friend of the Conservative leader in particular and of sportsmen and men with power mixing. Raymond Illingworth had only become captain of England a year before because Cowdrey was injured; a chunk of English cricket wanted Cowdrey back once Illingworth failed - or even if Illingworth kept doing well. Thus Cowdrey as the premier playing English cricketer appeared on the BBC radio Today news programme on Saturday morning, May 16, before Kent began a match against Warwickshire at Gravesend. The interview, besides characteristic Cowdrey, summed up where cricket stood. He gave a hint of Christianity ('we all hope and pray there will be integration and multi-racial cricket there', he said of South Africa). He was wavering ('one doesn't like this form of blackmail but the fact is that the pressures are mounting'). Cowdrey wondered aloud what was in the best interest of cricket yet could not help thinking what 'playing under tension' would feel like for himself ('I saw it in the West Indies and Pakistan and India and no-one could say it was enjoyable cricket'). He sounded fatalistic ('one hopes and prays that it will not be quite as difficult as we all anticipate'). It was as if those few in authority in cricket, having worn blinkers for months, were now set on a kamikaze crash into the actual tour. John Thicknesse in the Evening Standard of Friday, May 15 reported that the Cricket Council was 'sticking to their guns'. It was all very well for Enoch Powell to say in a speech at Shrewsbury the next day that 'it is no business of the government who is invited to sports competitions. If we don't like particular people, let us deal with it under law.' The Bishop of Bristol, Oliver Tomkins, showed more realism. He told his diocesan conference at Swindon that the longer it took to cancel, the more it looked like giving in to violence. "Unfortunately this is true," he said. "But it is never wrong to do what one believes is right, even though some people believe it to be right for the wrong reasons." Those 'people' were 'extremists'; like Powell, Tomkins saw a 'dangerous road' if a minority broke the rules to get its own way. He even called it 'the biggest issue threatening not only England but contemporary civilisation'.

EW Swanton had attended the Thursday Commons debate. He began an article in the next day's Telegraph with the 'ironical paradox' that the 'party of controls' (Labour) insisted on cricket making its own decision, 'while the party of personal initiative and free enterprise' (Conservative) wanted the Government, if anyone, to cancel the tour. Swanton, like Boyle in the Commons, paid his tribute to the MCC ('most venerable and respected of games institutions'). It had 'access to the best brains'; perhaps a polite way of saying those at Lord's were not brainy, but knew people who were. Swanton's point was Tomkins': "If we give in here, where does it end. But that, if you like, is a political, not a cricket question." He hoped the Cricket Council had the 'moral courage' to call off the tour: "After many misgivings I felt before the situation had reached its present pass that perhaps the risks were worth taking. I believe now they are not and that the consequences might well do irrevocable harm to cricket."

Swanton, like Arlott, was one of the major commentators on English cricket; as an impeccable conservative ('one of the elders of the game', Arlott wrote approvingly on the following Monday), Swanton's change of mind carried more weight. As if he knew he would anger others, he set out a defence. He reminded readers that for a year he had called for a 'multi-racial tour', of 30 players, enough for a first tour and an 'A team' of 'non-Europeans'. He implied that SACA had had a chance to show 'White goodwill', and chose not to take it. Significantly, in his later autobiography Sort of a Cricket Person, Swanton saw no need to alter his risk-based argument, while remaining endearingly gentlemanly (or an old-fashioned sexist). The tour 'had simply become impracticable'; grounds would have become a 'battlefield, to which no-one would take women or children'. In the News of the World on Sunday, May 17, Frank Butler made the same point, that indeed Swanton quoted three days later. "Would you be happy to send your schoolboy son with one of his pals armed with a packet of sandwiches and a flask of milk" - a slice of social history there - "to watch one of the South Africa games?" Butler declared the tour 'doomed'.

On Friday, May 15, the International Olympic Committee voted 35-28 to expel South Africa. It had taken 11 years, since the Soviet Union began a campaign for cynical political reasons, that newly independent African nations took up. If you wanted to go to the Olympics, as every athlete did, you would not dare play South Africa at an Olympic sport. In the Sunday Telegraph, Harry Raven commented: "The South African sporting story seems to be nearing an end." While the IOC was only making definite what had been awkward for years - South Africa had not gone to the previous two Olympics, in Tokyo or Mexico City - the lesson for cricket was clear. Just as the Olympic movement had had to choose between South Africa, or the rest of Africa, sooner or later MCC would have to lose South Africa or the countries South Africa never played at cricket. Dennis Brutus of SAN-ROC said cancelling of the tour was more likely. The Observer of May 17 in an editorial noted a lesson for protesters too: Brutus had succeeded by 'patient lobbying' and none of the STST violence.

The trouble was that the set times of the Commonwealth Games and cricket tour demanded a decision. The Glasgow Herald in an editorial of May 16 felt 'the judgement of a sporting Solomon is badly needed in the next few days'. Something, Games or tour, would have to suffer. Swanton too had noted a 'balance of evils'. Ted Dexter had come out against the tour in his column in the Sunday Mirror. The BBC then invited him on the radio programme The World This Weekend. There he said: "Quite honestly the growing opinion of a lot of sensible people and a lot of responsible bodies seems to me to sway the argument against the tour." He showed some bravado. "Those of us who have played abroad have played to a continual cacophony of sound, people shouting, rioting, and we have got on with quite well." What about mirrors shining in the eyes? "Oh, that has been happening in India and Pakistan for donkey's years," Dexter replied. "Cricket goes on quite happily."

What Dexter or 'sensible people' or anyone said, and where they said it, no longer mattered. Just as in August 1914 surprisingly few people decided whether Europe went to war, only the two dozen or so in the Cricket Council could decide. "I know them to be a very fair-minded body of men," Dexter said, reasonably, "and very broadly representative of the country as a whole," which was laughably untrue. "I would have thought that one or two of them just like me perhaps must have had a change of opinion in relation to recent events." Dexter sounded unsure, but was right. Jack Elliott, the Nottinghamshire committee man, a new member of the Cricket Council, said he would not watch South Africa at Trent Bridge: "I want no part in dealing with a racially selected team from a country where people are treated like animals because of the colour of their skins."

At the very least, the Cricket Council would no longer be unanimous.

On Saturday, May 16, the season's fifth round of three-day county matches began. Four more rounds, three weeks to the day, and the South Africans began their first match. The tourists were even closer than that; they would land in 17 days. At Middlesbrough for the Yorkshire-Glamorgan match, Bill Bowes reported a 'feeling' among the two teams that the tour would be called off, and quoted the explicit breaking of ranks by Jack Elliott. As the Glasgow Herald put it, 'a battle of nerves' was under way, between the cricket authorities and its opposition. Just when the politics of sport had become sharpest, reports about it were becoming disturbingly vague; or, the men in authority would not comment at all, as on May 11, when Gubby Allen and Aidan Crawley for the Cricket Council went to the Jamaican High Commission in London, to hear from eight diplomats, mostly from the Caribbean and notably India and Pakistan. The West Indian cricket board of control stated on May 15 that the tour would result in 'irreparable harm'. At the Cambridge Union on May 15, Jamal Kedwal of the Indian High Commission in London warned that India 'might' sever cricketing relations if the MCC insisted on the South African tour. Lord's was having to learn diplomacy on the job; in this case, working out what words meant, and who spoke for a country; its high commission, the cricket administrators it might meet every year or two, or some politician?

In a few days at the end of July and early August 1914, when kings, ministers and generals in a few rooms found themselves on the brink of a momentous event, from which (for better or worse) the world as far as 1970 sprang, those most powerful men in Europe had found themselves paradoxically hemmed in – by the diplomatic agreements of 20 years, centuries of culture, even railway timetables. So it might prove for the Cricket Council – if they ever met; because unlike in 1914 the tour was already going ahead; a decision would have to be unmade. Few made such a stark international comparison in 1970 because they did not know how true it was.

* * *

Howard Hanley was an Englishman who loved cricket; even in old age in Australia, he umpired. As a young man he went to the United States, became a scientist, and around this time flew to the Soviet Union. At Moscow airport, where he had to change 'planes, he went into a waiting room, 'basically for foreigners; and there was a huge amount of stuff in English, propaganda and magazines and things. Now I had nothing much to do and I looked at some of them.' He knew, then as now, that the Soviets were preaching to him. Some articles were about the South Africa tour. As Hanley recalled in 2018, while 'the Russians didn't give a squat about cricket', they knew that some Africans and Asians passing through did. "The theme of these articles was, basically, look at the capitalist bastards putting down the poor downtrodden black guys in South Africa. Why do you guys want to support America and England, or Europe." Hanley, 'a rather conservative English person, to be honest, in those days', realised something he had not seen in print before. The tour, and cricket since the D'Oliveira affair, was "an international event, and the context was nothing to do with the cricket. It was simply whether or not England, part of the capitalist world, was going to support the underdogs. This was an issue which actually involved the most high-level politics, way beyond cricket, and way beyond South Africa and England."

The shock to Hanley was that the Soviets were using the tour as a piece of Cold War propaganda, seeking to win Nigerians, Kenyans and the like to their side; and the western world, let alone Lord's, knew nothing about it.

Chapter Ten

The last week

Political memory lasts about a week, professors say. Political foresight stretches about another week ahead.
                    CP Snow, The State of Siege, 1968

Monday, May 18
While newspapers could not hunt every piece of news, it looked as if they, and their readers, preferred what they already knew. The tour gave newspapers an ideal story; it would run and give easy copy; the time and place of the climax were in the office diary; editors could get worked up. "The Cricket Council must stand firm," the Daily Telegraph editorial said. "The MCC is about to perpetuate the greatest farce in the history of sport," said the Yorkshire Post.

Talking of farce, strangely little was coming out of trade unions, usually one of the most powerful forces in the country, and thus hated by conservatives. Over the weekend, the Association of Broadcasting Staff 'opposed' the tour, according to the Times, for one. In fact, for all the fine things the union said – it opposed racial discrimination and apartheid – it would do nothing. If any members would not film the tour, the union would support those with a conscience. The cameramen chose not to even threaten as a union to blank television screens; because they knew they would be too unpopular; and they wanted their wages. The National Union of Journalists, typically high-minded and wordy, had decided the same weeks before. A few campaigners tried; such as Paul Foot of Private Eye, nephew of Labour MP Michael, who got the central London branch of the NUJ to vote 16-15 for a boycott of the tour (sports journalists voted against). Foot proposed the same motion at the NUJ annual conference, at Harrogate on April 21, 'to give practical expression to feelings on apartheid'. Foot evidently felt it was professional for journalists to censor the news; NUJ members voted him down.

The last week

At the weekend, Billy Griffith had trailed that the Cricket Council would meet within the week, which prompted speculation. John Arlott in the Guardian supposed some 'face-saving formula' would let Lord's cancel the tour.

Other speculation was over. At 5pm Harold Wilson visited the Queen at Buckingham Palace to formally ask for a general election. Hain looked back in his 1971 book: "We were now in the field of high powered party politics."

Most, 26, of the Cricket Council's 28 members made it at Lord's for their crucial meeting. One not attending was Colin Cowdrey, as Dennis Amiss in Warwickshire's second innings was keeping Kent at bay on the second day of their three-day match at Gravesend. "The other members know my views on the tour so I will not be travelling up," he said. Even those few words revealed that Cowdrey had made his mind up, regardless of what he might have heard at the meeting; was that true for those in the room? The Council chairman Maurice Allom began as if members wanted a full picture, with a review of various meetings: with Frank Cousins, the trade unionist chairman of the Community Relations Commission; with Sheppard and his Fair Cricket Campaign; Gubby Allen, Aidan Crawley and Griffith's meeting with high commissioners of Asian and Caribbean cricket-playing nations; a May 13 meeting with Walter Winterbottom, as director of the Sports Council, and Sir John Waldron; letters from the former Archbishop of Canterbury Geoffrey Fisher, and the Chief Rabbi, Dr Emmanuel Jakoborits; and a conversation between Griffith and Douglas-Home. Set against most of those, the 'vast majority of cricketers and cricket followers in this country' were still in favour of the tour, Allom said. Thus Allom, no doubt in line with Crawley and Allen - who had done much of the work, whereas other Council members merely turned up for the meeting - framed the debate to stand by the tour.

Then members had their say. Allen said the views of overseas countries were politically motivated. He was 'convinced' Pakistan and India would 'pull out' – that is, of cricket against England – 'at least temporarily'. If West

Indies did also, it meant 'complete separation of black and white countries': 'awful if so'. Hubert Doggart sounded set against the tour, citing 'cannot do justice to the cricket', and the risk to 'Commonwealth cricket' and 'race relations'. Wilf Wooller was having none of that. "Where will it stop?" he asked. He saw greater problems ahead, and used the Desmond Donnelly argument; if South Africans were good enough to trade with, and fight and die in the war, they were good enough to play.

As Rowland Bowen wrote in the summer edition of his journal, The Cricket Quarterly, if by playing South Africa, England were to lose three Test-playing countries, the tour 'ceased, manifestly, to be in the best interests of English cricket', and everyone at the Cricket Council meeting must have known it, 'no matter how stupid they were'.

Tuesday, May 19
The Council would announce their decision at 7pm. Some assumed, and some in the press printed their assumption, that the Council would call the tour off. Arthur Latham,

Birmingham Post article of May 19, showing Edgbaston behind barbed wire, and warning of financial catastrophe for county cricket.

Labour MP for Paddington, for example, had been one of a deputation of several MPs due to visit Lord's, only to have it called off because of the Cricket Council meeting, evidently at short notice. John Kay speculated that cancellation was 'imminent' and the Manchester Evening News made it their front page lead.

Instead, Wooller and his kind got their way, 'by a substantial majority', Griffith said. He would not give the exact voting figures. The cherished single voice of cricket had cracked. Lord's felt it could only stand by South Africa with a compromise; it told SACA 'no further Test tours .... until South African cricket is played and teams are selected on a multi-racial basis in South Africa'.

Otherwise, the Council did not concede anything to anybody. As for the Commonwealth Games, the Council felt 'deep regret' and hoped boycotting countries would think again (in other words; none of Lord's' business). When it suited the Council, it did make the outside world its business; it claimed to share 'growing concern' in Britain about 'the unacceptable apartheid policies' of South Africa. Cricket, so the Council reckoned, was making 'an outstanding and widely acknowledged contribution' to good relations 'between all people among whom the game has been played'. As for the dangers to the tour, they came from a 'minority group'. Perhaps with the election in mind, Griffith said: '.... as shown by the outcome of recent opinion polls, it is clearly the wish of the majority that the tour should take place'.

What was the Cricket Council playing at? It was keeping loyal to South Africa, the only people delighted. For a body supposed to stand for the national game, the Council had an odd air of battening down the hatches. Anything uncomfortable – such as the Commons debate, that at least showed that Lord's could only count on most of one of the two main political parties – the Council had ignored. The Daily Telegraph reported the next day how Griffith made it clear 'that it was the Council's final decision'. As a grim-faced Griffith put it: "The argument is over .... Now there is no point in further delegations coming to see us." The Manchester Evening News – perhaps embarrassed by guessing wrong the day before - called those very words 'arrogant'. The rest of the press would not thank Lord's either. Brian Johnston recalled his fellow journalists were 'stunned'. He had said on the BBC all day as late as the 6pm TV news that the tour would go on. Johnston had what he later called the 'one and only scoop' of his career. Despite the personal and commercial rivalries, journalism is a surprisingly herd-like job; it had taken self-belief for Johnston to keep his 'lone stand' – and a 'Mole' inside Lord's. Johnston recalled he couldn't resist giving him a wink. "I hadn't asked him for direct information when I rang him early on May 19. All I said was: 'How many marks out of ten would you give me if I said the tour was going to go on.' 'Oh,' he replied after a short pause, 'about nine and a half.' That was good enough for me." Johnston was a good enough journalist to protect his source, while he reminisced in his 1991 book Forty-Five Summers. Or had Johnston given readers a clue – to keep

Brian Johnston; the cake-loving stalwart of Test Match Special in truth had to be an accomplished journalist to hold down a live broadcast career at the BBC.

up the joke, characteristic of the man - by printing a picture of Griffith and Allom? In a world where we learned even who was the 'Deep Throat' of Watergate (eventually), it's typical of English cricket that it keeps its secrets.

Lord's was about to learn a basic fact of politics and diplomacy; while you saw delegations, and at least pretended you might do as they wished, they had to be civil. Once you made a 'final decision', you freed them to say anything. 'Ecclesiastics are pontificating' said a droll Special Branch report dated May 19. Lord Constantine – the former West Indian all-rounder Learie, turned quangocrat, as a member of the Sports Council, Race Relations Board and BBC governor – saw 'no saving grace' in the Cricket Council making future tours multi-racial. Race relations were 'precarious' now, he said. Peggy Holroyde, a member of the Yorkshire committee of community relations, wrote to the Yorkshire Post that the Council 'had made a real bosh job'. She and plenty of others saw the condition that SACA had to make future tours multi-racial – but not this one – as illogical. 'An error of judgement,' the Glasgow Herald called it.

Mild by comparison, Sir Herbert Brechin, Commonwealth Games chairman, said he was 'disappointed'. He revealed how false were the Council's hopes for Edinburgh: "Now there is no doubt that the threat of withdrawals by countries will become reality."

The Council had invited the politicians to gain publicity by making an election issue of something already on front pages for weeks. On ITV's This Week, the Liberal Party leader Jeremy Thorpe said the Council, by inviting South Africa, behaved 'as stupidly as any body of men or women can'.

At least cricket was finding out who its friends were; in print, not so many. The Daily Telegraph praised the 'victory for liberty'; the Leicester Mercury noted 'the gate daubers, pitch poisoners and mole manipulators [presumably it meant actual not journalistic moles, as weapons against cricket fields] have failed to cower the solid, sensible gentlemen of Lord's'. The Birmingham Post on its front page complained of 'wrong piled on top of wrong'; after the double insult by South Africa over the D'Oliveira affair, English cricket's response should then have been 'instant and final'. EW Swanton, glaringly less triumphant than the Telegraph's editorial page wrote: "Conflict and travail lie ahead and all that remains in doubt is the degree thereof."

Around the corner from Lord's, Pauline Matthews of Grove End Road was planning to send her daughter away during the tour matches. "I was in Jamaica during the cricket riots a couple of years ago, I know what tear gas is like." Another local resident, Lady Catherine Archibald, a daughter of the Conservative prime minister Andrew Bonar Law, took a petition to Lord's, urging them to call off the tour. The Yorkshire Post, even before the Council's decision, deplored a 'Tour de Farce' under 'siege conditions'. Civic leaders, usually glad to host a Test match that brought trade and publicity, were turning against the game. In Leeds, the city council watch committee chairman, Alderman Harold Jowitt, told the Post that Leeds chief constable James Angus had told him the tour games at Headingley – a Test, and the county game that Yorkshire moved from Sheffield – would need 1400 police, from across Yorkshire. Headingley was only prepared to pay for its usual 15. The Post reckoned the city council would have to pay half of a £105,000 bill for police; the Home Office would pay the other half. Left unsaid was the fact that someone would have to pay it all. "We didn't ask for these matches," Jowitt complained. Organisers of STST in Leeds, the Rev Neville Wright and Maureen Baker, handed a 5000-signature petition into Headingley. Trent Bridge meanwhile had to remove signs placed on the entrance doors, saying 'whites only' and 'non whites', presumably put there by protesters to brand cricket as part of apartheid.

While each ground had to face such protest alone, the TCCB in a letter to counties recommended that legal action against demonstrators should be 'co-ordinated', through the TCCB's solicitor.

Of the 30 or so letters sent by protesters to West Indian and Asian players in English county cricket, urging them to stand publicly against the tour (or else), only five replied, either that they would not play (Intikhab Alam and Younis Ahmed of Surrey), or their teams were not due to play South Africa anyway (John Shepherd, Asif Iqbal and Roy Marshall). That most replies came from Pakistanis may have been because the Pakistan board of control had written to its players in England. As Asif Iqbal put it, while the letter did not 'expressly forbid a Pakistani cricketer from playing against the tourists', their homeland plainly wanted them to cry off. Geoffrey Howard at Surrey said defensively: "Neither player has approached us yet and there is nothing I can say until they do." If anybody did not want to play South Africa, Surrey would 'respect their feelings', Howard said.

By cable to MCC, the Pakistan board withdrew from the under-25 tour – due to play counties and an England under-25 side between June and August – without giving a reason. If world cricket faced a split on racial lines, thanks to the tour, Lord's had some crucial diplomacy to do. How well did it know Pakistan? Was that withdrawal the worst, or a start? An intriguing report from the British High Commission in Pakistan to the Foreign Office in February might suggest that the Pakistanis were bluffing. A diplomat in Rawalpindi, DM March, noted 'remarkably little comment' on the tour there. He reviewed recent cricket history. Pakistan was 'now starved of first-class cricket'. After the 'deterioration of the political situation' cut short the MCC's tour in early 1969, the New Zealanders had visited briefly after their tour of England in October and November 1969 (their third and final Test match, March could have added, cut short by a pitch invasion). Pakistan had no prospect of any international team visiting 'in the near future'; they could not afford to pay guarantees to Australia and West Indies. Thus if Pakistan were to break off with the MCC, 'they would in fact be cutting themselves off from their best link with first-class cricket'. March had asked the FO's 'posts' in Karachi, Lahore and Dacca (then still part of Pakistan) if they had heard of 'any political movement' against the tour: ".... there is no evidence to suggest that the MCC need be concerned". Besides, MCC had some credit in Pakistan, March suggested, for carrying on with their last tour, 'until the unfortunate riot at Karachi made further cricket impossible', as he diplomatically put it.

Also in February, an equivalent report went from New Delhi to the FO. It reported no public discussion of the South Africa tour to England; 'indeed the press has watched with interest the South African victories over Australia in South Africa'. Apartheid was however 'an emotive subject here'. A proposed MCC tour of India in the English winter of 1968 had come to nothing because India refused to release the necessary foreign exchange; in other words, due to politics. The report noted Indian cricket had 'no influential friend in government circles' because the minister for education, who had most to do with cricket, was 'totally undistinguished'. Similar reports reached the Foreign Office from the Caribbean, of island cricket administrators at most talking of a break with Lord's. If the FO was making the well-being of English cricket its business, did the FO pass those reports to Lord's, whether formally or in a conversation at a gentleman's club? Nor was it a passing interest. On April 6, the FO in Rawalpindi noted that the Pakistan Sports Council statement against the South African tour was 'largely for the record'. Pakistani selectors were travelling to Lahore to pick the under-25 team for England that summer.

Lord's could guess the hand-to-mouth finances of other Test-playing countries because it knew its own. Was Lord's relying on Pakistan and West Indies sticking with England only for the money from tours? Leaving aside the cynicism that would let relations be so soured, Lord's had to reckon with the possibility that just as English cricket was preparing to hurt itself, financially, reputationally and perhaps physically for the sake of South Africa, so might Pakistan, West Indies and India act irrationally, for the sake of principle.

The Foreign Office's job was to gather all these ideas, and weigh them for British interests. From South Africa, the ambassador Sir Arthur Snelling on May 5 had written expecting a 'sharp deterioration in relations'. "We are still far and away South Africa's biggest market despite all the nasty things her ministers say about us …. So this cricket business could affect our trade adversely." Might South Africa, too, punish Britain, and itself, economically, in return for the hurt of a cancelled tour?

* * *

Race relations were even harder to fathom than the political and economic effects of the tour, whether cancelled or carried through. Then, let alone now, how could you read what was inside people's heads? Newspapers carried downright rude letters. In July 1965, after a letter in the Western Daily Press from Paul Stephenson, secretary of the West Indian Development Council, about that summer's South African tour, six letters followed. One said the South African cricketers were invited; 'that's more than can be said regarding many coloured immigrants in this country'. South Africa generally provoked plenty of letters. The fact that some praised apartheid would suggest that such views were acceptable. In another Bristol newspaper, the Evening Post, in 1965, one letter even sounded fascist ('equality and democracy are not synonymous' and 'two races only have created civilisation – the mongolid and the caucasoid'). That did not make the country racist. We can feel sympathy for Godwin Matutu, a student from what we now call Zimbabwe, in front of Oxford magistrates after the on-field protest against Wilfred Isaacs' tour in July 1969 – 'this is a court of white people', he complained. 'In South Africa there are people in detention without trial, and their only crime is to be born black.' If Britain were like South Africa, why was Matutu free to say such things?

In April 1969, David Sheppard ended an article in the Sunday Telegraph on the D'Oliveira affair: "We have our own racial problems in this country and we are not doing very well at them." Sheppard was part of a larger Anglican anxiety that race relations might be 'strained', as Michael Ramsay, the Archbishop of Canterbury, put it in an April 1970 speech. Even if so, English cricket – if only when overseas tourists came to town – was one of the few places where immigrants felt able to assert themselves. In July 1969, reviewing the Saturday of the Lord's Test match against the West Indies for the Evening Standard, Timothy Raison saw a 'respectable' West Indian spectator boom 'sit down' to other West Indians dawdling past, and blocking the view. "What is this colour problem that has so bedevilled British politics over the last few years," Raison, a future Conservative MP, asked rhetorically.

By hiring non-whites, first-class counties, let alone northern leagues, were far ahead of parliament – Constantine was the first black peer – the armed forces and police, professions, even other sports such as football. The stereotypical MCC clubman, who hardly ever saw a black face, except perhaps a passing bus conductor or the Black and White Minstrels on TV, applauded a Sobers or D'Oliveira.

The sheer naivety of Jean Morris, a columnist for the Press & Journal in Aberdeen – about the furthest city from the immigrant districts of the 1960s – was revealing, when she wrote about apartheid in November 1969 before the Springboks played in the city. "Unlike the people of Wolverhampton and elsewhere we haven't had to think, how would I like to have coloured people as my neighbours. How few of us even in the Church have seriously thought about how we would like to have them as part of the family – enough for the family of God – but acceptable to ours? That's really why the majority are quite prepared to let the Springboks come and to go and watch them play." Or, as she added, were people simply ignorant, of apartheid and race alike, and saw the rugby tourists simply as entertainment?

As a typed flier for a public meeting at Bristol University student union in December 1969 against the Springboks put it: "Merit not race should be the basis of selection. That's how we play the game in Britain." To be charitable, English cricket had sound principles; if it had a fault, it was too naively trusting of white South Africa. So were others; Britain had a 'fund of goodwill' towards South Africa, the

Birmingham Post stated in an editorial of May 16. South African discrimination made the 'situation', not Britain, the Post pointed out. Sheppard, while passing on the gist of his meeting at Lord's to Howell on May 5, said he had raised 'community relations'. Gubby Allen replied that 'if this was put to us by the proper people, this should be something we should have to consider'. Did Lord's have to be told to consider the community? Or was Allen's reply reasonable; were 'community relations' truly unfamiliar? Faults in others are easy to find; and what can be more hypocritical than calling others hypocrites? Yet the Sunday Telegraph had a point in their editorial of May 17, that accused the anti-apartheid movement of playing 'a kind of game'. Just as sport was a substitute for war, so protest could be a substitute 'for accepting personal responsibility for neighbourly race relations at home'. You looked good on newspaper front pages if you pestered the Cricket Council by holding a placard beside the Grace Gates; it did not make you a good person.

Wednesday, May 20
In South Africa, Wilfred Isaacs gave a private dinner to the tourists at the Wanderers club, eleven days before they would set off. Wives were not allowed on tour. Valerie Lindsay, wife of wicketkeeper Dennis, admitted the competing tugs of loyalty and concern: "I won't be surprised if the tour is cut short and I won't be sorry. I think there will be trouble. The team is thrilled so I am thrilled for them. I would not have been sorry if it had been called off." The tour manager Jack Plimsoll said he was packing his bags.

Journalists felt the same tugs. Brian Bearshaw of the Manchester Evening News admitted he was selfishly 'itching' to watch South Africa. He quoted the former Lancashire captain Ken Grieves, now the professional for league club Milnrow, who could be franker because he did not have a county or MCC employer to please. He had gone on BBC television months before: "I said then that if the tour did start it certainly wouldn't finish!"

Lord's could only pretend it was business as usual; Jack

Bailey stated that Lord's might change the starting date of the first Test, which now clashed with election day, Thursday, June 18. If Lord's felt it had nothing more to say or hear, that left the field to STST. At their press conference, Peter Hain explained away the movement's recent quiet - 'we held our fire in the last few weeks because we expected a courageous advance', from Lord's. That neatly passed over STST's failure to put numbers on the street, and even blamed Lord's for it. According to the organisers, protest appeared to be something they could turn on like a tap, for Hain promised 'the greatest demonstration against apartheid in sport ever seen in this country', on Monday, May 25 in London.

Jim Callaghan had one of the most thankless days that a Home Secretary can endure; a visit to the annual conference of the Police Federation, at Llandudno. A thousand of the bolshiest police grumbled ('for years we have been eyeball to eyeball with the fanatics, the lunatics and the hooligans', said their president, Reg Gale). Oddly, police felt unloved and not listened to, while making one-sided demands (more pay, a return to hanging) and enjoying the power of having one of the most senior politicians in the country say kind things to them ('we are in for a long, hot summer', Callaghan said, promising his 'support'). Callaghan had already taken the initiative against the Cricket Council by calling them to a meeting at the Home Office the next day. He claimed to 'want to hear from them their reasons for going on with this tour'. He said they would have a 'full discussion, at my invitation .... I would be failing in my responsibilities if I did not meet them. I will simply ask them if they have considered the consequences of their action'. He denied that he would put any pressure on the Council; which was, like so much in life, a matter of opinion.

Callaghan's grip contrasted with comments by others, perhaps feeling pressure. Lancashire Chief Constable William Palfrey accused 'my lord bishops' of making 'a holy crusade' and wished they would march to church instead: "If they would do that I would put the police band at their head." Roy Edey, a Greater London councillor and Kent county club member, wrote to the Queen, appealing for royal intervention to stop the tour. If people in authority were so bad-tempered, hysterical or plain silly before the tourists landed, what would they be like later?

Thursday, May 21
Reporting for the Guardian, John Arlott at the Oval commented on the 'discordant note' made by the coiled barbed wire around the Oval the day before. After Gary Sobers made 160 out of 235 and Nottinghamshire were all out for 281 on the Wednesday, the Surrey opening bat Mike Edwards made a square cut on the Thursday morning. Brian Bolus stopped the ball inside the boundary rope, only to run into the wire. While a fellow fielder untangled him, Edwards and Younis Ahmed ran four, before they chose to stop. In the Yorkshire Post, sports writer Richard Ulyatt called the event symbolic; 'not cricket'; 'it seems to me unreasonable on the part of the cricket authorities to expect first-class cricketers to chase to the boundary with the barbed wire looming ever nearer and nearer.' A mile away, on the other side of the Thames, those same authorities were about to run into the political equivalent of barbed wire; Jim Callaghan.

He had rung Harold Wilson the night before, at 10.30pm, 'to discuss the line we would take'. In privacy, the politicians' 'line' sounded far harder than what Callaghan had told the public through the press. Callaghan would tell the Cricket Council that 'on grounds of public policy the Government considered that the tour should not go ahead'. The reasons would be 'potential damage to race relations', and the Commonwealth Games; and 'the burden on the police, without making it clear that they would if necessary be able to deal with any situation that arises'. Callaghan would still insist that he wasn't trying to pressurise them; he was only doing his duty, to 'draw their attention to the wider considerations outside the interests of cricket'. He would not take no as an answer from Maurice Allom, the Council chairman, but would insist if he had to on meeting the whole Council.

The last week

Boundary view of Kensington Oval, south London.

A May 1970 afternoon's cricket at the Oval; inside the barbed wire around the boundary.

Wilson agreed; hardly surprisingly, as Callaghan had covered all the main issues. Perhaps only for the sake of having something to say, to show who was prime minister, Wilson suggested that Callaghan might 'also refer to the burden on the taxpayer of maintaining law and order if the tour were to go ahead'. If Callaghan did comment on that – Lord's, and the likes of Headingley and Wooller, had shown themselves happy for taxpayers to pay for police so far – it went unrecorded. Instead, Callaghan revealed that he had discussed it with Sir Leslie O'Brien, governor of the Bank of England, who Callaghan would have known from his years as Chancellor of the Exchequer. According to O'Brien's contacts – a telling sign of the links between Lord's and City money-making – there was 'a good chance' that the Cricket Council would respond to such an appeal.

Callaghan and Wilson had another telephone call the next morning, at 11.35am. Some of it went over the same ground, agreeing to the vague yet hard to resist phrase 'public policy'. For whatever reason – did Wilson feel cricket hated him, thanks to his alleged inciting of people to demonstrate? – the two agreed to keep the prime minister out of it. They spoke at length about 'press and television handling'. If the Cricket Council did call the tour off, Callaghan would see the 'press and television people' that evening, to 'get the angle right'. Critics accused Wilson, and later leaders, of taking more trouble over the media than actually doing things. Wilson however did not overlook details; in this case, if the Council asked for compensation. Callaghan would not bring it up; if the Council did, Callaghan would say 'he would consult his colleagues'. Surely this was cynical, as Callaghan was already consulting his most senior colleague. In fairness, Wilson did think 'such a request should be treated sympathetically'. And if Wilson and Callaghan did not take trouble over the media, the Tories would; the two men spoke of going 'into the attack on the Tory attitude', particularly Reginald Maudling's speech of the night before as reported in that day's newspapers, which claimed Labour was pressurising cricket.

The actual meeting went much as Wilson and Callaghan

had planned; hardly surprisingly, as Callaghan had scripted it, and the Cricket Council hardly knew enough about the police or race relations to argue with him. Callaghan said he could not refuse to let in the South Africans as aliens; it followed that he could not prevent the tour without the consent of the Cricket Council. Callaghan had shown his hand; he wanted the tour stopped. "He asked whether the Cricket Council would regard their previous decision as irrevocable in the face of such a request." Maurice Allom replied that if such a request were made, 'it would be virtually impossible for the Cricket Council not to accede to it'. Allom, on purpose or not, had walked into the trap that Callaghan had set; and Callaghan closed it. "The Home Secretary said that he now made such a request."

They agreed that Callaghan would write to Allom. The meeting broke up while Home Office officials drafted a letter. Callaghan signed it, and handed it to Allom. They agreed that the Home Office would publicise the letter at 3pm, and Callaghan would then meet press and TV.

Allom was sharp enough to raise cricket's loss of receipts from spectators and the BBC. Callaghan replied that the Government could not indemnify the clubs, 'but he would be willing to discuss with his colleagues whom he had not consulted [strictly true, although he and Wilson could easily have been more forthcoming] any request for limited assistance'.

It had not taken long. By 12.30pm, Griffith was reading Callaghan's letter over the 'phone to Cheetham in South Africa. Callaghan duly made his case to the media. He stuck to his 'line' that he 'put no pressure on them at all'; although Callaghan had enforced his power by making the Cricket Council visit him. Times reporter Peter Evans asked Callaghan pointedly how he would reply to the charge that he was bowing to a minority and interfering with freedom. Callaghan posed as a neutral between cricket and its protesters: "I shall be accused of many things. The umpire always is." Also with some reason, Callaghan separated the actual protesters (a minority) from the cause ('one of the

The front page of the Evening Argus in Brighton on Thursday afternoon, May 21, 1970, reporting Jim Callaghan's demand to the men of Lord's.

few issues of recent times where public opinion has been divided right down the middle'). Tories such as Quintin Hogg replied predictably, deploring how Wilson and Callaghan had 'bowed to threats and yielded to blackmail'.

Even before the official reply from the Cricket Council, the news of Callaghan's letter was enough to convince everyone that Lord's would give in. At the Police Federation conference in Llandudno, they cheered. Prince Philip had been to a Lord's Taverners party. When asked afterwards if he thought the tour would be cancelled, he said with a smile: "Which tour? We [he and the Queen] have just been on one [to Australasia for two months] – it's too late to call it off." India and a dozen African countries said that they would attend the Commonwealth Games after all. Michael Stewart in a telegram to the embassy in Pretoria had to explain as best he could how 'developments' led the British Government to break its word, and seek to influence MCC: 'Events have moved very fast ... and it has been impossible to give the South African government more warning'.

In an editorial that morning, the Daily Telegraph had asked what new argument could Callaghan put to the Cricket Council. More to the point was a chess analogy that Ali Bacher used in a BBC radio interview. Callaghan had 'manoeuvred the MCC into the position of checkmate' and the cricketers had been 'pawns'.

Friday, May 22
About 200 Oxford students, shouting 'apartheid out' set off in the morning on a four-day march to London, due to stop overnight at High Wycombe, Uxbridge and Notting

Birmingham Post front page article on Friday morning, May 22, listing the men, mainly ageing and from Oxbridge, due to decide on what next for English cricket.

Hill; on Monday they would pass Lord's and reach Trafalgar Square in the afternoon for Hain's promised 'greatest demonstration'. As their slogan and banners suggested, the marchers had demands beyond sport: they were against Britain investing in South African 'slavery', and wanted political prisoners freed; Vorster and the Rhodesian leader Ian Smith were 'Nazis' and Hastings Banda, the leader of Malawi, a 'traitor' for hosting Vorster that week.

The Cricket Council was meeting at Lord's to consider Callaghan's letter at 2pm, giving members from afar time to travel. As Cowdrey drove through the Grace Gates – he was free that day, before beginning a match at Leicester on Saturday – he told waiting reporters: "I never thought it would come to this." What did Cowdrey mean by 'this'? The Evening Standard, according to its headline, claimed the tour was still a 'riddle'. In truth it was only a riddle because to the end those in authority met in secret. EW Swanton, reporting from Cardiff on the Glamorgan-Hampshire county match – Glamorgan's defence as champions was faltering already – wrote later that the Cricket Council had 'no tenable option' left. The Daily Telegraph, editorially as fierce as ever, asked 'what a Home Secretary is this, who pompously hectors and browbeats the law-abiding in an attempt to induce them to submit to violence and intimidation before it has even occurred'. The Telegraph once more called on cricket to stand firm, 'with a clear conscience'. In the Birmingham Post that morning, a Council member, Edmund King the Warwickshire chairman, commented that the Council was 'now duty bound' to abide by Callaghan. King's sense of duty was all the more striking because he sounded bitter and was 'naturally very distressed' by the Government. "It has come down formally on the side of the demonstrators and anarchists and against the clear thinking and sporting cricket administrators." King was certain cancelling would only strengthen apartheid; the demonstrators would lose, he said; not that they would worry: "They can now start on something else."

After an hour and a half, Allom replied to Callaghan so briefly as to be rude. "The Cricket Council today considered the formal request of HM Government to withdraw their invitation to the South African Cricket Association to tour the UK in 1970 contained in your letter of May 21, 1970. The Council were of the opinion that they had no alternative but to accede to the request and are informing the SACA accordingly."

Press questions after Tuesday's 'final decision' to keep the tour had been barbed; 'now there was only an air of sadness and sympathy', the Sunday Telegraph reported. Callaghan replied even more briefly than Allom, appreciating the prompt response.

Chapter Eleven

'The foul stink of success'

Whatever may be the changes produced by man, the eternal round of the seasons is unbroken.
                    John Fenimore Cooper, The Deerslayer

In the television room of the University of Glasgow's student union, they cheered the news of cancellation. Peter Hain - pleased, naturally – spoke with remarkable composure. He gave credit to 'the massive show of public feeling', something far from true. If the tour were dead, Hain trod on the corpse to make sure: "There cannot be another tour by an apartheid team to Britain, and possibly the rest of the world. We have seen racialism rejected in sport. If another apartheid team shows its face in Britain we will be very quick to step down on it." Hain looked at once to the future: "I hope this will be seen as a beginning and not an end in itself. Eventually apartheid must be rejected in all of its forms." In his 1971 book, he admitted that the 'sheer stupidity' of the Cricket Council's decision of May 19 to keep the tour had depressed him. Like a sportsman who has reached a season's or a career peak, Hain found the success hard to take in: "I felt curiously flat and tired." Just as the record-breaker has to carry on the match, so Hain carried on the protest. He wrote to the 15 South Africans competing at the Wimbledon tennis fortnight, asking them to declare against apartheid, or face demos. An 'Anti Demonstration Association' - the kind that never says how many, if any, members it has, yet is seized on by the press – condemned Hain 'and his mob of terrorists'. Police guarded the courts and Wimbledon was peaceful. Besides, Hain as a Young Liberal had work to do in the election. At a press conference he made the crackpot demand for schools 'to be democratically controlled by all', students, teachers and dinner ladies.

Sir Herbert Brechin beamed with relief and called it 'an

'The foul stink of success'

"Who's going to break the good news to Henry?"

The Jak cartoon in the Evening Standard of May 23 and a cartoon in the next day's Sunday Telegraph summed up how cancellation denied protesters the enjoyment of a demo.

257

An unflattering Daily Mail cartoon from May 23. A king-like Peter Hain seated on an upside-down soap box receives humbled Harold Wilson and Labour ministers, such as Jim Callaghan wearing comically small policeman's helmet. 'And now what do you suggest we do next, Mister Hain?' Wilson asks.

extremely wise decision all round'. Because countries had not formally withdrawn from the Commonwealth Games, Edinburgh did not even have to send new invitations. Players deep down were glad, Norman Yardley said in his weekly column. "But they are also bitter that they and this great game of ours have been used as a political doormat for a battle that should have been waged in Downing Street if it had to be waged at all." Jim Kilburn, the scrupulous cricket correspondent of the Yorkshire Post, while sorry that South Africa would not tour, wrote that the game would not be 'tormented' by disruption 'as distasteful to me as is the principle of apartheid itself'.

Many cricketers past and present reacted more like Yardley, against 'the dirty deed done'. 'One of the blackest days in English cricket', Tom Graveney called it. Raymond Illingworth said the Cricket Council had had no alternative, 'with a gun being held at their heads with threats of riots by militant demonstrators and pressure from the government'. Brian Close said the cancellation left him 'a very bitter and disillusioned man'. He saw it as a double blow: "This could have been the tour to put cricket firmly back on its feet as a drawing power and money spinner. And we could have beaten the South Africans. It's disgusting to think that people cannot go out in a free country and enjoy themselves by watching cricket." Others sounded more regretful, such as Basil D'Oliveira, who said he had been willing to play the South Africans: "At the same time I appreciate that this has grown into an issue with complications beyond the boundaries of the cricket field." Some combined these reactions. Gloucestershire captain Tony Brown said his whole team would be 'bitterly disappointed'. Illingworth called it a 'sad end'; Quintin Hogg and the Glamorgan president Jack Clay, a 'sad day'. After a May 14 letter from a Miss Monica Morton who, as a niece of a former Derbyshire player, deplored the tour, Donald Carr replied as late as June 9: "It is sad that cricket got involved in a matter of this sort which caused so many strong feelings from varying points of view."

Few of those who wanted the cancellation gloated, whether because they did not want to spark more anger or, like the News of the World, they too saw the story as 'sad and sorry', except they saw Lord's as 'well meant peace-makers' who had been giving in to the South African 'bully'. More at a distance, the Irish Times could welcome a 'happier ending'. From Cape Town, John Miller reported in the Daily Telegraph on May 28 that the tour 'debacle' had done 'untold harm to the cause of the sane and sensible opponents of apartheid who have to live in South Africa's strange society'. The British consulate in Cape Town reported a dozen abusive 'phone calls, mostly aimed at Harold Wilson, taken by the caretaker. In the Green Un in Leeds, David Swallow wondered about the 30 English cricketers, including Don Wilson and Barry Leadbeater of Yorkshire, making a 'good living' each winter in South Africa, coaching boys and club players. Wilson said he was under contract to the Wanderers club in Johannesburg; where, he might have added, another Yorkshireman, the former batsman Willie Watson, had emigrated to manage it. Wilson said he had grown fond of the country: "I am waiting to see what happens. It could be that .... English cricketers will no longer be welcome I

OPINION
Sick of rabble-rousers

Because of widespread violent round cricket grounds many people will give qualified assent to Mr. Callaghan's "persuasive" request to the Cricket Council that the South African tour shall be abandoned.

At the same time let no one mistake what has happened.

THE GOVERNMENT HAS SURRENDERED TO THREATS OF VIOLENCE.

The would-be tour-stoppers are many kinds of people. They include responsible and sincere leaders of public opinion who have the cause of racial harmony at heart.

BUT WITH THEM MARCHES A MOTLEY ARMY OF COMMUNISTS, BOTH OVERT AND DISGUISED ANARCHISTS, AND BLOODY-MINDED FOLK BALANCING ALL MANNER OF WEIRD CHIPS ON THEIR SHOULDERS.

They are those whose main target is not the South African team but the disruption of our society by any means which seem the most promising, including violence.

IT IS TO THIS RABBLE THAT OUR GOVERNMENT HAS CAVED IN.

The lost tour was integrated in a vital election issue — law and order.

We believe the bulk of our people are sick of hooligans, vandals, and violence.

They are sick of professional protesters. They want to see more police, more severe penalties.

And a sterner social climate.

"As the demonstrators said to the Cricket Council, mate — 'If there's any violence it'll be your fault.'"

An angry Leeds Evening Post front page editorial of Friday, May 22 said the Government had 'caved in' to a 'rabble' of 'professional protesters'.

certainly won't hold the club to my contract."

Apartheid's politicians, predictably, barked. Vorster said: "During the whole controversy I purposely did not say anything because I did not want to give anybody any excuse for cancelling the tour. I would like to say this; every lawyer will tell you that if you once pay a blackmail, you will have to meet increased demands as time goes on .... It is not cricket or sport that loses, but it is the forces of law and order which suffer a heavy defeat." Politicians or any of us seldom act more strongly about something than in our first reaction; and none of Vorster's words suggested that he would bite. Sure enough, in January 1971 in his review of 1970, the British ambassador Sir Arthur Snelling recalled 'an incredible amount of Press coverage in this sport-mad country' and 'deep and widespread resentment'. Snelling however also noted: "The exclusion of South Africa from a growing number of international sports is resulting in some domestic pressure for relaxation of the colour bar but only in the sporting field and so far without producing any significant change in government policy." Lord's had cancelled for purely British reasons; not to influence South Africa. Some in South Africa took the hint anyway. EW Swanton found it 'most important' that Ali Bacher, a supporter of the Progressive Party, critical of apartheid, appealed for a broader attitude to multi-racial sport, 'the first unequivocal statement from a responsible figure in White South African cricket'. Bacher, like his country, was beginning a 20-year wriggle out of a straitjacket that they had tied themselves into.

By contrast, politics in Britain soon passed over the cancellation. Jeremy Thorpe wrung what he could out of the news, saying 'the only tragedy is that the Cricket Council could not have faced the obvious earlier'. Reacting to the cancellation, the Leicester Mercury said, 'who would have thought cricket could become an election issue?'. In truth, the tour, once dead, was also dead to the politicians. Thus Harold Wilson, touring the Commonwealth Games stadium in Edinburgh, when offered the chance to say he was glad about the cancellation, said instead: "I have nothing more to say on that other than what I have already said publicly many times." Some on the other side felt the same. The Bishop of Leicester, Ronald Williams, one of the patrons of the tour fund, would only comment 'less said the better'. Some let off anger at the main characters. The Daily Telegraph columnist Peter Simple asked for any legal reason why Hain should not be deported to South Africa. The answer, if Simple were truly interested, was that Hain was as British as he was. Percy Fender wrote to the Telegraph that 'instead of having MCC on the mat', Callaghan 'should have summoned Hain and his fellow travellers to the Home Office and said to them, 'although Ahr Arold ['our Harold'] has given you his permission – indeed incited you – to demonstrate, do not forget the thin white line marked breach of the peace'. Having slandered Hain as a Communist and mocked Wilson's Yorkshire accent, so the 77-year-old former Surrey and England all-rounder went on, laying into Labour as 'weak kneed' and 'double talking'. Another former county captain writing to the Telegraph, RH (Dick) Moore of Hampshire, asked cricketers to wear a black tie on June 18, 'in memory of cricket as it was enjoyed before 1970'. The metaphor of mourning was telling. To Moore, cricket was the victim; except, it lived on. Everyone accepted the tour was dead. As Hain wrote in his 1971 book, the Conservative Party's role had been 'squalid', yet a Conservative government would have had to seek cancellation. Conservatives and Liberals alike found things to deplore. Where was the Government's moral support to those threatened by the demonstrators? asked the Yorkshire Post. The conservative historian Sir Arthur Bryant began an article in the equally conservative Illustrated London News pompously: "The surrender to the threat of violence that put finis to the South African cricket tour is an episode which any lover of this country's history and free traditions can only view with disquiet." Yet even he had to admit that after the D'Oliveira affair, Lord's invitation to South Africa was 'open to doubt'. In a private letter to Lord's, Herbert Brabin, secretary of the Constitutional Club, while disappointed, wrote: "We feel that the MCC did a staunch job but realise that the final outcome was inevitable." Maurice Allom said much the same to the TCCB at its first meeting after cancellation, on Wednesday, May 27; at such short notice, the chairman Cecil Paris had to give the committee time to read the agenda. Allom had to explain why the Cricket Council had swung from the TCCB's unanimous view of December 1969 and February 1970 that the tour should proceed. He 'doubted whether any sport had ever been faced with problems containing such wide ramifications'. He blamed 'events' of the previous week, that 'had moved so quickly that it had been impossible to refer the matter to the board [TCCB] before taking the inevitable decision to accede to the requests of HM Government. He knew everyone concerned was deeply sorry for South African cricket." Some were more than concerned. EJ Gothard, there for Derbyshire, took issue with the May 19 statement that had ruled out future tours until South African cricket was multi-racial: "He suggested that it would have been preferable to have left the position open to more flexible negotiation." In other words, Gothard – aged 65, the stereotypical old amateur captain – wished for some way to keep playing South Africa. Allom 'assured the meeting the Cricket Council had considered that'. Until eight days before, everyone in authority in English cricket was set on playing South Africa; now Allom was as adamant about the opposite. This was pure totalitarianism, as satirised by George Orwell in 1984, when one minute Oceania was at war with Eurasia, and the next at war with Eastasia.

The Sheffield Morning Telegraph had commented sourly after cancellation, 'the cricket fields of England can revert to their customary near-bankrupt calm'. The TCCB meeting showed how commercially naïve those in charge were. Gloucestershire asked for a 'purely domestic county programme for 1970', as if the game could do without tour income. Bernard Coleman, chairman of the TCCB's public relations sub-committee, reported 'two substantial offers of sponsorship' for the Rest of the World series, from cigarette firm John Player, and car maker Ford. As Coleman warned, the TCCB would have to re-negotiate the TV contract, and the £70,000 from the BBC for the South Africa Tests would likely be 'reduced considerably'.

Coleman's friend and fellow Surrey committee man was Raman Subba Row. "I am not a crystal ball gazer," Subba Row had said on cancellation, "but if minority groups are allowed to take the law into their own hands I would not be surprised at anything that happens." It did not occur to Subba Row that the 'minority group' that had changed policy - so suddenly that it did not have time to answer the dismay of many, and consider the costs - was the very cricket authority he belonged to.

* * *

In October 1970, as chairman of England selectors, Alec Bedser reported that 'in spite of the problems at the beginning', the 1970 Test season against the Rest of the World was 'probably the best seen in England for some time'. Among others a sense of decline, even dread,

May 1970: the Oval has its barbed wire taken down.

lingered. On cancellation, the Sunday Telegraph journalist Peregrine Worsthorne compared the 'humiliation' of the MCC to the fall of the Bastille, and Callaghan to Louis XVI. Less grandiose but as political, Edmund King the Cricket Council member feared 'not only for cricket but our whole way of life and our liberties'. Some harked back to a better past, such as Dick Moore in his Telegraph letter ('the golden era of the 1930s'). What to some was welcome, even necessary, such as sponsorship, to others was demeaning. So wrote the classics professor Harold Harris, in a 1975 book, Sport in Britain. He singled out the 1970 series, when 'the title Test match .... was bestowed on exhibition games by 22 hirelings advertising stout'. The brewer Guinness was sponsor. Strikingly, besides ageing conservatives – Harris died aged 71 in 1974, days after finishing that book – young left-wingers hated the game, as old-fashioned and apartheid-supporting. In between the extremes, Bill Bowes the former Yorkshire fast bowler turned sports journalist warned in May 1970 'that immediately you accept sponsorship you lay yourself open to 'direction", such as TV telling you when to play. Bowes – as informed about the game as any man of his time – had aired what would become the most profound problem for any sport, and indeed any broadcast entertainment. More pressing after cancellation was what the Yorkshire Post called 'the vicious militants', who the newspaper feared would 'grow heady on the foul stink of success'. In the July issue of The Cricketer magazine, EW Swanton noted two extremes; the violent demonstrators of the left, and the 'elderly skinheads of the right'. He was hinting at angry Telegraph readers who sent him vulgar letters, having turned against the tour. The June 1970 general election, while also a passing affair, likewise showed Britain to have two camps; each defining itself against the other. Thus the novelist RF Delderfield in a July 1970 column wrote that he had voted Conservative, for (among other things) 'the rule of law as against the unremitting squawks of the banner waving demos'. On cancellation, Raman Subba Row among others feared that Australia's next tour in 1972 might be a target for protest, because Australia was fighting in Vietnam, or over the injustice against Aborigines. Society was indeed at the mercy of protesters, except they had so many wrongs to choose from; what about John Player, whose cigarettes gave smokers cancer? One letter in The Cricketer in August 1970 asked acidly if Arlott would refuse to commentate for the BBC on the John Player Sunday League, 'as a matter of conscience'.

If cricket people feared the worst – the apartheid issue 'can bring sport to its knees', Illingworth had said on cancellation – that was partly because they saw cricket as fragile. Derek Birley in his 1979 book The Willow Wand, recalled the 1970 tour as 'the most serious and sustained argument there has ever been about sport, certainly in Britain'. Was it a coincidence? he asked. Cricket, he suggested, was a 'symbol of values'. Birley had unerringly missed the point; cricket had merely been a prize for the demonstrators, who had seen its practical vulnerabilities. In his 1980 memoir Runs and Matches, the Kent amateur batsman turned journalist Tony Pawson recalled seeing in Italy at the end of the Second World War in 1945 how ordinary civilians were 'always the ones to pay'; the 'aggressive extremists of right or left are forever forcing their theories on the rest of us'. The war had stamped Pawson, like so many of the men in this story – Arlott, Swanton, Wooller – who had become middle-aged by 1970. While their attitudes differed, they were altogether more worldly-wise than snobs like Harold Harris, whose 1975 book complained 'that most of what passes for top level cricket today is the wrong kind of cricket played by the wrong kind of cricketer to titillate the wrong kind of spectator'.

Peregrine Worsthorne began his article on cancellation by claiming that 'the protest industry' had won 'a famous victory, its most significant to date in the civilised world'. To the Leicester Mercury, county secretary and captain spoke alike: Mike Turner feared more demos, and Raymond Illingworth felt cricket had created a precedent that could spread to other sports. The Mercury in editorials, too, saw cancellation as a 'dismal watershed', that had only postponed society's 'inevitable clash' with anarchy. The Yorkshire Post meanwhile saw 'the hint of a right wing backlash threatening the kind of dangers we thought had disappeared after the 1930s'; in a word, fascism. The Western Daily Press columnist Jean Blackmore said she had no interest in cricket and 'the South African cricket controversy has been too long and too painful to bear further comment'. Like any good columnist, she went ahead anyway. She said she felt 'uneasy for the future'; what if militants went after hunting, medical science for experimenting on animals, or butchers selling meat? Another commentator, Sir Arthur Bryant, saw the same threat to freedom, only in more high-flown terms ('age old British right' .... 'gross impertinence'). The mightiest protesters in 1970s Britain proved to be strikers. In June 1970 pickets at a factory in Cumbernauld lined the gate and lay in the road to keep traffic away. They foreshadowed the famous miners' siege of the Saltley depot in 1972 and indeed the petrol delivery drivers' blockade of 2000. A few organised workers could paralyse an employer; even society.

The day after cancellation, a front page cartoon in the Sheffield Morning Telegraph showed two wild-haired men tearing up posters saying 'Stop the Tour'. One said to the other: "Ah well, back to Vietnam!" While that belittled unfairly the convictions of some, it did prove true; protesters could always find other causes; and the anti-apartheid movement faltered. Written on the archived Bristol AAM folder for 1971 and 1972 are the words 'very quiet'. The obvious next targets were South African sportsmen, whether playing tennis or golf singly, or cricketers with counties or the Rest of the World. In December 1969, Menzies Campbell recalled running a race in Los Angeles in 1967 alongside Tommie Smith and John Carlos (of 1968 Olympics black glove salute fame) and the white South African Paul Nash. Campbell recalled shouting back at some of the crowd shouting 'racist' at Nash: "It was intolerable to expect an individual to answer for the collective policies and attitudes of his country." On cancellation, Mike Procter said several friends had urged him not to play for the Rest of the World, and 'phone calls had threatened him with protests unless he

South Africa and Gloucestershire all-rounder Mike Procter.

signed a declaration against apartheid. He said he would not sign, and would turn out for the Rest of the World, if selected: "I should try to help the MCC after all the problems they have had to contend with in the last few weeks. I believe the cricketer's job is to get on with the game and not get involved in politics, whatever the threats." Why did protests against such players come to nothing? The answer lay in the fact that Procter was playing for Gloucestershire against the Cavaliers, ironically the team standing in for the South Africans. Procter, Richards and other South Africans were already playing peacefully with West Indians in county cricket, just as they played under Sobers in the Rest of the World series. Any protester still finding fault with Procter would have to take on all English cricket.

Anti-apartheid protesters had begun branching out from sport early. In November 1969, Special Branch in Edinburgh reported to colleagues in London that Edinburgh students intended to attend an exhibition at Olympia and place false orders with South African companies there. On June 4, 1970 Special Branch reported anti-apartheid organisers, still recovering from their 'unexpected victory', had demonstrated the previous week at the Rothmans tennis tournament at Surbiton. The police's insider reported that the movement had decided against demonstrating outside Barclays, because it would not make news. Instead, they would target the South African embassy, or ambassador. The two dozen protesters outside Lord's on May 19 - 'mainly teenagers', police reported – were already looking beyond cricket, to judge by their leaflets. One read: "British firms prop up apartheid and rake in large profits from the muscle of black workers. And all that Harold Wilson says he is against apartheid, he has carefully protected the stake of British big business." The leaflet ended in capital letters, in case anyone were losing interest: "TO STOP THE CRICKET TOUR IS ONE WAY TO STRIKE AT THIS EVIL RACIALIST SYSTEM AND ITS BRITISH BACKERS." What the leaflet avoided saying was that British jobs relied on apartheid; the very nature of trade made it hard or even foolish to separate good economic connections from evil. The Tories saw they could harm Labour. After cancellation, the Conservative Party chairman Anthony Barber asked Wilson rhetorically: "Does he now back the same demonstrators in their direct action against British companies with commercial interests in South Africa?" As early as May 25, the Yorkshire Post noted that the anti-apartheid movement would try to win over trade unionists at the many Bradford textile firms that depended on South Africa for wool and mohair. This ethical appeal got nowhere. Not that British workers were more self-interested than any others. In April 1970, BJ Rogers of the Foreign Office wrote to the Board of Trade about a possible black African and Caribbean boycott of South Africa, like the Arab world's boycott of Israel that was of 'considerable nuisance value'. Rogers suggested Barclays Bank would be a 'test case'. This was not a new idea; one of the organisers of the demo in Leicester against the Springboks, Stuart Roach, had a conviction for damaging the window of a South African bank in August 1969. Time would tell how thankless any campaign against banks for links to South Africa would be. How could you tell it was working; and even if it did, wouldn't some other bank take its place? Going after sport was easier, and more exciting; in May 1970 New Zealand students ran on the field during trials in Wellington for the rugby team to tour South Africa. When the Springboks toured Australia in their winter of 1971, the same cycle of demos, barbed wire and brutal policing played out. Australian rugby, and society generally, evidently stood by apartheid, despite Britain's experience. It took a brave and alert Sir Donald Bradman to have Australian cricket uninvite South Africa, on September 8, 1971, several weeks before they were due. Only then, as Ali Bacher put it, was the final nail in South Africa's cricket coffin; at least until apartheid was over. Even then, as Barry Richards put it in his 1978 autobiography, 'a long-term separation seemed unlikely'. The Britons of the early fifth century must have felt the same about an end to Roman rule.

* * *

The banners at the first demo against the Springboks,

at Twickenham, set the tone. The largest, made from a bedsheet, said: "Magdalen students – no apartheid – no Springboks." The campaign sought a negative; no tour. In his 2012 memoir Peter Hain recalled his decision, announced on the night of success, to wind up STST. Hain had shown remarkable maturity again; how few leaders voluntarily give up power! As Hain said, STST had 'a very specific purpose' and he believed that success 'was not sustainable'. Hain knew his movement. Sheffield University in late May went on a one-day strike against the Americans in Vietnam. One postgraduate complained in a letter to the Sheffield Morning Telegraph that some protesters launched 'toilet rolls from the upper stories of the Arts Tower'. As frivolous were the callers to BBC radio in Nottingham who had threatened to take Nottinghamshire chairman Jack Baddiley hostage; until they put in a call that they had had so much publicity, they had achieved their object. Most demonstrators were trifling with causes. They were only good for mischief, with other people's property and well-being. Contrast them with how English cricket even in defeat doggedly chased compensation from the government. On June 2, in a letter to the MCC secretary ('Billy'), Raman Subba Row wrote on his public relations consultancy notepaper that he was glad to hear of a letter from Denis Howell about compensation: ".... can I just emphasise the point that our bargaining position might be much weaker after June 18 than before if I know anything about politicians." In other words, after the election, whichever party was in power would feel less like pleasing English cricket. So it proved. On July 9, the Conservative new sports minister, Eldon Griffiths, wrote to the new Foreign Secretary, Alec Douglas-Home that the Cricket Council had put in their bill: "It's a whopper!"

That set the unfriendly tone among ministers, who were in fairness in charge of public money. Politically, the Tories did have more in common with Lord's than Labour. A draft letter of March 1971 from Douglas-Home to Griffiths gave the government's view that 'contact offers the best prospect for promoting change there [South Africa]'. However, the letter later admitted that Communist countries in sport did not require British teams to be Communist, whereas South Africa segregated spectators under apartheid, which was illegal under Britain's Race Relations Act. On March 31, 1971, Griffiths announced that cricket would get £75,054; Lord's said it fell 'well short of expectations'. That hid months of arguing beforehand. Ted Heath told ministers in January: "I don't see that anything I or others said in Opposition commits us to pay a penny." The government would pay, only to honour Labour's undertaking ('this must be made clear'). The £75,000 amount came from 'abortive expenditure incurred' and the difference between what the BBC would have paid for the South African tour, and what it paid for the Rest of the World. Junior Treasury minister Maurice Macmillan suggested a 'small meeting' with Griffiths and other ministers before a home affairs committee meeting; in other words, to agree what to do before the meeting proper. These ministers were taking such care because, as Macmillan put it in a letter to Chancellor of the Exchequer Reginald Maudling, the issue was 'highly political'. Other sports might invite South Africans, run into trouble, and bill the government. Griffiths at the 'small meeting', on January 25, set out four alternatives. Pay nothing; pay cricket's whole claim, of £200,000; pay the £13,674 Lord's spent on the tour; or that amount plus the loss from television. The Attorney General, Sir Peter Rawlinson, gave the legal view; the government did not have to pay. Griffiths gave a cricket view; the 'financial plight' of first-class counties that had made a loss of £176,000 the previous season. The South African tour would probably have brought in £150,000. Griffiths said the Cricket Council had behaved 'extremely well and with restraint'; in plainer English, Lord's was not making a fuss. As a sign of how publicity-conscious the Conservatives were, a 'recent leak in the press' was blamed on the Yorkshire club, and not the Council. The ministers agreed to let cricket have 'an accountable amount'; that is, not the round figure cricket had invented.

The physical traces, of the tour that never was, soon went. The barbed wire at Headingley had to stay for the Roses match the weekend after cancellation; as a precaution, the boundary line was marked several yards inside. Most counties pulled up the artificial pitches and re-turfed, the TCCB heard in October 1970. The board hoped all counties would; and if not, those pitches were not for use in county cricket.

Little remained to be said. On legal advice, Lord's had to write to those who gave to the 'Support The Seventy Tour' fund, to offer them their money back. Billy Griffith, ever the gentleman, wrote a letter on June 4 to Sir John Waldron, the Met Police Commissioner, thanking him for his help 'in these last few trying months'. Waldron replied kindly a week later. The planning had been a 'useful exercise', he said. "It was a great shame that matters outside the control of cricket led eventually to the disbandment of this Test series because the South Africans are a wonderful side and would have given great pleasure in this country by their forceful and enterprising cricket. However such things shall be." In a June 1970 letter to Donald Carr of the MCC, Arthur Coy of SACA praised Basil D'Oliveira, 'who has reason to feel bitter yet as a great gentleman pleads for the tour to go on'. His letter, and Carr's warm reply, sounded like messages between Britannia and Rome, as the Roman Empire fell in the fifth century, or conversations on the bridge of the sinking Titanic. All sides could draw on a shared, civilised past; except that however much they pretended, something was ending.

Chapter Twelve

Verdict: the dreamers of the day

What's coming? I ask the taxi driver in Memphis. And he says: "…. Fifty years from now everybody will be grey anyway, Jews and Germans and French and Chinese and niggers, and who'll give a durn?"
Robert Penn Warren, Segregation: The Inner Conflict in the South, 1956

"Looking back one cannot quite believe that it all happened," Wilfred Wooller wrote for the 1971 Surrey county club yearbook. He wondered at 'the mysterious hysteria' between the South African tour of 1965, and 1970. Wooller could explain nothing because he had learned nothing; or rather, he would not admit that other people's beliefs were as valid as his.

He was one of what TE Lawrence towards the beginning of The Seven Pillars of Wisdom called 'the dreamers of the day'. All men dream, Lawrence wrote. The dreamers by night wake, and can tell their dreams are vanity. The dreamers of the day 'are dangerous men, for they may act on their dream with open eyes, to make it possible'. Peter Hain, like Lawrence himself, was one of the 'dreamers of the day'. As Hain put it in his 2012 memoir,

Good, that's got that out of the way — I never think sport should interfere with politics.

Birmingham Post cartoon on Saturday, May 23; as Jim Callaghan carries news of cancellation, Harold Wilson wearing trademark macintosh and painting a 'Vote Labour' sign, comments: 'Good, that's got that out of the way – I never think sport should interfere with politics.'

STST became 'one of the very few British protest groups to have completely achieved its objectives'. In his 1971 book, he was already reminiscing that for many people STST was 'unique and stimulating'. Perhaps in politics, like love, the first experience is the sweetest.

Oddly, both sides – anti-tour, and the anti-antis – wanted to fight on, and got nowhere. By July Simon Hebditch as London organiser of Action Committee Against Racialism, the new STST, was boasting of contacts inside factories of firms with holdings in South Africa. Peregrine Worsthorne in his comment on cancellation warned that protesters as the new mob had beaten the rule of law; 'nothing will be the same again'. Worsthorne was exaggerating. He had forgotten that the mob had won earlier, by shouting down Michael Stewart at Oxford, and preventing Enoch Powell from speaking (not for the last time) at Dundee in January 1970. Some in the three main political parties, having leapt on the tour as an issue, did not want to let go; even after cancellation, some MPs called for a Commons emergency debate before Parliament dissolved. Partly, this was because they agreed about so much else; entering what was then called the Common Market, for instance. Putting it another way, John Fisher in the Yorkshire Post described the election as 'fundamentally about philosophy'; the kind of society you wanted to live in; a competitive one, or one with social justice. There the tour, and South Africa, belonged, and it duly featured early in the election campaign. The Labour candidate in Chorley, Derek Forwood, in his adoption speech laid into the Conservatives for using the tour as a stick to beat the Government. Someone asked Labour candidate Ron Truman in Burton upon Trent if he agreed with cancellation. "Yes. I am a cricket fan but South Africa forfeited my consideration when they stopped D'Oliveira going to South Africa." The Tory candidate for Westminster, Christopher Tugendhat, threw every cricket cliché he could at Harold Wilson: ".... whatever bumpers he sends down or no ball that he bowls, we are going to hit him for six right out of this constituency." Quintin Hogg at an election meeting raked over the tour, 'something we naturally take rather to heart in Marylebone'. The issue quickly faded. Politicians talked instead about the 'cost of living'; the old favourite; what mattered to you.

* * *

Towards the end of his biography of Churchill, Sir Martin Gilbert quoted the great politician's verdict on Eden's failed Suez invasion in 1956: "I would never have dared, and if I had dared, I would never have dared stop." Like Suez, the Seventy tour was a double failure by Lord's: arranging it in the first place, and then giving in and looking weak. Cancellation was not inevitable, although it's tempting to see signs it was. In mid-April, when explaining in the Guardian why he would not broadcast on the tour, John Arlott wrote that it was 'destined to failure', even if the matches were completed. As early as the Springboks' match at Leicester in November 1969, a South African journalist had cabled home that the cricket tour had little chance, if the young showed so much hostility to apartheid. As Foreign Secretary Michael Stewart's speaking notes - in case of a tricky conversation with Dr Luttig the South African ambassador - put it after cancellation, there were 'changed circumstances' since October 1969, thanks to protest. In the Birmingham Post after cancellation, Alan Smith commented: "I suppose it was inevitable that in a pre-election period the Government would not like scenes on television that would demonstrate that they cannot keep law and order." While true enough, had Wilson held the election in the autumn, and had the Commonwealth Games been outside Britain – as they were otherwise, from 1962 to 1982 – the 'circumstances' for cancelling would not have been there.

A future Conservative MP, in 1970 a Birmingham alderman, Anthony Beaumont Dark, on the eve of cancellation said he was sure that people were prepared to pay 'the price of liberty'. He complained that demonstrators would realise that as long as Labour were in power, 'they could get their way if they shouted and protested long and vigorously enough'. Days before, the Yorkshire Post had also spelt out that central principle; violence and disruption, 'used as a means of political argument'. Labour and Tories were arguing over whether 'direct action' was valid; they could not wish it away. Many people - more liberal and neutral, or merely indifferent? - according to the Yorkshire Post 'would heave a sigh of relief' if Lord's or the South Africans would call the tour off.

Cricket felt, as Raymond Illingworth put it afterwards, 'caught in a crossfire'. As Alan Ross put it as acting editor of The Cricketer in January 1971, the English game felt 'exploited', 'by those who have absolutely no concern for it'. Hain in his 1971 book by contrast claimed British sports officials had been exploiting their position, to defend white South African racialist sports bodies. At least arguably, then, cricket and rugby were not victims, but had chosen to take a stand, and found themselves in conflict with society. Numbers on either side did not matter, because it never takes many to upset the peace that sport, or theatre or trade, needs. It only took one end of terracing closed and massed police for Bill McMurtie, at the Springboks' match against Scotland in December 1969, to report 'an unreal atmosphere'.

Sport went on during the widespread rioting in England in August 2011, because rioters wanted to loot, not take on sporting crowds. By contrast, a single crossbow bolt fired onto the Oval field in 2017 led to armed police and a police helicopter, and an abandoned match. It showed more than the authorities' extreme fear of terrorism in 'crowded places' (if that jargon can apply to the county championship). People in authority have a mania for avoiding safety and other risks, in case customers are hurt, complain, and sue; which would jeopardise the jobs of those in authority. Cricket, sport and society generally have gradually taken more notice of risk; for instance, motorcycle helmets and seat belts became the norm, like helmets for batsmen, from the 1970s. Some in 1970 did speak of risk, notably EW Swanton in his important article of May 15 turning against the tour. The Brighton Argus on January 1, 1970 reported that 'no matter what they [the

Verdict: the dreamers of the day

"Voluntary collection? We didn't even pay to get in!"

One of the funniest cartoons about the affair, from the London Evening Standard. As MCC types rattle tins, skinheads respond: 'Voluntary collection? We didn't even pay to get in!'

TCCB] come up with, guarding vulnerable property like cricket grounds is a risky business'. A memo of November 1969 by JH Waddell of the Home Office saw 'great risk of injury to demonstrators at the hands of the crowd' and risk of police 'being identified with one side or another'. Those examples cover all the risks that the tour threw at cricket: physical, financial, and reputational. English cricket made the fundamental mistake of ignoring risk and instead thinking and acting only in terms of principle. The Bishop of Bristol in mid-May 1970 warned that to dismiss the protesters as thugs or Maoists was 'to run the risk of being blind to the element of truth in their protest'. The men of Lord's set out their ideals in the leaflet for the 'save the tour' fund, that boiled down to standing by South Africa, and against 'mob rule in our public life'. Each side saw that STST was about greater stakes. So, according to Rowland Bowen, were factory strikes, and the student movement worldwide. All were against the 'blatant hypocrisy' of life, and for social justice. Conservatives, by politics and nature, rallied. The diarist of the Derbyshire Advertiser weekly newspaper, Rosemary Meynell, wrote in May 1970 why she gave 'ten bob' to the tour fund. "I don't approve of apartheid and I am not very interested in cricket but I am sick of being told by moralists which athletes should be allowed to come here and which should be excluded." Lord's stood its ground, John Woodcock recalled in 2017. "I suppose you could say it was damned if it was going to be told what to do about anybody, it was perversity as much as anything, as much as principle." Bowen, too, saw at Lord's the 'wish to give orders always'. For the exact motive for Lord's, and its downfall, we should turn to the supreme satire on modern power, 1984. George Orwell wrote that no change can ever be admitted: "For to change one's mind, or even one's policy, is a confession of weakness." Even in April 1969, when the MCC had to admit, after newspapers broke the story, that Vorster had told a go-between that D'Oliveira would be an unacceptable tourist – sheer cheek by a foreign politician, which Gubby Allen hid from almost everyone – the Lord's statement did not admit to any mistakes. To David Sheppard, this was typical MCC: 'decisions behind closed doors', and 'whenever a storm develops, you sit tight until it blows over'.

Such a self-serving attitude belongs as much to a political movement seeking to overthrow authority as to anyone in authority. In the conservative magazine The Spectator in April 1969, Simon Raven pointed to the threat: "Nothing, nothing at all, is to be allowed except what is strictly allowed by the fanatics to rearrange the world just as they want it." The nightmare of 1984 as imagined by Orwell arose because the Party had the power to ignore reality – to alter the past, and enforce the thought that two plus two equals five. People survive, even when crossing the road, by knowing what's what. As David Sheppard said in April 1969 of the (eventual) selecting of D'Oliveira to tour, the selectors making 'a difficult decision' needed 'all the available evidence'; Gubby Allen denied it them. In this story, fanatics on both sides in denial of reality made bad decisions and false predictions, besides blatant lies. John Jackson, the 'Support the Seventy tour' campaigner, in mid-May 1970 claimed wrongly the tour would be the central theme of the general election. Jackson denied his campaign, launched in Leeds Conservative Club, was party-political. He dismissed the £100,000 cost of policing the protest in Leeds 'because of the principle involved'; naturally, because he would not have to pay!

At the beginning of the STST movement, in November 1969, a leading article in the Times set out the central question, 'whether any group with strong political views has the right to veto lawful events which the majority ... desire to take place – and show that desire by paying gate money'. The Times denied there was such a right of veto, unless 'the conscience of a vast number of people' was affronted. This story proved the Times wrong; the force that STST had to show was less than vast; and as those in authority have become ever more cautious about risks, even a threat of trouble may do. Police routinely will not agree to cover pre-season football matches between rivals – a veto, in effect – in case of hooliganism; universities ban invited speakers; theatres close controversial plays. Or more likely, clubs, universities and theatres censor themselves in the first place. However cowardly, each generation has to wrestle with the nature of liberty – what to allow, and how to define what you don't like, such as 'hate speech'. It's basic politics. Jim Parks in April 1970 deplored that 'the majority of English enthusiasts are to be deprived of the pleasure of watching' the South African cricketers; why blame them for their country's government? he asked. As soon as he used the word 'government', Parks was bringing politics into sport whether he liked it or not. So was Colin Milburn when he wrote in an April 1970 column, 'what I do know is that politics should be kept out of cricket'. Milburn in any case spoiled his argument by suggesting 'the Government should foot the bill for police protection of the grounds ... it isn't up to cricket authorities to pay for law and order'. As soon as anyone talked of the police, and who paid for them, wasn't that political, of interest to tax-payers?

Newly free countries were already bringing sport into politics; again, whether you liked it or not. In March 1969, the British High Commission in Nairobi reported 'high feeling' in Kenya and that it threatened to break off athletics relations with Italy, Switzerland and West Germany if they sent teams to South Africa's Olympic-style Games in Bloemfontein. The British embassy in Pretoria in November 1969 reported home that at a world gymnastics tournament in Ljubljana, where South Africa appeared, the United States, Canada and others walked out. Britain did not. Countries were having to take sides, for or against South Africa. Lord's, even if you could hardly expect it to follow gymnastics in Slovenia, would have to choose too. Some saw this in good time. In October 1969, Tom Taylor, a former chairman of selectors at Glamorgan, told his fellow finance committee men to consider the possibility of next summer's South African tour being abandoned because of demonstrations. The committee agreed (unanimously, needless to say) that Glamorgan 'would like to see the South Africans play cricket in this country'. That was one more denial of reality,

A South African stamp to mark their Olympic Games-style tournament in Bloemfontein in 1969, rather dubiously using the Olympic Rings and flame.

fit for 1984, thanks to Wilfred Wooller. Taylor may have spoken out because he was about to resign; he died soon after. In his 1971 book, Hain recalled it was 'impossible to communicate' with the men in charge of English cricket, 'let alone reason with them …. the rugby world is even more out of touch with the social consequences of its actions'.

Lord's was not short of critics. In December 1968, Christopher Hollis in The Spectator said Lord's handled the D'Oliveira affair 'about as ham-handedly as possible'. Ken Grieves in May 1970 called it a mess, 'right from the start'. As a good newspaperman, John Woodcock recalled in 2017 that the story 'gathered pace as it went along'. Nottinghamshire chairman Jack Baddiley assured his committee at a meeting in April 1970 'that the police were prepared to take every precaution to ensure that the cricket would be played without interruption'. Someone had raised the 'feeling' – that is, the opposition – against the tour. Even that small, typically vague piece of minute-taking showed how the cricket authorities did not want to face reality. Irresponsibly, they left hard work to others. They made insulting assumptions. An undated memo at Lord's noted that "as no trouble will occur in member occupied stands, it is waste of money to have row of police facing them. At rugby grounds the police around members stands have been unoccupied." That at least showed Lord's could observe reality – and had watched the Springboks. What would it look like to everyone else, behind barbed wire – that members were trustworthy, and they were not? Feeling, assumptions and reputation, all intangible, are hard to measure. At a Glamorgan committee meeting on May 19, Trevor Billing reported that about 30 members had resigned over South Africa; and 20 had joined, to support South Africa. Those numbers were tiny compared with the total membership of about 7000. What, if anything, did it mean for cricket's reputation? No-one was asking.

* * *

In Janaury 1970, the Irish Times journalist Dennis Kennedy, home from South Africa, concluded that apartheid was not

A 1965 portrait photograph of Robert Menzies, sent to Harold Wilson.

only evil, but uniquely so, 'mainly from its enshrinement in a legal system', besides Christianity. Among conservative politicians with a legal background who condemned STST for 'threatening – and successfully, threatening – the rule of law', was the most distinguished of his kind, the retired Australian prime minister Robert Menzies. For Menzies and his kind, the law, or 'the rules' at a club, trump politics; at the same time the law gives some power to the petty official, the power to enforce; and denies it him – the power to bend the rules. It unites the white-coated Lord's steward of old, as late as the 1990s, who would not allow a journalist up the stairs to the press box without a jacket and tie, and the district governor in Tolstoy's Resurrection, who said 'in my position I do not permit myself to swerve an inch from the letter of the law, just because I am a man and might be influenced by pity'. Rules were weapons for the likes of Wilfred Wooller at Glamorgan and Gubby Allen at Lord's; those men made other people keep to the rules, while they made up rules as they went along. This explained why Rowland Bowen in his Cricket Quarterly could rage at the men in charge at Lord's as stupid, and evil. Their 'officer versus troops complex' meant that they resisted reasoned appeals and STST, but accepted Callaghan's order. They were guilty, 'of the purest political cynicism seen in this country since the Tory party first started drilling in opposition to the elected Government of the day, over Ireland in 1914', and, we might add, seen again over Brexit, from 2016. They failed, thanks to their failings. For we must not fall for the dangerously common belief that dictators are efficient; that, to put it another way, the Fascists made the trains in Italy run on time. Bowen judged that Lord's had 'endangered their entire strangle-hold control of cricket, largely', he added in

Colin Cowdrey has put £1 on his son's future.

We're adding to his score.

We fancy ourselves as fairy godfather. And we reckon it's never too soon to start planning your children's future.
Opening a Lloyds Bank savings account is one very good way. Just £1 is all you need.
You can add to it every birthday and Christmas, and every year we'll add to it as well.
So, as they grow, your children will have a nice little nest egg growing with them.
They'll have their own savings book, and when they're old enough, can draw up to £20 from any of our branches.
It's a super sort of independence to give a child, right from the moment it's born.
Come and talk to us about it now. You don't even have to wait for the christening.

Lloyds Bank helps you to plan

Advert for Lloyd's Bank, Sunday Telegraph, September 1968. English cricket was (and still is) bankable (pardon the pun) for big business; both in their own way happily invested in apartheid South Africa

glee, 'through their own ghastly incompetence'.

Robin Knight looking back in 2018 drew the same moral: "The MCC history is littered with this, and it goes on to this day. It's the way the MCC on the one hand has survived 200 years, and on the other hand it's why the MCC has lost control of the way cricket was run." For each man (to repeat, no women allowed) in authority, apartheid was at the same time a private reckoning, and cemented or spoilt his relations with others. For the connections between the men of cricket, while varied, were many. While this story has no trace of Freemasonry, many - Cowdrey, Allen, Brian Close - were Masons.

Robin Knight recalled Raman Subba Row was 'fatally compromised'. To the shock of David Sheppard - he and Subba Row overlapped at Cambridge for two years - although Subba Row was of mixed race, he put his ambition and career in cricket ahead of principle, according to Robin Knight.

Don Wilson called it a tragedy, 'that cricket lovers all over the world are not going to get the chance to see them', the South Africans; although as David Swallow, interviewing Wilson in the Leeds Green Un, noted, every county club (except Yorkshire) would mortgage its grounds to hire Graeme Pollock, Eddie Barlow, or Tiger Lance. By 1972, Mike Procter and Barry Richards were reporting that they were feeling stale after six years of all-year cricket; hardly tragic. Few credited Basil D'Oliveira as the only man who had had to leave his homeland to make anything of himself; let alone Mandela in prison. Young men like Procter and Richards understandably put themselves first; if they did not, who would? Older men, in authority, the stewards of the game, were supposed to think more widely, of 'the inflammatory influence' the tour was bound to have, as John Arlott told the Panorama debate. As the TV reviewer Pat Roberts saw, the pro-tour side 'avoided to a man the fundamental issues'; another sign of unreality.

For this story was not only about politics, let alone the law, but morality. Hain and his movement could stand on morality as a battlefield of their choosing, not of the men in political power and upholders of the law. Not that protesters had the field to themselves. As early as November 1969, Peter Jenkins of the Guardian gave a column over to his defence against 'many letters', accusing him of hypocrisy (why not ban Soviet ballet?), or of inciting violence. Jenkins also faced a left-wing argument; that protest against sport was an easy option, compared with a trade embargo. Jenkins might have said, why punish ourselves for the crimes of others? He might have admitted that it would be better to hurt apartheid on weekdays, rather than at weekends. Instead he wrote that rugby and cricket grounds were 'as good a place as any to start'. For protests, like politics, the law and anything human, are not morally perfect. That everyone in public, and whole countries, had their hypocrisy exposed – many of the Commonwealth countries threatening the Edinburgh Games discriminated by tribe, race or religion

– may explain why Hain wrote in his 1971 book that he, 'an almost fanatical' cricket follower, lost interest in the game. He could not tell the game apart from the people; the religion from the church-goers. Nor could some protesters separate South Africans from their country; in the United States some heckled and threw things at the golfer Gary Player; he had to eat and sleep under guard. The hecklers, the London teachers who on the eve of cancellation urged schools not to take children to watch the South Africans, and the Aberdeen reverend Thomas Howle, who told the General Assembly of the Church of Scotland that he went to see the Springboks at Aberdeen, 'because I believed profoundly that the game should take place'; all believed they had right on their side. Remembering that both sides in the two world wars told themselves that God was on their side, we are fooling ourselves if we ever believe that the winning side politically must be the right side morally.

Was it, in our story? Opinions differed, just as the demonstrators who invaded the Springboks match at Leicester in November 1969 'timed their interventions well – or badly, depending on one's point of view', as the Leicester Mercury rugby reporter Mike Wood put it. The demonstrators did not succeed purely on the merit of their case; how could they, when they never spoke a word to the rugby players? As the RFU secretary PT Rippon wrote in November 1969, police asked, if a demo held up play, 'that players should keep together and move to a clear space on the field'. Players, and spectators, were not to enter into 'any debate, discussion or physical skirmish'. The RFU would brief the South Africans likewise, 'although I would think that this would be pretty superfluous'. A 66-year-old man, who had 'many coloured friends' wrote in the Oxford Times in January 1970 of his disgust – that is, a moral reaction - at demos against the Springboks. On either side, some otherwise intelligent men claimed to find themselves lost for words. Bristol University's vice-chancellor, Prof Merrison, called the apartheid park bench and ambulance 'such a primitive assault on human dignity', that he could not understand it. While the Springboks were in Manchester in

November 1969, a local Labour MP Paul Rose said: "I cannot understand any decent sportsman wanting to have anything to do with a racially selected team that masquerades as South African." In December 1969 the Tory MP George Younger claimed that he found the demonstrators' aim of cancellation 'most incomprehensible'.

The fact was that those people, having made their mind up about the tour morally, were hardly going to admit that the other side had a point; why else was it at large? The West Indian protest leader Jeff Crawford said in cancellation week, 'as a black man there cannot be any compromise on this issue'. In August 1969, a student of Ruskin College, Oxford, told his local Bristol Evening Post that after he had a letter published in the Post on the evil of apartheid, he received 'a very strongly worded postcard from some crank in Bath, unsigned of course', that made him angry. The sort so quick to tell others they were wrong were oddly sure that they were right. For you do not have to be virtuous, to take a moral stand. Raymond Illingworth said, thinking of Crawford after cancellation, that the demonstrators' threats were 'hardly civilised'. Illingworth was complaining about methods, not the moral case. STST knew their case was morally stronger, and made much of it. Keith Morrell, the Labour candidate for Marylebone, weeks before cancellation called the tour 'an affront to the conscience of a civilised community'. Frank Ziandi, a law student from what was then Rhodesia, told a public meeting at Golders Green in London, on May 13, 1970 that 'history is on the side of the black African and one day he will take over'. By demonstrating, you were identifying with 'this inevitable process', and would one day feel proud, he predicted. Ziandi was using every trick he could – racial guilt (presumably the audience was largely white); flattery (clever you, picking the winner!); and a reward (costing the victors nothing). To Ziandi, might (eventually) was right. More impressive were those few like Peter Lever and Mushtaq Mohammed who objected to playing against South Africa for their county. They, like Martin Luther, and Martin Luther King, were of a moral character that made them take a path, no matter how lonely; even if it were the death of them. David Sheppard outside Twickenham in December 1969 said: "I wasn't going to come today, because I had arranged to preach at a wedding. But my conscience made me feel that you cannot let other people carry a banner for you. I told this young couple about my decision this morning and I shall go along to their wedding party this evening." Sheppard and others – few, compared with the indifferent millions - were bearing witness to the truth in the final words of Alan Paton's novel Cry, The Beloved Country. All, white and black alike, suffered under apartheid – 'the fear of bondage and the bondage of fear'. Even men who tried to make excuses for apartheid knew it stank. Richard Harrison, writing in the Express and Echo after the Springboks played at Exeter in December 1969, had to admit 'disadvantages' in the South Africa he had come from ('the obvious one is the morality of the system'). In the Glasgow Herald the same month, a businessman, 'appalled' by the reception for the Springboks, praised South African hospitality. He claimed to see (gradual) change for the better among the 'natives', 'while I am prepared to argue on the morality of the system'. Everyone with a conscience knew; what was anyone doing about it?

Or, to be kinder, what could anyone under the total system of apartheid do? Even if whites, South African or foreign visitors, wanted to play blacks at sport, or eat at the same table, would the other side dare, and would anyone in sight let them? Here was another scene fit for 1984, that left only lonely defiance, like Winston Smith's diary. Peter Lever said in January 1970: "The only thing to jolt them is to refuse to accept them. We have got to isolate them totally in sport." Lever would play Procter and Richards when with their counties Gloucestershire and Hampshire; but not South Africa. By July 1972, Procter seemed to agree. While praising progress in multi-racial golf and tennis in South Africa, he said: "The only thing that will really bring about a complete volte face [by his government] is the day the Springbok rugby team is ostracised internationally. Then I believe we will see some action."

Tories shouted humbug when they could. Chris Chataway complained in November 1969 that the British government would not let the Springboks play on Ministry of Defence fields, but did supply weapons to the Nigerian government for their war in Biafra. The Aberdeen Tory MP Patrick Wolrige-Gordon said apartheid was wrong and would end in disaster unless something changed, 'but two wrongs do not make a right', implying that the demonstrators were doing wrong also. In ignorance or on purpose, these men were avoiding the question. Contrast their meanness with David Sheppard, after the special meeting of the MCC in December 1969: "What is more important than votes is that ideas have been ventilated. Nothing will be quite the same in English cricket after the debate." Sheppard was vague for a reason; signs of change were few, and not instant. Rex Alston crassly ended his review of the meeting in Playfair Cricket Monthly with the 'political fates' that 'deprived' the tourists 'of the pleasures of the South African trip'. White hospitality had done the trick yet again. In a 1986 book, while apartheid was still dragging on messily, Mike Brearley in conversation with the like-minded John Arlott felt 'that we are trying in this country to be multi-racial in every way and it is also a symbol for black people in Great Britain that we don't play South Africa'. A symbol was better than nothing; a start. In November 1969 a half-coloured woman - so she called herself - wrote to the Manchester Evening News of how she was travelling home to Moss Side on a bus, when students marching against the Springboks held up traffic. The driver and two passengers complained about the students. Another two passengers were coloured. "I stood up and told him [the driver] what I thought of him and his ideas." The woman, disgusted by the driver - another moral reaction - had taken the chance given by the demo to stand up to the bigots. For what good? For all we know, the driver only became more bigoted. Even if so, it was a tiny exchange in the greater struggle that never ends, where every action or inaction, words or silence, weigh in a moral balance, that politics and the law but poorly express.

* * *

Cricketers are a very tolerant lot, Norman Yardley wrote after cancellation, 'but I don't think many of them will forgive ex-Test batsman David Sheppard for his part in all this.' In Tony Pawson's 1976 interview of Sheppard in The Cricketer, it sounded as if some had not forgiven. When Sheppard, now Bishop of Liverpool, found time to watch cricket, he went in the crowd, 'to avoid possible embarrassment for old friends in the pavilion' who disagreed with him over South Africa. Sheppard still believed he was right. As he had written in his 1964 autobiography: "I have never been to South Africa, but some things are right and some are wrong at any distance." The instinct of English cricket, like any group, was not to question itself, but to rally. Norman Yardley urged every real lover of the game (maybe one more dig at demonstrators) to 'arrange his own demo', and watch as much cricket as possible, 'in support of a game that has taken such an unfair bashing from inside and out in recent months'.

If STST took up all the time of its leaders, at least they had chosen it; not so Billy Griffith the MCC secretary. In April 1970, MCC appointed an administrator, Group Captain Ronnie Ford, to do day-to-day affairs to spare Griffith. Even though Griffith lived alongside Lord's, his wife Barbara told the Daily Express: "He often doesn't get back until nine or ten," too late for dinner. "But I have got used to that." John Woodcock recalled Griffith in 2017: "It was a very difficult job he had. He wasn't qualified for it." Woodcock meant well towards Griffith, who had been able enough to keep wicket for England and captain Sussex. Griffith turned 60 in the summer of 1974 and retired. David Frith, interviewing him for The Cricketer, asked which of all the crises was the most stressful. South Africa, Griffith replied without doubt:

'because it went on for so long .... one got no rest from it – sometimes seven days a week, 24 hours a day. I was often seen as the decision maker when after all one was merely the spokesman. It was very distressing that many people even close friends assumed that I had some sympathy for the policies of the South African Government, however often I stated otherwise .... All that time I received hundreds

of letters almost daily castigating me for all sorts of evil intentions and I cannot deny that this distressed me more than I can say.'

Basil D'Oliveira in his 1969 book praised Griffith at length: "Above all things he works for the good of cricket." D'Oliveira recalled Griffith spoke to him at Lord's, when Worcestershire played Middlesex there in the final match of the 1968 season; that is, days after selectors so upset D'Oliveira by not choosing him for South Africa. "No one has been more genuinely hurt by the whole story than Mr Griffith," D'Oliveira said. Griffith 'honestly, sincerely and fearlessly did what he thought to be right'. Left unsaid was what D'Oliveira thought of everyone else at Lord's.

* * *

In no time, at the TCCB's meeting at Lord's on May 27, the Wednesday after cancellation, Stuart Surridge proposed and Arthur Gilligan seconded the dates and venues for the Test matches against the Rest of the World – hardly surprising, as they were the same as the Tests against South Africa. Terence Harris, a Leicester alderman and chairman of Leicestershire Cricket Society, blandly told the Leicester Mercury that any cricket enthusiast would rather watch the Rest of the World in peace, than watch the South Africans disrupted. Reporters such as Jim Kilburn of the Yorkshire Post hoped for a new start: "Players now cloaked in public sympathy could win the more enduring quality of admiration if they played attractively and earnestly and unselfishly," he wrote, characteristically earnest himself. In Lancashire, county club chairman Cedric Rhoades was selfishly against releasing his overseas players Clive Lloyd and Farokh Engineer 'for what in all probability will become exhibition matches'. The cancelled tour gave cricket a brief chance to try something fresh. It only had old or plain bad ideas. Kilburn suggested North versus South, or Probables versus Possibles, as a Test trial; a domestic only summer, Colin Milburn urged.

This last-minute Rest of the World series, talked down by some, suffered from confusion from the start. According to the TCCB's rules, these were not proper Test matches; but to interest the BBC, they had to be. The TCCB bought off the counties by paying them £150 for releasing each Rest of the World man; £200 for Sobers as captain. Freddie Brown, as manager of the Rest of the World, asked his players if they wanted to play for their counties on the Sunday of the Tests. Hardly surprisingly, they wanted the day free, like other Test matches. The TCCB at their meeting on Wednesday, June 24 – the Rest of the World had won their first match by an innings on the Monday – voted 13-1 for those overseas players, nonetheless, to play in the Sunday League for their counties. The board voted nonsensically 13-2 for England players not to play on Sundays, even though they appreciated that it 'might be difficult to justify to the press and supporters of some counties', one rule for one team, and another for the Rest. In the end, both sides had Sunday off.

English cricket got the takings it deserved. The Glamorgan AGM in February 1971 heard that its share was £2230, £4000 less than expected from the South African tour. Glamorgan had a deficit of £10,000 on spending of £50,000. Wilf Wooller said the five shillings gate entrance price would rise to six shillings, 'or in modern terms 30 pence'. Wooller blamed rising costs. Several counties, he said, were 'very short of money indeed', and he 'would not be surprised to see one or two go out of action by the end of the decade'; thanks partly to him.

South Africa was still there. Scottish sea anglers applied for a Sports Council grant, for their air fare to compete in South Africa. The new Conservative sports minister Eldon Griffiths put his view on paper within government; as it was in the national interest to trade with and invest in South Africa, Britain worked with its navy, and people holidayed there, 'it would in my own view be illogical to boycott South African sports teams whether coming to this country or playing against our teams in South Africa'. The Government could not stop British teams going, or South African sportsmen coming, to Wimbledon tennis for example, 'though people like Peter Hain may seek to stop them by protest'. Hain – plainly still well informed - duly placed a letter in the Guardian, flagging up that the Sports Council would meet to decide on the grant. The Council, purely for sport reasons, recommended the grant; only for Griffiths and fellow Foreign Office and Scottish Office junior ministers meeting in February 1971 to decide against. As shifty as Labour, the Tories agreed that the Scottish Office would 'quietly' inform the anglers. Griffiths told the meeting 'it was an unfortunate fact that international sport was now closely involved in international politics. This was a fact that the Government had to reckon with.' Hain had gotten under the skin of politicians.

It made little sense that the Tories, plainly itching to support South Africa, did not do so. On ITV on April 30, 1970, Ted Heath had said: "I have come to the conclusion that there is no instance in modern times whereby by ostracising a regime one has been able to bring them to the opposite point of view." Such was the thinking behind détente with the Soviets. In June 1971, the defence and oversea policy committee of ministers debated a paper on international sporting exchanges. On paper beforehand, the Foreign Office wrote of ".... the Government's belief that contact offers the best prospect for achieving change in South Africa .... providing South Africa accepts our teams without question (as should be the case after the recent concessions in sporting policy announced by the South African government)". That appeared to open the way for tours to resume to South Africa, which as the FO admitted blandly "will not necessarily satisfy all those in this country and overseas who are concerned about apartheid in sport". Another paper before the committee spoke of a 'less interventionist' government; except it also had to be consistent, and 'defensible'. The British government subsidised trade missions to South Africa, whose members stayed in racially segregated hotels; hardly 'defensible', and another sign that the touch of apartheid could only corrupt. Politics - what made ministers look good, and what they could get away with - counted. Any change had to be worth doing; a British boycott of the Communist bloc, for instance, 'would achieve little'.

The 'recent concessions' arose from a speech on April 22, 1971 by Vorster to South Africa's parliament. Like so much out of white South Africa and Vorster's mouth in this story, while the headline – 'Vorster allows mixed sport at top level' in the Daily Telegraph – sounded important, that was only 'by local standards', as the Times put it. In detail, let alone in practice, it meant less. The British Lions rugby team was due to tour South Africa in 1972. They could play 'Coloured' sides; which whites could not watch. That made no sense, as Sir William Ramsay, president of the Rugby Union, pointed out, because non-whites could watch white games (from 'enclosures'). Teams touring South Africa could bring who they wanted. A French coloured rugby player was about to prove it. Did that include D'Oliveira? Had Vorster put cricket through ructions since 1968 for nothing? Vorster did not say. Hain dismissed it as 'glossy wrapping around racially segregated sport'.

For apartheid would stay – no mixed trials, so all-white South Africa teams still. Weeks before, Jack Cheetham had said his government had refused to allow two non-whites in the team to tour Australia later that year. The next day, at a festival match between Transvaal and the Rest, after one ball the Rest walked off the field and came out again, and made a statement that they wanted non-whites on the Australian tour, chosen on merit. Frank Waring the minister of sport dismissed it as a gesture.

On Wednesday, April 28, 1971, Benny Green was one of the 300 or so at Lord's for the opening day of the season, when MCC played county champions Kent. With a few details he captured the anti-appeal of the game to the fanatical few; Mike Denness let the first ball from Ken Shuttleworth sail down the leg side on what John Woodcock called 'a crippingly slow' pitch. In the Long Room, 'the average age of the onlookers was between 80 and 90'. Sir Neville Cardus in a camel's hair overcoat had his back to the cricket, laughing in company. Green left through the Grace Gates at lunch, when Kent had made 56 for one after 39 overs, 'into

Sunday Telegraph advert for a chest cough medicine, May 1970.

Sir Neville Cardus.

the real world, which was, I had to admit, going about its business as though cricket had never existed'. Green had expressed a truth; that cricket, like any other sport, or the theatre, or art in a gallery, is as much about turning your back on the rest of the world as about whatever's created inside the arena. Green might have added that cricket, too, was going about its business; whether it ever toured South Africa again or not.

That night, a mile and a half away, a banner-holding crowd of Bangladeshis jeered as the Pakistan tourists attended a reception in Mayfair. When the team landed at Heathrow the day before, police took them out a back way, to avoid the protesters waiting in the international arrivals lounge. The Bangladeshis, angry at the war in what was then East Pakistan, shouted 'stop the murder, stop the cricket' at the Pakistan Airlines ticket desk instead. While the demonstrators at worst threw eggs, they were taking protest against sport a fateful stage further, as Peter Hain appreciated. When asked by the Bangladeshi students, he had advised them to beware of any demo; and not to disrupt matches. Were the Pakistanis prejudiced against Bangladeshis, in sport? "I don't think it has been proved,"

Intikhab Alam leads the Pakistani tourists off their PIA flight at Heathrow, Tuesday, April 27, 1971. Note towards the back in a pale jacket; an 18-year-old Imran Khan.

Hain said. In other words, the Bangladeshis were bringing their civil war to Britain, and British people could say; go home and fight it!

As a good host, Donald Carr had met the visitors at Heathrow. "I certainly hope that the tour will go smoothly. I think it will," he told reporters. The Pakistanis' manager Masood Salahuddin said: "We have come to play cricket." The South Africans would have said the same, a year before.

Chapter Thirteen

D-Day, sixth of June

The situation is fast becoming anomalous to a runaway truck gathering speed down a hill to Lord's on June 6 for a mass demonstration to stop the tour.
Peter Hain speaking at Lancaster University; quoted in the
Glasgow Herald, May 16, 1970

Most other people had moved on when AH Coy wrote to Lord's on June 24, 1970. 'And now this great country' – he was talking about Britain – 'led by a government that cringes to a Moscow-oriented minority' – South Africans never missed a chance to slander the protesters – 'has insulted an old friend' – meaning South Africa – 'rather than risk a policing encounter,' whatever that meant. And why? 'Because they fear facing some civil demonstrators.' On July 21 the ever-diplomatic Donald Carr sent a cordial ('I do hope you will find some good reason for visiting this country in the not too distant future') and gossipy reply, praising Eddie Barlow in the Rest of the World team ('what an enthusiast!'). The fact remained, as Coy admitted, that cricket between the UK and South Africa was 'now finished'. Coy could only console himself with settling the blame on others. How right was he? How sensible was the fear of demonstrators?

* * *

Billy Griffith may have invited demonstrators to do their worst. When Griffith faced the press on May 19 as Lord's stood by the tour for the last time, reporters asked him what if demonstrators halted play, day after day. 'If it is completely impracticable to play, then it is obvious the tour cannot go on,' Griffith said. Not that Peter Hain needed encouraging. On Saturday, May 2, during a thinly-attended protest outside Lord's, Hain had stood on a soapbox and said: 'My forecast is that Lord's will be a very different picture on June 6 to what it is today. We will protest then both inside and outside the ground. We will stop these matches.' As in war or sport, the first 'encounter' – the 'trial of strength', a Special Branch report called it on May 19 – would set the tone.

As early as March, according to a police report on the STST national conference at Hampstead town hall, a trade unionist from the printers' union Sogat had said that the June 6 demonstration 'should be of such proportions that it should effectually finish the tour'. Some said much the same in public. Peter Gilmore, of the north west London branch of STST, told his local newspaper in late April: "I don't think the tour will last more than a week." Other campaigners were assuming a longer haul. David Sheppard as chairman of the Fair Cricket Campaign spoke in early May of a 'massive demonstration' (as if there were any other sort?!) outside Lord's on June 20, the Saturday of the first Test match. Also around this time, as it dawned on all that the South Africans were due, Jim Callaghan told the Cabinet on April 30 that if there were evidence of STST concerting plans to interfere with cricket, 'this might lay them open to prosecution for conspiracy even before such plans had actually been put into operation'. However, the law was not nimble enough to save the politicians. As Callaghan added, a prosecution 'based on an actual breach of the peace' was more likely; that is, once the South Africans had landed. As June 6, 1970 neared, the uncomfortably warlike anniversary of the 'D-Day' invasion of France, it did look as if Hain and company (or conspiracy) would meet their match.

Police were assuming that the tour would happen, Callaghan told the Cabinet on May 7. With Callaghan's approval, police had written a 'code of advice on conduct of stewards', to be 'widely publicised in the hope that it may serve as a warning to potential demonstrators'. All sides were using the media to make their case, or prepare their followers. On May 20, Wilfred Isaacs gave a dinner at the Wanderers ground in Johannesburg to the South Africans about to tour. The rugby player Dawie de Villiers proposed a toast, and told the cricketers to 'go to Britain and prove that you are true sportsmen and not political animals'. He rather muddled that pure-sport argument by adding: 'This will be much more than a cricket tour,' and more ominously: 'It will be a challenge, and a challenge from which you do not run away.'

The tourists were due to gather in Durban on Monday, May 25 for a week's practice before they took off from Johannesburg at 4.30pm on Monday, June 1. Also on the flight would be six journalists and Mrs Duffus, presumably the wife of Louis, one of the journalists. They would land at Heathrow on the Tuesday at 10am and take a coach (with a 'discreet escort' by police) to the Waldorf Hotel in central London. At 6.30pm they were due at South Africa House for a reception. On Wednesday and Thursday morning they would practice at Lord's, until a 1pm lunch by the British Sportsmen's Club, at the Savoy on the Thursday. Club secretary TN Pearce had ruled out Wednesday, as that was Derby Day, a sign of the interests and spare time of club members, that included Prince Phillip and Peter May. TN (Tom) Pearce may be more famous for giving his name to festival and touring elevens (including to South Africa) than as a 1930s captain of Essex. He had written to the Metropolitan Police on May 13: "Last November we gave a similar reception to the South African rugby union touring team which attracted no interference of any kind but it is felt there may be more notice taken this time." Police had planned for the tourists to enter the Savoy by the Embankment entrance – that is, the back door. Such social events were traditional for sporting tourists. More intriguing was an offer in February of a cocktail party by the Constitutional Club in St James' in central London. The South Africans wrote to Lord's asking for advice. Lord's didn't give any, apart from saying the club was 'tied to some extent with the Conservative Party' and did not normally invite touring teams; which was presumably why the South Africans asked for advice in the first place. This may be one example of what Dawie de Villiers in his toast had called 'sports loving people in Britain .... who will make you welcome'. Other impeccable institutions and officials had shown where they stood. The Northern Cricket Society announced a dinner for the South Africans in Leeds on July 29; that is, the eve of the fourth Test. Dr Eric Treacy, the Bishop of Wakefield, would give the toast; Sir Cyril Hawker, president-elect of MCC and chairman of Standard Bank, would respond; and Brian Sellers, chairman of the Yorkshire county club, would preside. The lord mayor-elect of Leeds by contrast was refusing to give a civic reception. Most revealing of all, the Springboks were not visiting Buckingham Palace and the Queen was not going to Lord's for the first Test – or to be exact, she was not invited. As Billy Griffith put it, the MCC did not 'wish to embarrass the Queen' in case she saw 'a display of bad manners outside or even inside the ground'.

On the Friday, June 5, the South Africans would have more nets. At night, might the tourists have gone to The Mousetrap, at the Ambassadors Theatre, as their rugby counterparts did in November? Police anticipated a vigil would start outside Lord's on the Friday evening. North London Polytechnic would stay open to house arriving 'provincial demonstrators', maybe from as far as Glasgow; and offer a 'teach in' and folk music. On Saturday, June 6, the first day of the tour's first match, against Southern Counties, the vigil would end and the picket begin.

* * *

Before any event, those in charge routinely estimate numbers, to lay on enough staff and beer and so on. For police, estimating numbers before a demo matters even more: too many officers is a waste of money and can look foolish; though it's better to over-police than have anarchy. A Sussex member for 30 years, Douglas Collins, fumed in his local Brighton Evening Argus after the cancellation that the students ('a handful of unwashed long-haired layabouts') 'should have their noses in their books'. While early June was exam time, even dutiful students ought to take a break, and a summer Saturday in London must have looked more tempting than (say) Swansea in November. In his 1971 book, Hain spoke of tens of thousands, even

100,000, demonstrators. He would. That is not to deny what he and others had built. The weekend before cancellation, an STST conference in Leeds drew 300 – a huge number by regional protest standards – and expected '10 to 15,000' to demonstrate at Headingley. That group had bought 700 tickets, presumably for demonstrators to enter the Test match. Numbers at a demo, like at a day's cricket, may depend on the weather; except that once university student unions had booked coaches, filled or not, they had to go. The kinds of demonstrator also mirrored the cricket crowd; besides the card-carrying member, there no matter what, you had the more fickle sort who paid at the gate. Add, then, home counties teenagers, gawpers, and left-wingers like the future mayor of London Ken Livingstone ('almost every weekend we marched against the war or apartheid', he reminisced), and you would have thousands – 10,000, the police estimated; the same or more than had lately marched against the American embassy, over Vietnam.

★ ★ ★

The barbed wire was only the most obvious sign that Lord's was expecting the unusual. The Surrey secretary Geoffrey Howard wrote to Donald Carr on May 1 agreeing that it would be 'helpful' for the England team to sleep locally, and for the two Test teams to arrive at the ground

View of a full house at Lord's from the air, looking north east, undated. Note the cars parked inside the ground.

together; which implied a rendez-vous somewhere outside. Carr indeed had just written to the five Test grounds that the two teams would have to stay in the same hotels and be coached in; on police advice; presumably, one body of cricketers would be easier to protect than two. Also presumably for security reasons, the outer gate would not hold the Southern Counties players' complimentary tickets as usual; players would have to forward them to their guests instead. Whoever was picked would have to park at Lord's, make their way to the Clarendon Hotel in nearby Maida Vale, and be bussed in at 10am on the Saturday. The following Wednesday, the Northern Counties eleven would do the same from the Victoria Hotel in Nottingham, to Trent Bridge. Players would have to pay for their hotel stay out of their match fee of £45. Counties were careful to look for their money's worth from their overseas players; Nottinghamshire for example wrote to Lord's that Sobers' contract would not let him play for Northern Counties, even though the county had a blank few days in the County Championship then.

If it sounded thankless for the players, police would have an even longer working day. For a Springboks Saturday afternoon match at Twickenham in November 1969, police – some 32 inspectors, 87 sergeants and 662 constables – had paraded at local stations or at the ground from 11.30am. If cricket began at 11am, police would go on duty soon after breakfast. Or even before; the Met horses and riders had been ready to leave Hammersmith at 6.30am to do their duty outside the Springboks' match at Leicester, and returned to London after 9.30pm.

Would students be about on a Saturday morning?! For the match that never was they may have copied the more leisurely LSE students who had met at Waterloo station at midday to take the train to Twickenham in November 1969. Those student organisers had already – and correctly – suspected police informers, because they asked demonstrators to congregate in 'certain stands'. Where on the day, three men and a woman named on a leaflet (one found its way into Special Branch hands) would say. The leaflet advised students to wear 'respectable clothes' and 'not to appear to be in a large group'. We ought not to assume that all would be against the tour; going to Twickenham that November were four coaches from Sussex University outside Brighton, including members of the uni's rugby club, who favoured (so Special Branch presumed) the Springboks.

In a beautifully-detailed technical drawing, the police drew up exactly where and how many officers would stand on duty at Lord's, such as a pair at the main entrance of the members' pavilion and some even inside. A 'process centre' behind the Mound Stand would handle arrests. Lord's gave police space for a canteen, for senior officers to park their cars, and 20 coaches to bring the coppers. It meant less car parking for everyone else. The MCC proposed the head groundsman's house at the East Gate as a temporary police station.

On the rugby tour, police had patrolled the ground at Leicester for a week before the match. Police knew to divert buses and traffic on the day. A leaflet (as first used around Grosvenor Square before the anti-American march of July 1968) delivered to ten streets around Lord's advised the 5,000 residents (including the Beatle Paul McCartney) not to leave their cars parked in the street; in case police towed them away.

Police would brief stewards inside the ground. Stewards could not act as vigilantes (which implied that was exactly how some saw themselves). If demonstrators got on the field of play, stewards had to call for police; likewise stewards had to report anyone shouting slogans, flashing mirrors or throwing things. Police from the five Test grounds and South Wales met at Nottinghamshire Police headquarters in April to agree tactics, such as asking caterers to pour drink into plastic beakers; because broken bottles could be nasty weapons, or thrown on the field. Police would not even allow beer cans in case demonstrators used the ring-pulls as knuckle-dusters. Police wanted long-handled shovels and buckets of water to hand, in case of smoke flares; and bolt cutters, because on the rugby tour demonstrators had chained themselves to things. Birmingham and Nottingham would have about 150 stewards. Those at Lord's would wear badges; at Birmingham, white coats and armbands; at Nottingham, different coloured armbands each day - alive to the risk that, just as crafty spectators might take a pass-out ticket one day and try to use it another, so demonstrators might spot the stewards' armband colour one day and copy it the next. By May 21, Edmund King at Warwickshire was saying that only 100 'volunteer stewards' would be on duty for the eight days the South Africans were playing at Edgbaston. While you could understand that few club members wanted to be on their feet all day, risking a roughing-up by younger men, for no pay and not much chance to see the play, cricket was clearly looking to the police to protect it. The senior police at that unreported April meeting reckoned each match would need one or two thousand officers - a colossal number in one place, as all England and Wales had about 91,000 police.

At least police had time to prepare and months of practice. Among the ideas at Lord's was a 'watch committee' and a policeman on each turnstile, presumably to deny entry to anyone who looked like a demonstrator, because also proposed was an 'appeal room' outside the ground where those refused could argue their case. An 'appeal committee' could demand a £5 deposit; or ask questions for the 'applicant' to prove their interest in cricket. Whoever had that idea naively assumed that anyone who knew cricket would not want to disrupt it. And what if someone, refused entry, waited five minutes then told the turnstile he had passed the appeal?!

Some sports grounds, such as Welford Road in Leicester, had enough room for police to enforce two ticket checks, one at the entrance to the car park and another at the turnstiles; Lord's could not. In case of smoke bombs, Lord's proposed to obtain some and try to put them out with sand and water. As pass-outs would be an 'extra burden' on police, Lord's agreed not to offer any.

At any South African match, police on horses would have

controlled the crowds. As early as the Leicester rugby match in November 1969, the city's chief constable John Taylor had praised the Met's horses that 'performed with their usual expert efficiency'. The 15 horses at the Coventry match in January 1970 were 'stretched to the limit', Met Commander John Gerrard reported afterwards. While the police's job of impartially (as they put it) protecting the field of play and allowing peaceful protest was obviously harder over a seven-hour day of cricket than for two hours of rugby, the bobby would put in a day's shift for either, and needed feeding the same. On duty he would only have time for a packed lunch, that he would bring, with his name, rank and number on the box. Afterwards, he would have a cooked meal, no doubt something plain that hundreds of people at a time have to expect; at Leicester in November for example steak and kidney pie, potatoes and peas, apple tart and cream, and roll, cheese and tea; as evocative of England (for better or worse) in 1970 as anything in this story. Less cosy, yet belonging also to the story, an 'Anti Demonstration Association' said it planned to photograph demonstrators and send a dossier to police, besides taking offenders through the civil courts; although those vigilantes did not say how they proposed to put names to the faces. The association also claimed it had recruited a 'freedom force' of ex-servicemen. Police would never have allowed such a challenge to their authority – if it had appeared; such groups that the press in this era credulously and irresponsibly kept featuring may merely have been a bigot beside a telephone. In any case, police on June 6 may well have copied the 'arresting squad' in each corner of Bristol rugby ground in December 1969. Rather than officers leaving their posts, squads of ten constables and a sergeant would catch pitch invaders; and if those squads had too many to give each the caution, noting any reply in the pocket book, and detaining the prisoner until he was photographed and charged, an officer could take a Polaroid photo, write his arresting officer's name on the back, and return to duty. Police, then, were ready for whatever STST had thrown at them so far; but were police ready for everything?

* * *

An informant told Special Branch in late April that STST supporters were keeping the main gate at Lord's 'under observation', to see what commercial vans went in; STST hoped to use one on June 6, 'and if possible drive across the wicket, causing serious damage'. Three blocks of flats overlooked the ground, such as Century Court behind the Tavern pub. Special Branch warned it would be 'quite simple' for demonstrators to trick their way past the caretakers, to 'launch an attack on wickets or players' from the roof.

The Met Police knew weeks before that the June 6 march would begin at Speakers' Corner and wind through Marble Arch, Oxford Street, Portman Square and Gloucester Place, into Park Road before turning left for Lord's. Plain-clothes besides uniformed police may well have accompanied it, because they did at an anti-Vietnam War march in Glasgow the winter before; as came out in court in the case of a drunk bystander who swore and threw a lighted piece of paper at the procession. Outside Lord's, police proposed a cordon of 600 officers down the centre of St John's Wood Road, and mounted police at the gates. Presumably demonstrators would have stood on the city side of the cordon, while the match ticket-holders walked on the other side. Demonstrators and Springbok spectators walking the same way had bantered insults. After months of argument, on STST's D-Day, the two sides may well have been tenser. In his 1971 book, Hain wished organisers had had more time to arrange 'teach ins' and street theatre, which may have lightened the mood; the May 2 protest outside Lord's included what the press called 'satirical playlets' on the pavement; and some demonstrators understood they were on a stage. Outside Exeter rugby ground in December 1969, when a three-deep cordon of police would not budge, protesters left until only two youths and a girl were there. One youth grinned and shouted, 'Look out, we are going to rush you!' and then walked off. However one of the best known ugly truths of modern life is that people in an anonymous crowd (the internet above all) behave less civilly than they would face to face. Inside Twickenham in November 1969, for instance, protesters threw pennies and fruit whenever players came near. If Hain's mid-May likening the affair to 'a runaway truck gathering speed' was threatening, his call for a 'mass demonstration' was believable. After cancellation, Ray Illingworth wrote: "If the tour had gone ahead, there could have been bloodshed." That too was believable. The Leicester match in November 1969 had seen several youths injured, and a policeman bitten by a dog; a 68-year-old bystander broke his collarbone. Insurance did show how cricket's occupations rated. A player was worth £15,000 if dead and £3000 if he lost an eye, hand or foot; an umpire if killed only £2000. The media were probably safest, as the general manager of BBC Outside Broadcasts, Peter Dimmock, remarked in a May 21 letter to Met Police Commissioner Sir John Waldron, asking for 'half an hour for a discussion' on security:

I suspect however that the demonstrators may leave us alone simply because they may hope to take advantage of the communications medium as a shop window for their demonstrations. Nevertheless we must clearly be able to satisfy our staff that we have taken all reasonable precautions to protect them and our equipment.

Dimmock did not seem to wonder whether television were truly a 'shop window' for demos, and if so, whether it was ethical for the BBC to grant it.

June 6 would probably have looked like anti-apartheid and other protests of the previous weeks. Outside Lord's on May 2, about 30 demonstrators – outnumbered by police – chanted, paraded with banners and handed out leaflets to those entering to watch Middlesex and Hampshire on the first day of the County Championship season. Most of the leaflets went in bins. The Saturday after, an anti-Cambodia war rally headed for Grosvenor Square, peacefully until about 600 broke away and rushed a police cordon. Some ran down Regent Street, scaring shoppers. In his book Hain admitted the 'aggressive chanting, blowing of whistles' and 'Sieg Heils' by demonstrators at the Springbok rugby matches, besides 'constant scuffling on the terraces'. In other words, angered rugby supporters fought back. Hain recalled the 'venom' of some. If the meek shied away from the D-Day at Lord's, Nazi salutes may have riled even mild-mannered middle-aged cricket watchers. June 6 might have become as notorious a scrap as the mass picket at Saltley coke depot in Birmingham in 1972. For the sake of an industrial, or political victory, miners' union leader Arthur Scargill and his kind put lives at risk, simply because so many volatile people were in a small, perhaps confined, space. Frank Williamson the inspector of constabulary had seen it at Leicester in November 1969, when demonstrators tried to force a way through or outflank the police cordons. Had they reached the rugby ground, the match would have been abandoned, he reported: '... and it is not idle conjecture to express the view that the reaction of some 10,000 spectators would have been so strong as to create an extremely serious public order problem'. Outside the ground, rugby fans rescued a policeman who 'almost fell under the wheels of a bus'; a youth on the ground got kicked in the head; demonstrators, including girls, were crushed against cars at a standstill. Rugby fans turned on demonstrators that police let go; and cried 'lynch them' at the long-haired ones that police did arrest. In a court case after the Leicester match, a 25-year-old postgraduate denied and was cleared of a public order offence – refusing to move when he was sitting in the road, linking arms with others. He spoke of a 'very confused' scene, and people 'being thrown on top of one another'. Another Leicester University student, in court after the Springboks' match in Manchester in December 1969, said a van had to brake sharply to avoid knocking him down, as he too sat in the road, arms linked. Many other court cases showed the risks to life: of demonstrators being choked as police took them into vans, or police hurt as those arrested lashed out. As likely, a tragedy would have come by accident: a trip under a horse, or a head broken on the kerb. At the meeting of Jim Callaghan and chief constables on November 24, 1969, someone recalled the 'Bolton disaster' of 1946, when football fans were crushed to death.

Peter Hain had told the Oxford Union, 'we have rejected the smooth approach and adopted the effective one'; tellingly he then denied that 'direct action' would mean disorder. Either he did not understand, or did and chose to go ahead anyway: once protest broke civilised norms, anything could happen. At least some of those chanted, sworn or hooted at would react violently; some protest would take a more violent turn; and so on. An echo of Hain's irresponsibility as leader was the reckless shoving of people, 'and forcing them, demonstrators and spectators alike, down the terracing into the struggling, jostling mob against the police officers', that Met Police Deputy Assistant Commissioner John Lawlor reported after the first Springboks match, at Twickenham. The fences and barbed wire around cricket and rugby grounds would stop protesters invading the pitch, like the barriers at football grounds against hooligans; except, it left the crowd fenced off from the police. As early as 1969, an official 'working party on crowd behaviour at football matches' heard of 'the possibility of a major catastrophe'. For that reason the crushings to death at Hillsborough in 1989, or somewhere else another day, were inevitable.

Some protesters, denied one route, were resourceful enough to find riskier ones, like the 19-year-old Coventry student at the Leicester match who got onto a rugby ground roof, 'to voice my opinion. I was quite orderly about it,' he told magistrates, who bound him over for a breach of the peace. He had understood that the closer protest could get to the thing protested against, the better; inside the ground was better than out. As Hain admitted to the Oxford Union, after the rugby tour, demonstrations outside grounds had proved a 'tactical failure'.

For June 6, then, STST wanted something new, whether a noisier or greater number of demonstrators, or a novel tactic. Given that, as the Birmingham Post noted on May 20, 'one small boy walking in front of a sightscreen is enough to halt a cricket match', the newspaper shuddered to think of 'what sort of ingenuity' the militants had prepared. STST had aired in public, all along, plenty of ingenious possibilities, whether to inform supporters, to frighten spectators into staying at home, or because STST's leaders couldn't keep their mouths shut. On Panorama in April, Hain had claimed the main protest would be 'to run on the pitch and stay there'. At the STST launch event in September 1969, someone had suggested letting off coloured balloons. Fareed Jafri, writing in the Pakistan Times (dutifully sent to the Foreign Office by diplomats) gave as long a list of possible tactics as any: letting rabbits loose, extra fielders, a bogus 12th man with drinks, the crowd refusing to return the ball; extra balls thrown on the field; slow hand claps; and mirrors. Lone stealth could work too; the only arrest at the Bristol rugby match in December 1969 had been of a 45-year-old man in a shabby raincoat, who strolled onto the field at half time, and spread pins and nails. More drastically, a black South African exile working as a translator, Oscar Faku-Juqula, wrote to his local MP Quintin Hogg in April, warning that he would pour petrol over himself and set it on fire at Lord's, in protest against apartheid. Mr Faku-Juqula wrote likewise to Lord's. Hogg passed his letter to police who took it seriously enough for an inspector to call. He reported to Sir John Waldron that the man seemed sincere, 'but he stated he would give notice of any future possible intentions'. That strange case is one more example of how whatever the campaigners did, or threatened, was for a purpose, to provoke a political change; and politics implies dialogue, even with an enemy. For their own reasons, the police wanted to liaise with the STST organisers, as the April meeting at Nottingham agreed. Demonstrators would want to approach reasonably near to the entrance of cricket grounds; 'police should compromise'. After the cancellation, Tom Graveney grumbled that 'now Hain, Sheppard and company have got their way, the only people to suffer are the coloured South African cricketers and the vast majority of cricket supporters in this country'. Some of what the former England batsman said was absurd – how were coloureds in South Africa, denied their rights, made any worse off by the end of all-white tours? – but Graveney had spotted the anti-tour movement was in pieces.

At least three strands of protest would have converged

on Lord's on June 6: the polite Christians like Sheppard; the louder students under Hain; and what UA Titley in Country Life magazine after the Springboks tour had called 'a raucous minority caucus of professedly anti-apartheid young agitators, many of whom know quite remarkably little about apartheid and many of whom as several authorities alleged bore a striking resemblance to the front rows of those demonstrating against quite different things'. As early as November 1969, in notes for Jim Callaghan before his meeting with chief constables, JH Waddell the deputy under secretary of state at the Home Office wrote that many demonstrators were sincerely against apartheid, as were most people in the country: 'However as on other occasions the processions of demonstrators are often taken over by other bodies like anarchists who are seeking other objectives which include confrontation with the police and the introduction of violence.' It not only suited government to blame 'anarchists'. After meeting Sir Edward Boyle, the former Conservative minister behind the 'Fair Cricket' campaign, Callaghan told the Cabinet on May 7:

.... the moderate opponents of the tour intended to draw up a code of conduct for demonstrators. This would be widely publicised and it should help to separate the moderate faction from the more radical elements associated with the Stop The Seventy Tour, which were believed to have been in touch with extremist coloured organisations. There was no doubt that some degree of disorder must be expected if the tour proceeded.

The longer that STST ran, the more banners and stunts for the television cameras, and irresponsible speeches to thrill the enthusiasts ('I am not suggesting you throw bricks at policemen, but you must demonstrate', Solly Sachs told a public meeting in Golders Green in May 1970, thus planting the idea in everyone's head of throwing bricks), like any idealists STST would face Arthur Koestler's 'Law of Detours'. Either the radicals, anarchists, extremists – whatever you wanted to call them – took charge by force, or the peaceful idealists had to crush the radicals, in the name (paradoxically) of moderation, and lost their ideals.

Some outsiders saw it. EW Swanton met Hain and Dennis Brutus confidentially at the offices of The Cricketer, that he edited. Swanton found the men sincere; 'but however fervently these two might say that they were committed to "non-violent action" there were others who would stop at nothing'. Other movements – women's suffrage, Irish and other nationalisms – had faced the same dilemma. The demonstrators wished to lead public opinion, said an Oxford Times editorial in January 1970: "So be it – public opinion is there to be led ... but if in their innocence they think it can be *driven* then they are likely to be disillusioned."

That said, politics was rarely as perfect as STST; the demos would either 'stop the tour' or not; there lay the appeal. Usually politics meant give and take; 'some degree of disorder'; and, as Callaghan also reported to the Cabinet, the disorder could be 'contained'. One ingredient of June 6 would have been out of anyone's control; the weather. Yet a rainy day and no play would have only put off the 'trial of strength', and perhaps made it even more fraught when it came. In fact June 6 was fine; Surrey and Essex had a full day at the Oval. June 6 had all the ingredients – the venue, the occasion, the time of week – for the biggest protest yet. At the other extreme, the Springboks match in Ebbw Vale on a midweek November night – a ground physically easy to defend, far from universities and anarchist squats – had passed without trouble. Callaghan told the Cabinet on April 30 that Sir John Waldron was confident that the Met Police could deal with any demos in London; but, Callaghan added, that 'might be too optimistic a forecast'.

After Lord's confirmed the tour for the last time, Sir John Johnston of the Foreign Office had speculated to the British ambassador in Pretoria, Sir Arthur Snelling, that 'a deterioration in Anglo-South African relations' was 'odds on'. Sir John further saw 'a distinct probability' of a match 'prevented, or one of the South Africans molested'. South Africa might call its players home. "Yet another alternative is that the tour will struggle on, each match being interrupted for some of the time with the result that feelings on both sides will get more aggrieved ... meanwhile your posture of the low profile if unheroic is entirely sensible and right."

Having chosen the heroic, high profile, cricket would have to manage it. Demos could have spread to any grounds whose county cricketers had played the tourists. Kent's secretary Les Ames had told Lord's on May 20 that Kent players were free for 'Southern Counties', as Kent had a bye in the Championship then; and Ames asked for them to play for Kent in the Sunday League. STST might in that case have gone to Tunbridge Wells on June 7. Then what? When South Africa went to Bristol in July 1965, the local protest organiser Peter Gregory had said: 'We would like to continue the picket through Monday and Tuesday but this is proving difficult to arrange as we all have our jobs to attend.' Would students have had such scruples?! Who else in their right mind would want to watch South Africa, except those who had to be there – John Arlott had said he would be at Lord's on June 6, to report for the Guardian, though somewhat hypocritically he would not

A newspaper advert for matches that never were; the Northern Counties warm-up, and second Test against South Africa, at Trent Bridge.

broadcast for television. As news broke of the cancellation, Nottinghamshire county club secretary Jack Baddiley was admitting that Trent Bridge had sold hardly any tickets for the second Test match, starting on July 2. The Rest of the World match in its place made a loss. The final, ironic image of a summer of the all-white South Africans on tour is of grounds filled with banners, whistles and hoots – not unlike the typical 21st century Test match – and the only income from spectators coming from demonstrators. The contest between the stamina of those protesting, and the slow tempo of the game of cricket, may have been as watchable as whatever the two teams were able to create on the field of play.

If your business is with Africa the mountain will come to you

And save you a lot of time and trouble.
Standard Bank is big in Africa, with over 1,200 offices in 19 countries of that big continent. Each office has an intimate understanding of local conditions and regulations and is ready, at a word from us in London, to help speed up whatever operations your business plans involve.
And you don't have to 'go to the mountain'. The mountain will come to you. Just drop the word to our Business Development Division at Head Office, 10 Clements Lane, London, E.C.4. (Telephone 01-623 7500). We will call on you, help formulate your plans and then get the strength of our local organisation working for you.
There are great advantages in having Standard Bank at both ends of your African operations. For a start, you don't need to get up from your desk.

Standard Bank

The Standard Bank Limited The bank that builds business
A member of Standard and Chartered Banking Group

May 1970 advert for Standard Bank; another bank that did not advertise its investment in apartheid.

Chapter Fourteen

After the end

By now you must be absolutely sold on the idea of touring.
Karen and Gary Hawkins, Bicycle Touring in Europe, 1974

For the rest of this story, the South Africans were like the Britons after Roman rule ended around 410, or the Jacobites after 1688. *We* know that their cause was lost; *they* had to find out. After cancellation Norman Yardley said that 'the real way to help the whole situation was to keep on playing South Africa'. Many cricketers did; only, not on official international tours. In his 1976 autobiography, John Snow recalled how the crowd rose to salute Derrick Robins' touring team in the autumn of 1973, that included the Pakistani Younis Ahmed and West Indian John Shepherd. Did black lives improve? Snow answered his own question: "No. It will take more than isolating South African cricket ...." While Snow, a contrary man, was right enough, he did not see that sport could only do so much; if others did not play their part, that was not cricket's problem.

As early as the Cambridge Union debate of November 1969, Denis Howell pointed out that every concession from South Africa was 'the result not of association but of protest'. In other words, touring as if South Africa were as normal as Australia, as if players magically sprinkled liberal dust, was 'a formula for inertia'. John Woodcock seemed to agree. In The Cricketer in May 1970 he wrote that 'for far too long far too little has been done by the white South African Cricket Association to recognise the moral and technical claims of non-white cricketers'. Disappointed by cancellation, D'Oliveira believed some contact was essential, 'if we are to have any influence'. D'Oliveira was not the only Coloured South African athlete in England however. The weight-lifter Precious Mackenzie, working in a tannery in Bristol, was about to represent England at the Commonwealth Games. Before cancellation he hoped enough countries would boycott the Games to make them flop.

Anti-apartheid began to claim victims, besides apartheid. Gary Sobers was about to go through what he called in his 2003 autobiography 'the worst period of my cricketing life'. After Sobers captained the Rest of the World in the summer of 1970, 'a team of liquorice all sorts in complete harmony', as Sobers' biographer Trevor Bailey put it quaintly in 1976, Sobers took up an invitation to partner Ali Bacher in a two-day, double wicket competition in Rhodesia. The easy-going Sobers – 'I couldn't see for the life of me what all the fuss was about' - had fallen for white southern African hospitality. Some felt genuinely angry that Sobers was enjoying himself while whites oppressed the black African masses. Many more, Bailey added, 'simply used the affair for their own ends'; on both sides. Tory newspapers such as the Daily Express praised Sobers, politicians on rival West Indian islands wanted an apology, or else. On October 30, 1970 JAB Stewart speculated to the Foreign Office

Gary Sobers batting for the Rest of the World in the 1970 season; Alan Knott keeps wicket for England.

from the British High Commission in Barbados that Sobers was 'got at', 'most likely by his wife', to apologise, and so 'averted the crisis in West Indian cricket'. Stewart called it 'a miserable tale'. At least Sobers learned his lesson; in his autobiography he recalled several invitations to play in South Africa, 'but I refused them all'.

* * *

If a woman splits from an unfaithful husband, it's not enough for the man to change his ways to win her back - the woman has to trust him again. For South Africa to play international cricket again, apartheid had to fall; or, show enough change; and even then, enough of the spectrum of outside opinion had to believe in South African goodwill. Some were suspiciously easily convinced. While still British ambassador in Pretoria, in April 1969 Sir Jack Nicholls wrote to the FO that Vorster's 'concessions' (evidently he kept offering them; years passed and nothing much changed) might appear 'inadequate', but were 'considerably in advance of his party, and public opinion in general'. Nicholls believed a boycott would be 'totally counter-productive'. At the other extreme, Imran Khan wrote in his 1988 autobiography that 'the Third World nations have a clear view on apartheid and believe there should be a complete embargo on South Africa'. Imran was the authentic voice of many more countries than Pakistan: with the pride of the newly independent, he was quick to take offence at the 'colonial and arrogant' English; although, or perhaps precisely because, he captained Oxford University at cricket.

Outsiders were assuming that South Africans knew, and would care about, what other people thought of them. On the brink of cancellation, Mike Procter showed this was not so. "I didn't realise how strong the feelings in this country were," he said. "I am quite certain people back in South Africa are not fully aware of the feelings despite the fact that they were fully aware of the events in the rugby tour." That implied, if cricket in South Africa were to undo the boycott, someone there would have to show some political leadership. SACA could not. As early as the winter of 1968-69, EW Swanton in The Cricketer had described it as 'an unimaginative, not to say timid body'. Even if - in a world without D'Oliveira - South Africa had toured in 1970, it would have come a cropper in the first World Cup, agreed in 1972, to run in England in 1975. Then South Africa - and West Indies, India and Pakistan - would have been like two aunts that will not talk to each other, that you had to keep apart at a family wedding. Even then, you would have to take sides by talking to one or the other. JL Manning, in the jubilee issue of The Cricketer in April 1971, correctly judged that cricket could not pay the price of retaining South Africa: "International cricket by definition must be multi-racial cricket. There can be no compromise." In his review of 1971 for the Times, John Woodock noted that South Africa's isolation had already 'intensified'. So had English efforts to break it.

Mike Procter in his 2017 memoir recalled a tour by an 'England Invitation XI' as 'a great opportunity missed'. In the English summer of 1971, D'Oliveira was 'naturally excited' and made 'quiet approaches to get his touring party together'. However SACA meeting in September 1971 refused the tour, 'with little explanation'. MCC had no winter tour in 1971-72 because India fell through. A few Englishmen - Norman Gifford, Richard Hutton, Bob Taylor and above all Tony Greig - featured for the Rest of the World in Australia. Otherwise, England's leading players had time on their hands. Colin Cowdrey did all he could to give them some South African hospitality.

* * *

After Cowdrey failed, Ted Heath's private office typed a letter in mid-January 1972 for the prime minister to sign, that regretted 'the breakdown of your negotiations to arrange a multi-racial cricket tour to South Africa this winter'. As any PM is a busy man - an enabling Bill for Britain to join the Common Market went to Parliament later that month - Cowdrey had gone through Heath's private office. Cowdrey evidently had Tory backing. On

January 11, the Foreign Office sent a message to the British ambassador in Pretoria, that Cowdrey was planning to tour, with D'Oliveira and three other non-whites, to play white, Coloured, Indian and black African teams. Cowdrey had an assurance from the Nationalist government that they could visit; would those various races' cricketing bodies agree? D'Oliveira had arrived in Cape Town, where his parents lived, before Christmas. Over the 'phone D'Oliveira told Cowdrey that Hassan Howa would ban Coloureds and Indians from playing Cowdrey's team. That would leave one three-day match against a black South African team, and otherwise matches against white teams. Cowdrey sensibly saw that was not multi-racial enough to work. Conversations between Cowdrey and D'Oliveira were even more tense because the D'Oliveiras had no telephone and D'Oliveira had to use a friend's 'phone. He cannot have liked to pay for an inter-continental call, when Cowdrey asked D'Oliveira to ring back. The crunch came at a meeting in Cape Town on Wednesday, January 12, when D'Oliveira and Howa faced local Coloured cricketers. At least some, like Howa, wanted nothing to do with segregated sport; and did not want D'Oliveira to, either.

Christopher Roberts of Heath's private office rang Cowdrey on the morning of January 11. He took Cowdrey to see William Wilson, a Foreign Office man working on southern Africa. The FO thought that Cowdrey 'should be encouraged to go ahead as planned'. Sir Alec Douglas-Home, Heath's Foreign Secretary, was 'inclined to think that D'Oliveira's proposal that he [D'Oliveira] should make a public statement' at the Wednesday meeting 'would not help matters'. Once again here was the standard Foreign Office view; the less you rocked the boat, the better your chance of doing a deal. In an earlier, January 7, call to Roberts, Cowdrey had passed on D'Oliveira's view that most Coloureds wanted the tour, but 'some of the more politically minded' did not. D'Oliveira asked Cowdrey for advice. Cowdrey rang Heath's office, asking for ten minutes of Heath's time. Heath initialled the page and wrote simply 'yes'.

Cowdrey's tour was serious, although 'of course an entirely

Kent and West Indies all-rounder John Shepherd.

private venture', as Roberts had told Heath in a memo. Cowdrey was also running out of time; he intended to go in February and March. His strikingly strong proposed team, as reported in the Guardian, had plenty of Kent men: Brian Luckhurst, Mike Denness, Alan Knott, John Jameson, Alan Ward, Derek Underwood, Geoff Arnold, Bob Willis, Pat Pocock, Tony Greig, Dennis Amiss or Keith Fletcher, D'Oliveira, John Shepherd, Harry Latchman, Asif Iqbal and Majid Khan. The Rest of the World were due to end in Australia at the end of January, giving Greig time to fly on. Names not there were as revealing; no Geoffrey Boycott, and no Raymond Illingworth, who reportedly had wanted to be captain. Cowdrey had already hurdled one obstacle. Rhodesia had asked him to visit too. Douglas-Home no less had stuck to the Foreign Office line; that Britain avoided contacts with the illegal Rhodesian regime. While Cowdrey and his team as 'private British citizens' had the right to go, their visit could prove 'an unwelcome embarrassment which would attract a great deal of attention'. Cowdrey took the hint. He could make the excuse that the tour did not have the time to include Rhodesia.

D'Oliveira, under pressure, cried off. Cowdrey issued a statement that he had not had enough time to 'prepare the ground', although he hoped to bring the tour about 'at the earliest opportunity'. In his 'Dear Colin' letter, Heath made plain that he stood by Cowdrey: "I am sorry that despite all your hard work this promising initiative has not for the time being come off. And I hope that it may be possible for a tour of this kind to be arranged at a later stage. Best wishes for '72, yours, Ted Heath." In a scribbled note, Heath revealed shocking nastiness towards D'Oliveira:

I always knew D'Oliveira would rat. It is one thing to have a willow in your hand and quite another to bend like a willow before every breeze.

Basil D'Oliveira.

* * *

In truth better chances would never come, because England resumed touring every winter. Likewise 1715 was a better chance for a Jacobite restoration than the '45, and the Battle of the Boyne better than either. The men who had done all they could to stand by white South Africa were still around; indeed, flourishing. Aidan Crawley for example became MCC president in 1972, nominated by his contemporary Freddie Brown. Crawley in his 1988 memoir singled out apartheid as an example where the president was more than a figurehead; he was 'the voice of cricket'. Wilfred Wooller retired after the 1977 season, when he was about to turn 65. Glamorgan were broke and near the bottom of the county championship. That was not Wooller's fault; nothing ever was, because he always had someone to blame. The weekend before cancellation, he reported from Worcester on the Worcestershire-Surrey county game for the Sunday Telegraph. He hailed 'this typical English scene which one felt would endure when the long-haired demonstrators had gone bald'. Who had been the more fanatical in this story; the protesters, or Wilfred Wooller? He had been happy to risk the bankruptcy of English cricket, and cracked heads of policemen and protesters. Blood is never on the hands of men like Wooller and Crawley. Indeed, as that dispatch from Worcester showed, Wooller and his kind dressed themselves in conservative ideas as respectable as their clothes. That made Wooller more dangerous to democracy than any planter of bombs or hijacker of aircraft.

* * *

Wooller and his kind were like the Romano-British landowners after 410; men in authority, whose power was passing, well within a generation, to new-comers. In May 1970, in a letter to the Portsmouth News, Mrs VE Chester of Warnford recalled how six years before Hampshire cricket club had 'asked us if we would entertain a team of cricket tourists from Mashonaland, in Rhodesia'. The small private ground – in that hilly stretch of southern England where cricket may have begun, near Hambledon – duly hosted the white farmers. "A good time was had by all and our villagers watched the match which was sponsored by my late husband." The Rhodesians had all fought in the 1939-45 war; their non-playing captain had lost a leg in action. "They told us theirs was the last country in Africa still flying the Union Jack and how proud they were of the fact." Compare that to 1977, when Sussex arranged for its second eleven to play the Willows, a South African side, at the Manor ground, Worthing. The Sussex club secretary Stanley Allen noted the Brighton Argus was 'rather sensationally reporting about possible demonstrations'. Allen was not happy about the Willows playing at Hove, 'because we wouldn't want demonstrations and possible damage'. The will to defy protest had gone. In August 1979, when Sussex's South African player Garth Le Roux was allegedly talking about a proposed tour to South Africa, a club committee told Allen to 'try and persuade him to keep his mouth shut'. Those who stood by apartheid were not reformed; only silenced.

Another Sussex player, Imran Khan, in his 1988 book contrasted how quick English cricket was to try to ban men for playing for Packer, with how those who went on tour to South Africa – some the same men – carried on for their counties, while serving bans from playing for England. Imran described apartheid as 'the yardstick by which commitment to human rights is measured'. Famous English cricketers went on tours to South Africa regardless, first in 1982, then 1990, ironically cut short by demonstrations. In July 1989, the new England Test player Angus Fraser was sitting in the dressing room at Old Trafford when 'one by one various England players used to come in to see Embers [Fraser's Middlesex teammate John Emburey], who seemed to be at the centre of things, and discuss with him whether they were going to South Africa'. Fraser like everyone else called the tours 'rebel' when in truth so many famous cricketers went, they were the norm. A 'rebel' was someone like Derek Randall, who was loyal to England, and did not take Packer's or apartheid's money. At a talk in 2017 I asked him if he had ever been asked to go to South Africa, and would he have gone? He began his reply talking about Packer, and I wondered if he was not listening, or was avoiding the question. I was under-estimating the man. He said: "Never even thought about it. Not South Africa …. may as well have gone and taken the money, because they treat you like rubbish, an ex-player. Sad, really." Of all the cricketers in this story, Randall showed the soundest moral compass; a man looked down on (if we are honest) as scatter-brained, and unrewarded.

* * *

John Woodcock, who reported on both 'rebel' tours, and who became 'a good friend' of Ali Bacher the organiser, recalled in 2017: "All to do with money. Every man has his price, as you saw in the days of Packer, and now anywhere, really." While Fraser did not deny the money – he smelled 'a mercenary attitude in the air' in 1989 - he hinted at a moral dimension, that had a tangible outcome. By putting money first, the 'rebels' put the England team second; they were not as competitive as Australia, which began a generation of thrashings of England. Perhaps the second-best England teams of that era were apartheid's last victim.

Or; perhaps England got what they deserved. The real victims, besides the obvious ones such as Nelson Mandela and others in prison, were the South Africans who unlike Basil D'Oliveira never became who they could have been. The Australian journalist Rohan Rivett in 1971 deplored how 'a coloured Bradman or Sobers will never be allowed to represent his country'. The BBC sports commentator Peter West, who visited an old school friend in South Africa in 1985, in his 1986 memoir complained that cricket and other sports there had become genuinely multi-racial, yet remained 'snubbed'. West however had to admit coyly that rugby was 'not yet so wholly integrated'. That did not stop him condemning governments as hypocritical for trading with South Africa. The hypocrites, to judge by the advertising boards around the grounds where the 'rebel' tourists played in 1982, were businesses, selling cigarettes, Dunlop tyres, and the like. Trade in cricketers, or what Imran Khan called 'collaboration', was widespread.

Tony Lewis gave a captain's report to Glamorgan's AGM in February 1971. Their bowler Malcolm Nash had suffered a hip injury the August before; he was 'relaxing in South Africa'. The trade was two-way; in 1977 for instance, from Western Province alone, Garth Le Roux, Peter Kirsten and Allan Lamb landed in England, seeking their fortune. They,

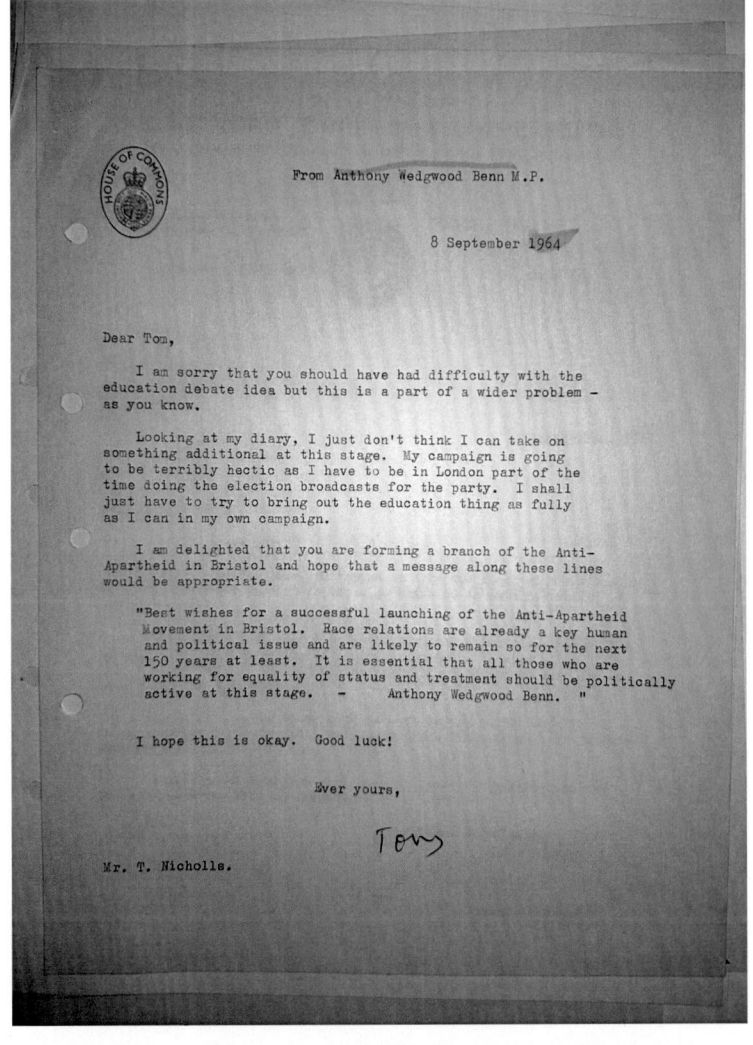

A September 1964 letter by Bristol MP Tony Benn, busy with Labour's campaign for the general election the next month, sending a 'best wishes' message to a local Anti-Apartheid Movement group.

and other white South Africans, plugged at once into the small world of world cricket, that gathered in England each summer. Bar Yorkshire, county clubs - seeking cheap, keen talent - gladly took them. English cities, meanwhile, were quietly segregating according to skin colour, besides wealth and social class. Sports grounds remained one of the few places where people of all colours mixed; provided they had the entry money. Apartheid in England, and in sectarian Scotland, because voluntary, would prove far harder to undo than in South Africa. Perhaps that is what Ron Press had in mind, when he sent a letter to Bristol's MPs in December 1969, ahead of the Springbok match and demo in the city. Two from Labour, Ray Dobson and John Ellis, signed and returned theirs. It said: "Together we can reverse the trend apparent in some quarters to accept, condone and introduce the apartheid system into Britain." Another Bristol Labour MP was the minister Anthony Wedgewood Benn. In September 1964 he sent a 'best wishes' message to Tom Nicholls, who was forming an anti-apartheid branch in Bristol. Benn wrote: "Race relations are already a key human and political issue and are likely to remain so for the next 150 years at least." We have less than a hundred years to go.

Burton upon Trent, January-March and August-November 2018

* * *

Thanks and sources

We have explored a subject which at first sight scarcely seemed to merit so detailed an investigation.
　　　　　　　　　　PJC Perry, Hours into Minutes (1966)

After finishing my biography of Brian Sellers, Yorkshire Tyrant, in the spring of 2017, I had the idea for Tour de Farce from reading Douglas Miller's biography of Raman Subba Row that summer. He covers 1970 on pages 123-4. As with my other books, I wanted to learn about a story that seemed forgotten. I began research at Worcester, during the 2017 conference of the British Society for Sports History (BSSH), where I appreciated ideas from Prof Dil Porter in a queue for lunch. Thanks to Raf Nicholson for sharing an article on women's cricket. At Worcester's library, The Hive, I read the local newspapers and Basil D'Oliveira's 1969 autobiography. Much later, in a charity bookshop in the city I bought Portrait of a Politician by the over-opinionated MP Sir Gerald Nabarro (1969, signed by the author). Evocative chapters on Africa and immigration revealed the Tory world-view.

A first stop was at Lord's, to go through the important MCC paperwork, thanks to librarian Neil Robinson. While some files about the tour are not open to the public, an advance since I last did research there is the online catalogue. Later MCC passed on my letter to Mike Brearley who sent me a kind and helpful email. At Trent Bridge, Peter Wynne-Thomas was as ever a help, not only providing the Nottinghamshire club minutes, but as a living encyclopaedia. Peter knew for example Rowland Bowen, whose Cricket Quarterly I enjoyed, on the shelves at the Trent Bridge library. Also useful were the Glamorgan club records at Glamorgan council archives, in the shadow of Cardiff City FC's stadium; and the Sussex club records, at The Keep, the Sussex county council archives outside Brighton. I was grateful to Stephen Hedges, the biographer of his father, the Glamorgan player Bernard, for discussing Wilfred Wooller with me. See throughout

Thanks and sources

Stephen Hedges' The Player from 'Ponty' (2019), for Wooller's background. For two of many views on Wooller, see AA Thompson in Cricket Banquet (1961), pages 115-6; and the essay by John Arlott in the Welsh anthology, Sport (2009), edited by Gareth Williams, pages 222-6. Wooller in his own words is in Cricket Voices: Interviews with Mihir Bose (1990), pages 107-126.

I went through Foreign Office, Home Office and Cabinet Office records at the National Archives at Kew. I gave a flavour in the May 2018 issue of the Magazine of the Friends of the National Archives.

Another main source were newspapers of the day. In order roughly from south to north, I went through The News, my old 'paper, at Portsmouth central library; the Express & Echo, at Devon county archives, Exeter, also housing Devon Life magazine that ran an evocative column by RF Delderfield; the Brighton Argus at The Keep; the Bristol Evening Post and Western Daily Press at Bristol central library; Salisbury Journal, Salisbury library; the Birmingham Post, and Sports Argus, Birmingham central library; the Western Daily Mail, Cathays library, Cardiff; Oxford Times, Oxfordshire county archives; Derby Evening Telegraph and Derbyshire Advertiser, the Magic Attic, Swadlincote; Leicester Mercury, Leicestershire county archives, Wigston Magna; Nottingham Evening Post, Nottingham central library; Sheffield Morning Telegraph, Sheffield library; Yorkshire Post, Yorkshire Evening Post and Green Un, Leeds central library; Yorkshire Evening Press, York library; Manchester Evening News, Manchester central library, where I read Peter Hain's book Don't Play with Apartheid on the shelves; and Lancashire Evening Post, Preston library. I read the Times and Guardian online as a member of Manchester libraries; and other national 'papers, the Daily Worker and the London Evening Standard, at the British Library at St Pancras. Local London newspapers I read at Holborn library; and City of Westminster archives.

Irish newspapers I read upstairs at the National Library of Ireland in Dublin on Tuesday, September 4, 2018. Thanks to my friend Donie O'Callaghan I better know the city's geography. Scottish newspapers I read in January 2018 while I was giving a pair of talks on Sellers to the cricket societies in Glasgow and Edinburgh. I read the Glasgow Herald at the Mitchell library, despite a mid-morning evacuation when the fire alarm went off; and The Scotsman and Aberdeen's Press & Journal at the National Library of Scotland in Edinburgh. After the Edinburgh talk, I won in the raffle and took away a useful bound volume of Playfair Cricket Monthly from 1968-69, also stocked at Trent Bridge. For an Australian view, the Canberra Times online is free to view on the Trove part of the National Library of Australia website.

It's striking how few of the people in this story were still going, near 50 years on. Robin Knight met me at the pub next door to Lord's in the summer of 2018. John Woodcock I met at his Longparish home in November 2017. After I broke off writing the book, Ruth Henig was kind in conversation. For the background to protest, Prof Joshua Bamfield was a help; he stood incidentally for Labour against Enoch Powell in the 1970 election. David Moore let me look through his old volumes of The Cricketer; if I had had as much good conversation elsewhere, I would never have got my work done. I gave a paper to the sports history group Spleish at the Crewe campus of Manchester Metropolitan University in March 2018; and at the 2018 BSSH conference at the University of Westminster, spoke on the might-have-beens at Lord's on June 6, 1970, only a stone's throw from that day's likely protest march route. The autumn 2018 journal of the Association of Cricket Statisticians carried my article, 'What Ted Heath thought of Dolly' about Cowdrey's failed effort to tour South Africa in the English winter of 1971-72, based on the Kew file Prem 15/1221. I appreciated a kind email afterwards from Bernard Whimpress.

An article in the Cricket Society journal of autumn 2018 courtesy of editor Nigel Hancock led to a 'phone conversation with Howard Hanley in Australia, who gave his intriguing story of Moscow airport. David Frith obligingly looked up the April 1982 cover of Wisden Cricket Monthly, that featured the 'rebel' English tourists in South Africa, and the advertising boards that showed western companies doing business with apartheid. In fairness, I did buy a copy at the time.

It's odd that the 1970 tour was front page news at the time, then has had so little written about it ever since; Peter Oborne for example in his history of the D'Oliveira affair passed over it on pages 234-5. Plenty of books from the time evoke the period, such as Michael Stewart's The British Approach to Politics (sixth edition, 1967) about how Britain's politics were supposed to run, and the more worldly Anatomy of Britain Today (1965) by Anthony Sampson, and The Body Politic (revised edition, 1971) by Ian Gilmour. Peregrine Worsthorne turned his Sunday Telegraph columns into a book, The Socialist Myth (1971), that from pages 130-37 significantly linked 'the problem of South Africa' and 'the race problem here at home'. While Cabinet diarists such as Tony Benn and Barbara Castle hardly mentioned the tours, that may say more about the editing later, because the first to publish his Cabinet diaries, Dick Crossman, did cover them; see volume three, pages 846, 878 and 908. See also Roy Jenkins' memoir A Life at the Centre (1991), page 297. Many books tried to explain protest, such as The Student Revolt (1970) by Colin Crouch; see pages 10-11 in particular. For where protesters stood legally, Civil Liberty: NCCL Guide to your Rights (1979) spelled it out, pages 152-53. Any number of books have a bearing on apartheid, race and sport, such as DJ Cameron's account of New Zealand's 1972 tour of West Indies, Caribbean Crusade (1972), page 50.

Most of the cricketers in this story brought out memoirs. Basil D'Oliveira's Time to Declare (1980) set out on pages 88-89 more frankly how he felt in 1970 than he did at the time. Mike Brearley in his On Cricket (2018) goes forensically into the non-selection of D'Oliveira for the South African tour of 1968-69; see selector Peter May's account in his autobiography A Game Enjoyed (1985), pages 190-91. Like others, what May did not write about – his cutting of an old friend such as David Sheppard, because they disagreed with over the Seventy tour – is as interesting as what he did write. Any number of works by and about cricket people before 1970 show how most people took South Africa for granted, as a normal destination, such as chapter 18, 'I meet the South Africans', in Godfrey Evans' 1951 memoir Behind the Stumps; and Christopher Martin-Jenkins' chapter on South Africa in his CMJ (2012). Alan Ross in Cape Summer (1957) was more uneasy; see the final page 252.

Some works shine an unflattering light, such as Stephen Robinson's biography The Remarkable Lives of Bill Deedes (2008). According to page 270, Deedes wrote to Vorster, asking him to cancel the tour. Even more surprisingly, Vorster wrote back, refusing. Hypocritically Deedes' Daily Telegraph condemned Labour for the tour's cancellation. As for rugby, Gareth Edwards does 'soul searching' about touring South Africa during apartheid at suspicious – uneasy? - length in his 1999 autobiography.

For authoritative, brief treatments of the D'Oliveira affair including 1970, see Arlott and Trueman on Cricket (1977), pages 112-14; David Frith's article in the 1986 edition of The World of Cricket, edited by Jim Swanton, pages 280-81; and Irving Rosenwater's, The South African Tour Dispute, in Wisden Cricketers' Almanack 1971, pages 128-141. Robert Winder in his history of Wisden, Little Wonder (2013) rather delicately describes this story as 'not Wisden's finest hour' (page 264). As Swanton features largely in this story and came out of it well, it's worth reading him further for background; in his memoir Sort of a Cricket Person (1989 edition), pages 221-23; and his chapter on Lord's, 'The Mecca' in his 1977 book Follow On. Swanton's biography of Gubby Allen, Man of Cricket, covers D'Oliveira, pages 288-93, including a photograph of Allen golfing with Keith Miller and Douglas Bader; significant as a meeting of like-minded friends of the wartime generation, with links to the press. For Swanton's influential May 15, 1970 article against the tour, see Last Over (1996) with David Rayvern Allen, pages 193-95. Another Telegraph man, Michael Melford, covered English cricket of the era as well as any in After the Interval (1990), and the tour on page 150.

For some background on the anti-Communist thinking of Aidan Crawley, see his essay in the significant collection Suicide of a Nation? An enquiry into the state of Britain today (1963), pages 94-104. For David Sheppard, see This Sporting Life: Cricket (1999), by Rob Steen, particularly pages 36-39. For Australia's cancellation in 1971, after a controversial Springboks visit, see A History of Australian Cricket (1993), by Chris Harte, pages 532-33; and Jack Pollard's history From Bradman to Border, Australian Cricket 1948-89 (1990), pages 241-2. An interesting Australian comparison is in The Aboriginal Embassy: an account of the protests of 1972, by Scott Robinson, a chapter in Terrible Hard Biscuits: A Reader in Aboriginal History, edited by Valerie Chapman and Peter Read (1996), pages 241-61. Sir Donald Bradman had the good sense to avoid most of the MCC's self-made and drawn-out troubles. Meredith Burgmann's story in Remembering Bradman (2003) by Margaret Geddes gave some background, pages 337-41. Another view – Tony Lock's, on his last day as captain of Western Australia – we can date and place exactly to Monday afternoon, March 1, 1971 on the WACA balcony, in Kirwan Ward's book Put Lock On! (1972). For Lock's anger at the cancellation, see page 109. As for Ireland, Kevin Myers does not mention his protest against the Isaacs tour in his memoir Watching the Door (2006); what he has to say about his summer of 1969 is on page 7.

South Africa was far more important and written about under apartheid than since. For another view of Grahamstown, see The Pilgrim's Way in South Africa (1928), by Dorothea Fairbridge, pages 152-53. One of many studies of white South Africans was Against the World (1966) by Douglas Brown, which touched on sport on pages 35-36. Donald McRae mentions the cancellation in his memoir Under Our Skin (2012), page 54. Volume two of The Cambridge History of South Africa (2012) touches on the place of sport in apartheid South Africa, pages 401-2. The final chapter of South Africa by Arthur Keppel-Jones (third edition, 1963) sets the 1960s scene as well as any; including an intriguing angle on the hospitality to English wartime visitors; it was 'often dangerous' to be in uniform in some Nationalist areas (page 197).

You have to stop somewhere, although various angles have a bearing on this story – the media reporting around 1970, less respectful of authority than before and more ready to give the time of day to protest; anti-apartheid's place in the larger and longer-running student protest movements; the policing of it all; how the Labour government and Tory opposition treated the issue; and how the tour mattered to race relations. To prove there's nothing new under the sun, We Refuse to Starve in Silence: A History of the National Unemployed Workers' Movement 1920-46 (1987) by Richard Croucher, showed that the NUWM were doing 'direct action' protests in London in 1938 (page 191). For proof that 'direct action' was common talk before Hain, see for example French Revolution 1968 (1968) by Patrick Seale and Maureen McConville, page 20. For two other tellings of the STST story by Hain not in this work, see Radical Regeneration (1975) and Sing the Beloved Country (1996), pages 50-61.

You can stop reading when you don't find anything more, which is never; note however that the tour had no mention in David McKie and Chris Cook's guide, Election '70 (1970). That suggested how the tour once cancelled died as a political issue, as Harold Wilson had wanted. For sources in full, visit my Wordpress site, markrowe.wordpress.com.

*　*　*

A note on words: this book uses 'white', 'non-white' and 'coloured' to describe the colour of people's skin. While these terms – as used in apartheid South Africa and Britain – are outdated and may offend, they were the ones used in 1970. As Mihir Bose put it in his 2018 book Lion and Lamb, 'reproduction of this language is necessary to faithfully represent events'.

Again as common at the time, in this story 'Springbok' is a shorthand name for the South African rugby team, and 'South Africa' for its cricketers. I sometimes use 'Lord's'

Thanks and sources

as shorthand for MCC and those in authority in cricket, although it can mean the physical place; and occasionally 'Twickenham' for rugby likewise.

* * *

Index

Abed, Dik 179
Aberystwyth 31, 33
Abrahams, Cec 179
Ackerman, Hylton 53
Ahmed, Younis 69, 242, 248, 315
Aird, Ronnie 11
Aitken, Sir Max 183
Alam, Intikhab 242
Aldermaston 7
All Blacks 62
Allen, Gubby 25, 61, 72, 77, 113, 179, 183, 184, 233, 236, 246, 278, 282, 331
Allen, Sir Philip 99, 100, 108, 175, 182, 193
Allen, Stanley 323
Allom, Maurice 184, 201, 202, 214, 236, 239, 248, 250-251, 254-255, 262, 263
Alston, Rex 38-39, 58, 288
Ames, Leslie 14, 222, 313
Amiss, Dennis 55, 236, 320
Angel, Graham 182
Anti-Apartheid Movement (AAM) 15, 17, 65, 107, 122-123, 267
Anti-Demonstration Association 256, 305
Archibald, Lady Catherine 241
Arlidge, Jack 195-196
Arlott, John 5, 6, 40, 41, 48, 74, 75-76, 77, 179, 194, 197, 201, 231, 236, 248, 265, 266, 275, 284, 288, 313
Ashe, Arthur 181
Ashe, GM 152
Ayer, Freddie 8

Bacher, Ali 178, 253, 261, 316, 324
Baddiley, Jack 210, 270, 281, 314
Bader, Douglas 125, 214
Bailey, Edward 29, 91-92
Bailey, Jack 23, 25, 77, 157, 177, 181, 184, 187, 221, 223, 224, 246-247
Bailey, Trevor 40, 316
Baker, Douglas 51
Baker, Maureen 241
Ball, MJ 19
Banda, Hastings 254
Bannister, Alex 17
Bannister, Jack 117, 183, 184, 214
Barber, Anthony 268
Barker, Jimmy 158
Barlow, Eddie 18, 51, 52, 117, 178, 284, 297
Barr, Grieg 81
Barrington, Ken 40
Bartlett, Gerald 85
Batchelor, Denzil 35
BBC 23, 44, 48, 49, 94, 116, 150, 156, 201, 229
Bearshaw, Brian 246

Beatles 31
Beaufort, Duke of 214
Beaumont Dark, Anthony 275
Bedser, Alec 214, 263
Bell, Ronald 112
Beloff, Nora 200
Benn, Tony 326, 330
Bennett, John 194
Benton, AE 9
Berlin, Sir Isaiah 8, 11
Best, George 187-188
Biggs, Cyril 67
Bijl, Vintcent van der 113
Billing, Ernie 163
Billing, Trevor 281
Birley, Derek 265
Birmingham Mail 9
Black and White Minstrel Show 53
Blackmore, Jean 266
Blake, Rev PDS 13
Bland, Colin 20, 73
Blenkiron, Bill 196
Blofeld, Henry 178
Bodyline 184
Bolus, Brian 41, 248
Bonham Carter, Mark 224
Bonham Carter, Violet 10
Bornman, Corrie 140, 147, 148
Bowen, Rowland 58, 70, 108, 119, 179, 198, 237, 277, 282, 327
Bowes, Bill 34-35, 211, 233, 264
Boyce, Keith 68
Boycott, Geoff 320
Boyd-Carpenter, John 225, 229
Boyle, Sir Edward 48, 217, 224, 225, 227, 229, 230, 311
Brabin, Herbert 262
Bradman, Sir Donald 44, 269, 332
Bramall Lane, Sheffield 17
Brearley, Mike 14, 57, 189-190, 288, 327, 330
Brechin, Sir Herbert 240, 256-257
Bristol Rugby Club 66
Bristol Tennis Club 64
British Lions 293
Brown, Freddie 153, 184, 291, 322
Brown, Tony 259
Brutus, Dennis 60, 65, 71, 152, 201, 232, 312
Bryant, Sir Arthur 27, 262, 266
Buller, Syd 15
Bullock, Alan 83
Burton, Jack 68
Busby, Sir Matt 214
Butler, Frank 221, 231
Byrne, Rev Patrick 138

Cabinet 45, 46, 202, 203, 206-207, 213, 214, 219

335

Index

Callaghan, James 33, 45-46, 75, 92, 97-98, 99, 113, 126, 182, 183, 184, 185, 187, 202-203, 207, 213, 214, 215, 218, 225, 227, 228, 247; telephone call with Wilson, 248-249; 250-251, 254-255, 273, 298, 311, 312
Cambridge Union 49, 315
Campbell, Menzies 130, 267, 286
Campbell, RMM 37
Canterbury 6
Cardus, Neville 13, 295
Carlos, John 267
Carr, Donald 11-12, 44, 130, 186, 190, 191, 196, 259, 272, 296, 297, 301
Cartwright, Tom 56
Castle, Barbara 44
Cavaliers 12, 52-53, 156, 165, 180, 181, 268
Cenotaph 34
Chalfont, Lord 49
Chapman, Ken 112
Charlton, Bobby 214
Chataway, Chris 288
Chatsworth 17
Cheetham, Jack 34, 74, 75, 148, 168, 177, 179, 180-181, 250, 293
Chesterfield 15
Chorley 274
Church of Scotland 12, 22, 33, 285
Clark, Geoff 148, 201
Clay, Jack 259
Clift, John 73, 76, 77
Close, Brian 112, 166, 210, 211, 214, 258-259
CND (Campaign for Nuclear Disarmament) 19
Cobham, Lord 61
Cohen, Jeff 101
Coleman, Bernard 263
Coleman, David 44, 180, 203, 208
Collins, Douglas 300
Common Market 274
Commonwealth Games 124, 202, 203, 207, 208, 213, 214, 218, 226, 227, 232, 238, 248, 252, 258, 261, 275, 284, 315
Compton, Denis 6, 40, 69, 113, 180
Conservative Party 45, 153, 202, 262, 269, 299
Constantine, Learie 17, 240, 245
Constitutional Club 262, 299
Cook, Roberta 27
Corbett, Ted 171
Cordle, Tony 33, 169
Corinthian Casuals 40
Corneal, Alvin 53
Cornford, Geoff 24-25
Cousins, Frank 236
Cowdrey, Colin 6, 56, 113, 180, 194, 214, 236, 254; and Ted Heath, 229-230, 318-321
Coy, Arthur 34, 44, 59, 72, 74, 75, 148, 178, 272, 297
Craft, Ruth and Michael 212

Crawford, Jeff 205, 286
Crawley, Aidan 72, 123, 217-218, 233, 236, 322, 332
Cresswell, Amos 30-31
Cricket clubs:

Blackheath 209
Derbyshire 17, 115, 117, 262
Eastbourne 63, 69
Essex 68, 312
Glamorgan 23, 60, 64, 94, 100, 101, 102, 117, 118, 137, 149, 150-151, 152-153, 157, 162, 163, 166, 170, 173, 176, 192, 211, 214, 216, 233, 254, 280, 281, 291, 325
Gloucestershire 17, 28, 37, 48, 158, 263, 287
Hampshire 215, 254, 262, 287, 307, 322
St Helens, Swansea 89, 152, 173, 192
Kent 222, 229, 236
Lancashire 75, 118, 166, 168, 177, 185, 216, 222
Leicestershire 86, 161, 191
MCC 11, 25, 57-58, 99, 116, 171, 198, 216
Middlesex 57, 190, 290, 307
Milnrow 246
Newcastle (Staffordshire) 160
Northamptonshire 53
Nottinghamshire 19, 26, 41, 61, 77-78, 102, 172, 185, 205, 210, 221, 232, 302
Somerset 155, 177
Standard Bank 69
Surrey 69, 117, 158, 171, 191, 215, 242, 273, 312, 322
Sussex 11, 24, 25, 39, 76, 100, 157, 160, 216
Wanderers, Johannesburg 193, 246, 259
Warwickshire 9, 27, 69, 162, 172, 174, 216, 223, 229, 236
Willows 323
Worcestershire 52, 61, 164, 290, 322
Yorkshire 25, 43, 112, 152, 153, 166, 171, 172, 211, 215, 216, 233, 271, 326

Cricket Council 25, 44, 46, 72, 73, 75, 156, 182, 184, 201, 202, 203, 207, 208, 214, 215, 217, 218, 219, 220, 225, 227, 228, 230, 231, 232-233, 235, 236, 237, 238, 240, 246, 247, 248, 250, 251, 252, 253, 254, 256, 258, 261, 262, 263, 264, 270, 271
Cricketer, The, magazine 7, 14, 19, 20, 24, 51, 56, 67, 70, 103, 117, 155, 167, 194, 204, 265, 276, 288, 289, 312, 315, 318, 329
Crockford's 125
Crompton, Frank 62
Crossman, Richard 43, 202
Cunningham, Marnie 139
Davidson, Brian 53
Davies, Oswyn 94

336

Index

Davis, Bryan 169-170, 176, 194
Day, Robin 201
Deakins, Leslie 9, 11, 20, 174, 223
Dean, Malcolm 199
Deedes, Bill 22, 31, 46
Delderfield, RF 15, 36, 146, 265
Denness, Mike 293
Dennis, Michael 78, 221
Denny, Michael 28, 105
Derby County 92, 94
Devlin, Bernadette 97, 107, 108
Dewar, Donald 122
Dexter, Ted 41, 45, 74, 180, 232
Dickens, James 11
Dimmock, Peter 307
Dobson, Ray 326
Dodd, EJ 27
Doggart, Hugh 40, 237
Donnelly, Desmond 224, 228, 229, 237
Douglas-Home, Sir Alec 57, 61, 62, 218, 219, 236, 270, 319
Duffus, Louis 299
Duke, Michael Hare 212
Dunwoody, Gwyneth 123

Eaks, Louis 158, 161
Ebbw Vale 97, 98
Edey, Roy 247
Edinburgh, see Commonwealth Games
Edinburgh, Duke of 218, 219, 250, 299
Edwards, Bill 151, 192
Edwards, Mike 69, 248
Elliot, Walter 62
Elliott, Jack 232
Ellis, John 326
Emburey, John 323
Engineer, Farokh 177, 222, 223, 290
Ennals, David 17
Ennals, John 107, 123
Eriksen, ER 28, 67, 70-71
Evans, Godfrey 14, 331
Evans, Peter 251
Ewbank, Colonel EV 10

Fair Cricket Campaign 217, 224, 236, 298, 311
Faku-Juqula, Oscar 310
Farley, William 84
Faulds, Andrew 228
Fender, Percy 261
Fisher, Geoffrey 236
Fisher, John 274
Fitzgerald, Garrett 140
Flack, Bernard 196
Fletcher, Keith 55, 320
Fluoride 33, 121, 124
Foley, Maurice 208, 218
Foot, Michael 92, 224
Foot, Paul 235

Football hooligans 31, 46, 66, 82, 99, 110-111, 191, 279
Ford, Ronnie 289
Fortune, Charles 5, 6, 177

Forwood, Charles 274
Frames, AS 64
Fraser, Angus 323, 324
Freemasonry 283
Frith, David 35, 289, 329
Frost, David 214

Gaby, Richard 176, 186, 190
Gale, George 33
Gale, Reg 247
Gavaskar, Sunil 7
Geach, Hugh 83, 90, 204
Gerrard, John 99, 137, 224, 305
Gibbs, Lance 51, 223
Gifford, Norman 318
Gilbert, Sir Martin 275
Gillette Cup 118, 166
Gilligan, Arthur 39, 41, 61, 119, 290
Gilmore, Peter 298
Gisby, John 96
Glasgow 12, 48, 300
Glassbrook Colliery 182
Gothard, EJ 262-263
Grace Gates 246, 254, 295
Grahamstown 5, 332
Graveney, Tom 51, 53, 117, 258, 310
Gray, GCG 177
Green, Benny 293, 295
Greenhill, Sir Dennis 76
Greenwood, Anthony 208
Gregory, Kenneth 117
Gregory, Peter 313
Greig, Tony 24, 318, 320
Grieves, Ken 246, 281
Griffith, Billy 11, 12, 35, 42, 59, 61, 62, 63, 68, 72, 73, 74, 75, 77, 78, 86, 99, 155, 164, 168, 174, 179, 186, 187, 190, 191, 193, 196, 197, 214, 216, 220-221, 222, 224, 236, 238, 239, 272, 289, 290, 297, 300
Griffith, Charlie 51
Griffith, Mike 194
Griffiths, Eldon 34, 114, 270, 271, 291, 292
Grigg, John 122
Grimes, Harry 13
Gross, SJ 137
Grosvenor Square 30, 146, 307
Group 4 174
Guy, Basil 212

Hackett, Tony 40
Hain, Peter 19, 21, 29, 30, 31, 32, 37, 45, 48, 64, 67-68, 71, 82, 86, 88, 89, 91, 92, 104, 119, 121, 125-126, 145, 147, 161, 162, 165-166, 170, 189, 201, 202, 204, 208, 213, 216, 236, 247, 256, 261, 262, 270, 273, 276, 285, 292, 296, 297, 300, 306, 307, 308, 309, 310, 311, 312, 328
Hall, Wes 51
Hamilton, Willie 227
Hammond, Wally 14, 44
Hanley, Howard 234, 329

337

Index

Harding, Judge Rowe 101, 152
Harris, Harold 264
Harris, Terence 290
Harrison, EE 25, 76
Harrison, Richard 287
Hart, Victor 131
Hartshorne, WP 123
Harvey, Bagenal 180, 181
Hastings Festival 18, 52
Hatch, John 115
Hattersley, Roy 80, 81, 149, 173
Hawker, Sir Cyril 48, 300
Hayward, Rev PN 12
Healey, Dennis 172
Heath, Ted 111, 229, 271, 292; and Colin Cowdrey 316-321; 329
Heathrow 8, 31, 109, 211, 295, 296
Hebditch, Simon 204, 274
Hedges, Stephen 327
Hell's Angels 146
Henderson, Roy 11-12
Herrmann, Frank 129
Heyhoe, Rachel 59, 214
Hicks, Gary 209
High Wycombe 253
Hill, Jimmy 40
Hillsborough 38, 129, 309
Hodgson, TCB 81, 109
Hogg, Quintin 24, 25, 122, 182, 183, 200, 206, 208, 215, 252, 259, 274, 310
Holroyde, Peggy 240
Hollis, Christopher 155, 281
Howa, Hassan 178, 179, 319
Howard, Geoffrey 69, 215, 224, 242, 301
Howe, Peter 57
Howell, Denis 41, 46, 49, 63, 74, 79, 80, 94, 113, 119, 125, 181, 182, 207, 208, 214, 217, 218, 219, 225, 226, 227, 229, 246, 315
Howle, Thomas 285
Huddleston, Trevor 10, 208
Hughes, Cledwyn 30, 33
Hutchinson, Jeremy 57
Hutton, Richard 40, 318

Ibadulla, Billy 223
Illingworth, Raymond 205-206, 229, 258, 266, 276, 286, 307, 320
Inch, John 129, 193
Insole, Doug 14, 40, 113-114, 153
Iona Community 12
Iqbal, Asif 222, 242, 320
Isaac, ST 151
Isaacs, Wilfred 28, 67-68, 70, 72, 113, 244, 246, 298
ITN 199

Jackson, John 121-122, 209, 210, 279
Jafri, Fareed 167, 310
Jakoborits, Dr Emmanuel 236
James, RA 72-73, 74, 75, 86, 99
Jameson, John 320

Jarman, Dr Francis 163
Jarrett, Mike 28, 158
Jazz 7
Jenkins, Peter 84, 284
John Player Sunday League 118, 166, 265
Johnson, Laurie 17
Johnston, Brian 20, 177, 178, 239
Johnston, Sir John 76, 208, 312
Jowitt, Alderman Harold 241
Judd, Frank 43, 226, 227, 229
Julien, Bernard 53

Kane, Jack 129
Kanhai, Rohan 223
Kaunda, Kenneth 219
Kay, John 118, 165, 238
Kedwal, Jamal 233
Kelly, Henry 70
Kemmy, James 140
Kennedy, Dennis 139, 281
Kent State 50
Kenyatta, Jomo 219
Kenyon, Don 196
Kerr, Anne 225
Khan, Imran 317, 323, 324
Khan, Majid 169, 320
Kilburn, Jim 258, 290, 291
Killick, Paul 179, 184-185
King, Cecil 229
King, Edmund 223, 254, 264, 304
King, Martin Luther 104, 287
Kirsten, Peter 325
Koestler, Arthur 311
Knight, Barry 55
Knight, Julie 172
Knight, Robin 57-58, 61, 283, 329
Knott, Brian 320
Kureishi, Omar 170, 181

Laithwaite, Bill 83
Laker, Jim 47
Lamb, Allan 325
Lance, Tiger 284
Lang, Sir John 156, 180, 181
Lansdowne Road 29, 97, 142
Latchman, Harry 320
Latham, Arthur 237-238
Law, Andrew Bonar 241
Lawlor, John 82, 98, 309
Lawrence, TE 273
Lawry, Bill 51
Leadbeater, Barry 259
Leese, Oliver 114
Leicester City Football Club 31
Leicester University Union 22
Lennox, Robert 137
Leonard, Bill 198
Le Roux, Garth 323, 325
Lever, Peter 168, 287
Levin, Bernard 17
Lewis, Tony 150, 170, 214, 325
Liberal Party 71
Lindsay, Valerie 246

Linley, Lord 211
Lipton, Marcus 225
Lishman, Gordon 32, 161
Lister, Joe 164
Livingstone, Ken 300
Ljubljana 280
Llandudno 247, 252
Lloyd, Clive 177, 223, 290
Lock, Tony 332
London Airport, see Heathrow
London Weekend Television 23
Longrigg, Bunty 191
Loosley, Michael 171
Lord's Taverners 252
Luckhurst, Brian 320
Luttig, Dr Hendrik 65, 105, 275

Mackenzie, Precious 315
Macleod, Ian 25
Macmillan, Maurice 271
Macrae, JV 42
Magee, Bryan 33
Mair, Norman 130, 134, 140, 147
Makins, Clifford 196
Malawi 254
Mandela, Nelson 7, 284, 324
Mann, Frank 113
Mann, George 113, 114
Manning, JL 69, 76, 115, 318
Marlar, Robin 57
Marshall, Eddie 185
Marshall, Pat 24
Marshall, Roy 242
Martin, Syd 180, 186
Mashonaland 322
Mattei, Barrie 85
Matthews, Pauline 241
Matthews, RB 137, 138
Matutu, Godwin 244
Maudling, Reginald 225, 229, 271
May, Peter 299, 330
McCartney, Paul 13, 303
McGarry, Joe 146
McGrath, Hugh 223
McKinnon, Atholl 186
McMurtie, Bill 276
McVicker, Norman 196
Melford, Michael 24, 27, 55, 70, 86, 90-91, 119, 177-178, 197, 331
Menzies, Robert 282
Mercer, Joe 214
Merrison, Prof Alec 115, 285
Meynell, Rosemary 278
Michaelson, Colonel BK 151
Milburn, Colin 55, 109, 113, 165, 279, 291
Millan, Bruce 208, 219
Miller, David 120, 121
Miller, Douglas 327
Miller, George 130, 131
Miller, John 259
Milnes, HT 26
Minor Counties Association 63
Miss World 35

Mohammed, Hanif 51
Mohammed, Mushtaq 53, 287
Monday Club 207
Montgomery, Bernard 114, 215
Moon, Norman 137
Moore, Dick 262, 264
Morgan, Elystan 182
Morgan, John 91, 96
Morrell, John 122
Morrell, Keith 286
Morris, Jean 245
Morris, Dr William 104
Morrow, John 104
Morton, Monica 259
Mott-Eadclyffe, Sir Charles 225, 226, 228, 229
Mousetrap, The 300
Mullens, Roy 163
Muller, Dr Hilgard 79
Murray, Deryck 53
Murray, Jed 88, 95
Murray, John 51
Murrayfield 12, 30, 37, 38, 96, 129-130
Myers, Kevin 70

Nabarro, Sir Gerald 327
Nash, Jack 116, 175, 210-211, 216
Nash, Malcolm 325
Nash, Paul 267
National Council for Civil Liberties 30, 109, 111-112
National Front 85, 143
National Union of Journalists 235
Newcombe, Barry 82, 83, 116, 134, 148
Newman, Colonel Charles 26, 214
Newton Abbot 32
Nicholls, Sir Jack 46, 49-50, 55, 61, 317
Nicholls, Tom 326
Nicholson, Geoffrey 138
Nicholson, Tom 170
'Night of the daubers' 156-160
Noel-Baker, Philip 224, 226
Norfolk, Duke of 19, 193, 214
Northam, Randall 208
Northern Counties 221
Northern Cricket Society 300
Nottingham Forest 94
Notting Hill 253
Nourse, Dudley 8-9

Oakman, Alan 14
O'Brien, Conor Cruise 123
O'Brien, Sir Leslie 249
D'Oliveira, Basil 10, 18, 38, 42, 51-52, 53, 54-56, 61, 179, 209-210, 222, 259, 272, 284, 290, 315, 318, 319, 320, 324, 327, 330
Olympic movement 112, 231-232
Ordia, Abraham 213
Orwell, George 278
Oxford College of Technology 28
Oxford Union 28, 30, 229, 309
Oxford University 8, 13, 38, 68, 81, 109, 317

Index

Paisley, Rev Ian 140
Pakistan 1971 tour 295-296
Pakistan under 25s tour 150, 242, 243
Palfrey, William 28-29, 247
Palmer, Gerald 11
Panorama 48, 156, 201, 284, 310
Pardoe, Jim 33
Paris, Cecil 74, 77, 100, 184, 191, 262
Parker, Grahame 48
Parks, Jim 14-15, 17-18, 19, 52, 117, 148, 203, 279
Pataudi, Nawab of 73, 180
Paton, Alan 287
Pawle, Tony 103, 104, 151
Pawson, Tony 67, 102, 265-266, 289
Pearce, TN 299
Pendry, Tony 15
Perry-Gore, Rev Noel 215
Philip, Prince, see Duke of Edinburgh
Player, Gary 285
Playfair Cricket Monthly 35, 38, 58
Plimsoll, Jack 15, 197, 246
Pocock, Pat 320
Polaroid 305
Police Act 99
Police Federation 28, 36, 247, 252
Pollock, Graeme 20, 51, 68, 73, 117, 284
Pollock, Peter 20, 51, 73, 117
Pope, George 115
Portal, Lord 214
Post Office 116
Poulton, Ron 77-78, 116, 174, 210
Powell, Enoch 167, 230, 274, 329
Pratschke, Anthony 139
Prentice, Reg 217, 225, 226, 229
Prescott, Robin 28
Press, Ron 37, 49, 64, 65, 67, 137, 326
Preston, Norman 166, 197
Price, Dai 92
Prideaux, Roger 55
Priestley, Jack 132-133, 140
Procter, Mike 117, 267-268, 284, 287, 317, 318
Progressive Party 261
Protests against sport: Aberdeen 105, 127-128; Bristol tennis 64-65, 211, rugby 110, 133-136, 138, 305, 310; Cardiff 143, 145; Coventry 137-138; Dublin 138-142, 148; Ebbw Vale 312; Edinburgh 96, 128-130; Exeter 37, 131-132, 306; Leicester 36, 84-87, 303, 307, 308, 309; Limerick 139, 142; Manchester 95-96, 308; Newport 89; Oxford University 68-69; Swansea 29, 89-95, 98; Twickenham 29, 81-84, 95, 98, 104-105, 143-144, 302-303, 306-307, 309
Protest, other 106-107, 121; if South Africans had played at Lord's 303-305, 306
Pugh, JA 26-27, 78

Race Relations Act 271
Raison, Timothy 245

Randall, Derek 323-324
Ramsay, Michael 244
Ramsay, WC 83, 145
Raven, Harry 231
Raven, Simon 61, 278
Rawlinson, Sir Peter 201, 202, 271
Rees, Geraint 111
Rees, Merlyn 208
Reid, Rev Ian 12
Reiss, Rev Robert 215
Rest of the World 73, 263, 267, 291, 297, 314, 320
Reynolds, David 124
Rhoades, Cedric 75, 118, 168, 185, 201, 222, 290
Rhodes, Harold 15
Rhodesia 6, 42, 50, 60, 123, 207, 286, 316, 320, 321, 322
Richards, Malcolm 73
Richards, Barry 7-8, 117, 269, 284, 287
Riley, Miss EM 42
Rippon, Geoffrey 123
Rippon, PT 21, 285
Risk 276-277
Rivett, Rohan 324
Roach, Stuart 86
Roberts, Christopher 319
Roberts, Pat 201, 202, 284
Robins, Derrick 53, 62, 69, 214, 315
Rogers, Miss BJ 124, 268
Romer, MN 70
Roope, Graham 40
Rose, Paul 286
Rosenhead, Jonathan 229
Ross, Alan 276, 331
Ross, Gordon 38
Rothmans 190, 268
Rowe, Lawrence 53
Rumsey, Fred 115
Russell, Graham 65

Sachs, Solly 311
Salahuddin, Masood 296
Saltley depot 266, 308
Sampson, Anthony 218, 221-222, 330
SAN-ROC 60, 62
Save The Seventy Tour 176
Savoy Hotel 299
Scargill, Arthur 308
Schoeman, Ben 27
Secombe, Harry 214
Securicor 68, 89, 174, 175, 190, 203
Sellers, Brian 153, 191, 196, 214, 300, 327
Sharpeville 10
Shepherd, John 222, 242, 315, 320
Sheppard, David 13, 14, 19, 20, 51, 57, 58, 61, 62, 79, 155, 201, 217, 218, 219, 236, 244, 246, 278, 283, 287, 288, 289, 298, 311, 330, 332
Shroot, Alan 48
Shuttleworth, Ken 293
Sibeko, David 202
Simmons, Jim 170

Index

Simon, Dr Glyn 137
Simple, Peter 261
Simpson, Bobby 51
Simpson, Reg 19, 78, 102, 221
Slovo, Joe 15
Smith, Alan 113, 275
Smith, Arnold 219
Smith, Ian 254
Smith, MJK 201
Smith, Tommie 267
Smuts, Jan 219
Smythe, Tony 111
Snelling, Sir Arthur 78, 208, 244, 260, 312
Snow, CP 125
Snow, John 315
Sobers, Gary 51, 73, 180, 205, 248, 291, 316-317
Solomons, David 176
Southern Counties 222
Soweto 13
Special Branch 31, 37, 66, 89, 105, 143, 176, 204, 209, 268, 298, 302-303, 306
Spence, Peter 22
Sports Council 226, 236, 240, 291
Sportsnight 44, 180, 203
Springboks 12, 13, 28, 29, 32, 36, 37, 38, 46, 47, 50, 51, 81-97, 105, 127-149, 156, 162, 170, 173, 186, 193, 201, 209, 210, 245, 269, 275, 281, 287, 302, 311
Sproat, Iain 122
Stable, Sir Wintringham 161
Star Trek 201
Statham, Brian 210
Steele, David 122, 227, 228
Stephenson, Paul 244
Sterry, RF 156
Stewart, JAB 316
Stewart, Michael 26, 30, 33, 50, 54, 79, 99, 123, 181, 182, 229, 252, 274, 275, 330
Stewart, Mickey 40
Stewart, Rev WA 13
Stonyhurst 10
Stop The Seventy Tour (STST) 21, 25, 31, 32, 37, 39, 67, 82, 83, 89, 92, 97, 121, 144, 145, 146, 154, 161, 162, 168, 186, 189, 199, 204, 209, 211, 212, 270, 274, 298
Stott, Bryan 102
Streeton, Richard 91, 92
Subba Row, Raman 23, 24, 77, 78, 79, 168, 178, 181, 184, 187, 202, 228, 263, 265, 270, 283, 327
Suez 275
Support The Seventy Tour 209, 210, 272, 279
Surbiton 268
Surridge, Stuart 191, 290
Sussex University 11
Sutcliffe, Billy 210
Sutton, DL 47
Swallow, David 259, 284

Swanton, Jim 40, 56, 59, 167, 194, 204, 215, 230-231, 241, 254, 261, 265, 266, 276, 312, 318, 331

Tarver, John 84, 108
Taylor, Bob 318
Taylor, Brian 68
Taylor, John 36, 84, 88, 95, 305
Taylor, Keith 209
Taylor, Reg 193
Taylor, Wilfred 130
TCCB (Test and County Cricket Board) 24, 25, 26, 60, 75, 76, 77, 86, 100, 101, 152, 155, 164, 165, 167, 168, 175, 177, 186, 191-192, 221, 241, 262, 263, 272, 277, 290, 291
Thicknesse, John 25, 26, 76-77, 170, 175, 230
Thomas, JBG 146, 149
Thomson, Ian 31
Thorpe, Jeremy 240, 261
Titley, UA 95, 149, 311
Tomkins, Oliver 136, 230
Townsend, WE 9-10
Trafalgar Square 7, 8, 105, 207, 253
Treacy, Dr Eric 300
Trueman, Fred 119
Truman, Ron 274
Tugendhat, Christopher 274
Tunbridge Wells 313
Turner, Mike 86, 161, 191, 266
Twickenham 22, 27, 29, 31, 36, 37, 81, 82, 83, 84, 95, 98, 104, 105, 110, 111, 116, 143, 146, 148, 149, 150, 156, 209, 270, 287, 302, 303, 306, 309, 334

Ulyatt, Richard 248
Up Pompeii 201
Uxbridge 253

Villiers. Dawie de 81, 298-299
Vinicombe, John 158, 161
Vorster, John 54, 55, 56, 61, 71, 84, 147, 179, 254, 260, 293, 317, 331

Wadell, JH 46, 277, 311
Walden, Brian 201
Waldorf Hotel 299
Waldron, Sir John 40, 155, 164, 165, 175, 193, 236, 272, 307, 310, 312
Walker, Peter 55
Walker-Smith, Sir Derek 224, 226
Ward, Alan 320
Waring, Frank 293
Warner Stand 175
Warwicker, John 43
Watson, William 62, 201
Watson, Willie 259
Way, Andrew 165, 174, 186, 190
Weatling, John Stuart 150
Webster, John 36
Webster, Martin 143
Webster, WCT 40

341

Welford Road 85, 86, 87, 304
Wembley 108
West, Peter 324
White, Crawford 117
White, FG 39
White, John 156
Wight, Peter 222
Wilkins, Chris 115
Willcox, Herbert 64, 65
Williams, Michael 149
Williams, Mike 65
Williams, Colonel Pat 24, 39
Williams, Ronald 261
Williamson, Dick 25
Williamson, Frank 29, 84, 87, 89, 90, 91, 98, 99, 106, 108, 308
Willis, Bob 40, 320
Wilson, Don 259-260, 284
Wilson, Giles 211
Wilson, Harold 23, 30, 43-45, 80, 99, 173, 199, 202, 203, 206, 207, 208, 209, 215, 218, 219, 236; telephone call with Callaghan, 248-249; 259, 261, 268, 273, 274
Wilson, William 319
Wilton-Godberford, David 212
Wimbledon tennis 256, 291
Winnick, David 63
Winterbottom, Walter 236
Wisden 17, 38, 119, 166, 179, 189, 197-198, 228
Wolrige-Gordon, Patrick 288

Women's Cricket Association 42, 59, 123-124
Wood, Jack 177, 216
Wood, Mike 285
Woodburn, Arthur 218
Woodcock, John 7, 13-14, 20, 54, 55, 56, 75, 76, 103, 114, 178, 278, 281, 295, 315, 318, 324, 329
Woods, Donald 115
Wooller, Wilf 23, 40, 41, 50, 60, 64, 66, 74, 81, 94-95, 98, 100, 101, 102-104, 117, 118, 119, 126, 137, 144, 149-150, 152-153, 160, 166, 167, 169-170, 173, 175, 176, 192-193, 201, 202, 214, 216, 237, 238, 249, 273, 281, 282, 291, 322
Worsley, Sir William 152, 215
Worsthorne, Peregrine 32, 45, 66, 215, 264, 266, 274, 330
Wright, Rev Neville 12, 241

Yardley, Norman 55, 71-72, 79, 122, 196, 258, 289, 315
Yarranton, Peter 27, 84
Yorkshire Evening Post 12
Young, Hugo 118
Young Liberals 32, 35, 37, 65, 68, 158, 161, 256
Younger, George 96, 286

Ziandi, Frank 286